12 Christmas Sermons

Charles H. Spurgeon

BAKER
A DIVISION OF
Baker Book House Co

Reprinted 1994 by Baker Book House Company

Published by Baker Books
a division of Baker Book House Company
P.O. Box 6287, Grand Rapids, MI 49516-6287

Printed in the United States of America

ISBN 0-8010-8391-5

CONTENTS

The First Christmas Carol

" Glory to God in the highest, and on earth peace, good will tow.rd men."—Luke ii. 14.

IT is superstitious to worship angels; it is but proper to love them. Although it would be a high sin, and an act of misdemeanour against the Sovereign Court of Heaven to pay the slightest adoration to the mightiest angel, yet it would be unkind and unseemly, if we did not give to holy angels a place in our heart's warmest love. In fact, he that contemplates the character of angels, and marks their many deeds of sympathy with men, and kindness towards them, cannot resist the impulse of his nature—the impulse of love towards them. The one incident in angelic history, to which our text refers, is enough to weld our hearts to them for ever. How free from envy the angels were! Christ did not come from heaven to save their compeers when they fell. When Satan, the mighty angel, dragged with him a third part of the stars of heaven, Christ did not stoop from his throne to die for them; but he left them to be reserved in chains and darkness until the last great day. Yet angels did not envy men. Though they remembered that he took not up angels, yet they did not murmur when he took up the seed of Abraham; and though the blessed Master had never condescended to take the angel's form, they did not think it beneath them to express their joy when they found him arrayed in the body of an infant. How free, too, they were from pride! They were not ashamed to come and tell the news to humble shepherds. Methinks, they had as much joy in pouring out their songs that night before the shepherds, who were watching with their flocks, as they would have had if they had been commanded by their Master to sing their hymn in the halls of Cæsar. Mere men—men possessed with pride, think it a fine thing to preach before kings and princes; and think it great condescension now and then to have to minister to the humble crowd. Not so the angels. They stretched their willing wings, and gladly sped from their bright seats above, to tell the shepherds on the plain by night, the marvellous story of an Incarnate God. And mark how well they told the story, and surely you will love them! Not with the stammering tongue of him that tells a tale in which he hath no interest; nor even with the feigned interest of a man that would move the passions of others, when he feeleth no emotion himself; but with joy and gladness, such as angels only can know. They *sang* the story out, for they could not stay to tell it in heavy prose. They sang, " Glory to God on high, and on earth peace, good will towards men." Methinks, they sang it with gladness in their eyes; with their hearts burning with love, and with breasts as full of joy as if the good news to man had been good news to themselves. And, verily, it was good news to them, for the heart of sympathy makes good news to others, good news to itself. Do you not love the angels? Ye will not bow before them, and there ye are right; but will ye not love them? Doth it not make one part of your anticipation of

3

heaven, that in heaven you shall dwell with the holy angels, as well as with the spirits of the just made perfect? Oh, how sweet to think that these holy and lovely beings are our guardians every hour! They keep watch and ward about us, both in the burning noon-tide, and in the darkness of the night. They keep us in all our ways; they bear us up in their hands, lest at any time we dash our feet against stones. They unceasingly minister unto us who are the heirs of salvation; both by day and night they are our watchers and our guardians, for know ye not, that "the angel of the Lord encampeth round about them that fear him."

Let us turn aside, having just thought of angels for a moment, to think rather of this song, than of the angels themselves. Their song was brief, but as Kitto excellently remarks, it was "well worthy of angels expressing the greatest and most blessed truths, in words so few, that they become to an acute apprehension, almost oppressive by the pregnant fulness of their meaning"—"Glory to God in the highest, on earth peace, good will toward men." We shall, hoping to be assisted by the Holy Spirit, look at these words of the angels in a fourfold manner. I shall just suggest some *instructive thoughts* arising from these words; then some *emotional thoughts*; then a few *prophetical thoughts*; and afterwards, one or two *preceptive thoughts*.

I. First then, in the words of our text. There are many INSTRUCTIVE THOUGHTS.

The angels sang something which men could understand—something which men ought to understand—something which will make men much better if they will understand it. The angels were singing about Jesus who was born in the manger. We must look upon their song as being built upon this foundation. They sang of Christ, and the salvation which he came into this world to work out. And what they said of this salvation was this: they said, first, that it gave glory to God; secondly, that it gave peace to man; and, thirdly, that it was a token of God's good will towards the human race.

1. *First, they said that this salvation gave glory to God.* They had been present on many august occasions, and they had joined in many a solemn chorus to the praise of their Almighty Creator. They were present at the creation: "The morning stars sang together, and all the sons of God shouted for joy." They had seen many a planet fashioned between the palms of Jehovah, and wheeled by his eternal hands through the infinitude of space. They had sung solemn songs over many a world which the Great One had created. We doubt not, they had often chanted "Blessing and honour, and glory, and majesty, and power, and dominion, and might, be unto him that sitteth on the throne," manifesting himself in the work of creation. I doubt not, too, that their songs had gathered force through ages. As when first created, their first breath was song, so when they saw God create new worlds then their song received another note; they rose a little higher in the gamut of adoration. But this time, when they saw God stoop from his throne, and become a babe, hanging upon a woman's breast, they lifted their notes higher still; and reaching to the uttermost stretch of angelic music, they gained the highest notes of the divine scale of praise, and they sang, "Glory to God *in the highest*," for higher in goodness they felt God could not go. Thus their highest praise they gave to him in the highest act of his godhead. If it be true that there is a hierarchy of angels, rising tier upon tier in magnificence and dignity—if the apostle teaches us that there be "angels, and principalities, and powers, and thrones, and dominions," amongst these blest inhabitants of the upper world—I can suppose that when the intelligence was first communicated to those angels that are to be found upon the outskirts of the heavenly world, when they looked down from heaven and saw the new-born babe, they sent the news backward to the place whence the miracle first proceeded, singing

> "Angels, from the realms of glory,
>   Wing your downward flight to earth,
> Ye who sing creation's story,
>   Now proclaim Messiah's birth;
> Come and worship,
>   Worship Christ, the new-born King.

4

And as the message ran from rank to rank, at last the presence angels, those four cherubim that perpetually watch around the throne of God—those wheels with eyes—took up the strain, and, gathering up the song of all the inferior grades of angels, surmounted the divine pinnacle of harmony with their own solemn chant of adoration, upon which the entire host shouted, "The highest angels praise thee."—" Glory to God in the highest." Ay, there is no mortal that can ever dream how magnificent was that song. Then, note, if angels shouted before and when the world was made, their hallelujahs were more full, more strong, more magnificent, if not more hearty, when they saw Jesus Christ born of the Virgin Mary to be man's redeemer—" Glory to God in the highest."

What is the instructive lesson to be learned from this first syllable of the angels' song? Why this, that salvation is God's highest glory. He is glorified in every dew drop that twinkles to the morning sun. He is magnified in every wood flower that blossoms in the copse, although it live to blush unseen, and waste its sweetness in the forest air. God is glorified in every bird that warbles on the spray; in every lamb that skips the mead. Do not the fishes in the sea praise him. From the tiny minnow to the huge Leviathan, do not all creatures that swim the water bless and praise his name? Do not all created things extol him? Is there aught beneath the sky, save man, that doth not glorify God? Do not the stars exalt him, when they write his name upon the azure of heaven in their golden letters? Do not the lightnings adore him when they flash his brightness in arrows of light piercing the midnight darkness? Do not thunders extol him when they roll like drums in the march of the God of armies? Do not all things exalt him, from the least even to the greatest? But sing, sing, oh universe, till thou hast exhausted thyself, thou canst not afford a song so sweet as the song of Incarnation. Though creation may be a majestic organ of praise, it cannot reach the compass of the golden canticle—Incarnation! There is more in that than in creation, more melody in Jesus in the manger, than there is in worlds on worlds rolling their grandeur round the throne of the Most High. Pause Christian, and consider this a minute. See how every attribute is here magnified. Lo! what *wisdom* is here. God becomes man that God may be just, and the justifier of the ungodly. Lo! what *power*, for where is power so great as when it concealeth power? What power, that Godhead should unrobe itself and become man! Behold, what *love* is thus revealed to us when Jesus becomes a man. Behold, ye what *faithfulness!* How many promises are this day kept? How many solemn obligations are this hour discharged? Tell me one attribute of God that is not manifest in Jesus; and your ignorance shall be the reason why you have not seen it so. The whole of God is glorified in Christ; and though some part of the name of God is written in the universe, it is here best read—in Him who was the Son of Man, and, yet, the Son of God.

But, let me say one word here before I go away from this point. We must learn from this, that if salvation glorifies God, glorifies him in the highest degree, and makes the highest creatures praise him, this one reflection may be added—then, that doctrine, which glorifies man in salvation cannot be the gospel. For salvation glorifies God. The angels were no Arminians, they sang, "Glory *to God* in the highest." They believe in no doctrine which uncrowns Christ, and puts the crown upon the head of mortals. They believe in no system of faith which makes salvation dependent upon the creature, and, which really gives the creature the praise, for what is it less than for a man to save himself, if the whole dependence of salvation rests upon his own free will? No, my brethren; there may be some preachers, that delight to preach a doctrine that magnifies man; but in their gospel angels have no delight. The only glad tidings that made the angels sing, are those that put God first, God last, God midst, and God without end, in the salvation of his creatures, and put the crown wholly and alone upon the head of him that saves without a helper. " Glory to God in the highest," is the angels' song.

2. When they had sung this, they sang what they had never sung before. " Glory to God in the highest," was an old, old song; they had sung that from before the foundations of the world. But, now, they sang as it were a new song before the throne of God: for they added this stanza—" *on earth, peace.*" They did not sing that in the garden. There was peace there, but it seemed a thing of course, and

scarce worth singing of. There was more than peace there; for there was glory to God there. But, now, man had fallen, and since the day when cherubim with fiery swords drove out the man, there had been no peace on earth, save in the breast of some believers, who had obtained peace from the living fountain of this incarnation of Christ. Wars had raged from the ends of the world; men had slaughtered one another, heaps on heaps. There had been wars within as well as wars without. Conscience had fought with man; Satan had tormented man with thoughts of sin. There had been no peace on earth since Adam fell. But, now, when the new-born King made his appearance, the swaddling band with which he was wrapped up was the white flag of peace. That manger was the place where the treaty was signed, whereby warfare should be stopped between man's conscience and himself, man's conscience and his God. It was then, that day, that the trumpet blew—"Sheathe the sword, oh man, sheathe the sword, oh conscience, for God is now at peace with man, and man at peace with God." Do you not feel my brethren, that the gospel of God is peace to man? Where else can peace be found, but in the message of Jesus? Go legalist, work for peace with toil and pain, and thou shalt never find it. Go, thou, that trustest in the law: go thou, to Sinai; look to the flames that Moses saw, and shrink, and tremble, and despair; for peace is nowhere to be found, but in him, of whom it is said, "This man shall be peace." And what a peace it is, beloved! It is peace like a river, and righteousness like the waves of the sea. It is the peace of God that passeth all understanding, which keeps our hearts and minds through Jesus Christ our Lord. This sacred peace between the pardoned soul and God the pardoner; this marvellous at-one-ment between the sinner and his judge, this was it that the angels sung when they said, "peace on earth'

3. And, then, they wisely ended their song with a third note. They said, "Good will to man." Philosophers have said that God has a good will toward man; but I never knew any man who derived much comfort from their philosophical assertion. Wise men have thought from what we have seen in creation that God had much good will toward man, or else his works would never have been so constructed for their comfort; but I never heard of any man who could risk his soul's peace upon such a faint hope as that. But I have not only heard of thousands, but I know them, who are quite sure that God has a good will towards men; and if you ask their reason, they will give a full and perfect answer. They say, he has good will toward man for he gave his Son. No greater proof of kindness between the Creator and his subjects can possibly be afforded than when the Creator gives his only begotten and well beloved Son to die. Though the first note is God-like, and though the second note is peaceful, this third note melts my heart the most. Some think of God as if he were a morose being who hated all mankind. Some picture him as if he were some abstract subsistence taking no interest in our affairs. Hark ye, God has "good will toward men." You know what good will means. Well, all that it means, and more, God has to you, ye sons and daughters of Adam. Swearer, you have cursed God; he has not fulfilled his curse on you; he has good will towards you, though you have no good will towards him. Infidel, you have sinned high and hard against the Most High; he has said no hard things against you, for he has good will towards men. Poor sinner, thou hast broken his laws; thou art half afraid to come to the throne of his mercy lest he should spurn thee; hear thou this, and be comforted—God has good will towards men, so good a will that he has said, and said it with an oath too, "As I live, saith the Lord, I have no pleasure in the death of him that dieth, but had rather that he should turn unto me and live;" so good a will moreover that he has even condescended to say, "Come, now, let us reason together; though your sins be as scarlet, they shall be as wool; though they be red like crimson, they shall be whiter than snow." And if you say, "Lord, how shall I know that thou hast this good will towards me," he points to yonder manger, and says, "Sinner, if I had not a good will towards thee, would I have parted with my Son? if I had not good will towards the human race, would I have given up my Son to become one of that race that he might by so doing redeem them from death? Ye that doubt the Master's love, look ye to that circle of angels; see their blaze of glory; hear their song, and let your doubts die away in that sweet music and be buried in a shroud of harmony. He has good will to men; he is willing to pardon; he passes by iniquity, transgression, and sin. And

6

mark thee, if Satan shall then add, "But though God hath good will, yet he cannot violate his justice, therefore his mercy may be ineffective, and you may die;" then listen to that first note of the song, "Glory to God in the highest," and reply to Satan and all his temptations, that when God shows good will to a penitent sinner, there is not only peace in the sinner's heart, but it brings glory to every attribute of God, and so he can be just, and yet justify the sinner, and glorify himself.

I do not pretend to say that I have opened all the instructions contained in these three sentences, but I may perhaps direct you into a train of thought that may serve you for the week. I hope that all through the week you will have a truly merry Christmas by feeling the power of these words, and knowing the unction of of them. "Glory to God in the highest, on earth peace, good will toward men."

II. Next, I have to present to you some EMOTIONAL THOUGHTS. Friends, doth not this verse, this song of angels, stir your heart with happiness? When I read that, and found the angels singing it, I thought to myself, "Then if the angels ushered in the gospel's great Head with singing, ought I not to preach with singing? And ought not my hearers to live with singing? Ought not their hearts to be glad and their spirits to rejoice?" Well, thought I, there be some sombre religionists who were born in a dark night in December that think a smile upon the face is wicked, and believe that for a Christian to be glad and rejoice is to be inconsistent. Ah ! I wish these gentlemen had seen the angels when they sang about Christ ; for if angels sang about his birth, though it was no concern of theirs, certainly men ought to sing about it as long as they live, sing about it when they die, and sing about it when they live in heaven for ever. I do long to see in the midst of the church more of a singing Christianity. The last few years have been breeding in our midst a groaning and unbelieving Christianity. Now, I doubt not its sincerity, but I do doubt its healthy character. I say it may be true and real enough; God forbid I should say a word against the sincerity of those who practise it; but it is a sickly religion.

Watts hit the mark when he said,

> "Religion never was designed
> To make our pleasures less."

It is designed to do away with some of our pleasures, but it gives us many more, to make up for what it takes away; so it does not make them less. O ye that see in Christ nothing but a subject to stimulate your doubts and make the tears run down your cheeks; O ye that always say,

> "Lord, what a wretched land is this,
> That yields us no supplies,"

Come ye hither and see the angels. Do they tell their story with groans, and sobs, and sighs? Ah, no; they shout aloud, "Glory to God in the highest." Now, imitate them my dear brethren. If you are professors of religion, try always to have a cheerful carriage. Let others mourn; but

> "Why should the children of a king
> Go mourning all their days?"

Anoint your head and wash your face; appear not unto men to fast. Rejoice in the Lord always, and again I say unto you rejoice. Specially this week be not ashamed to be glad. You need not think it a wicked thing to be happy. Penance and whipping, and misery are no such very virtuous things, after all. The damned are miserable; let the saved be happy. Why should you hold fellowship with the lost by feelings of perpetual mourning? Why not rather anticipate the joys of heaven, and begin to sing on earth that song which you will never need to end? The first emotion then that we ought to cherish in our hearts is the emotion of *joy and gladness.*

Well, what next? Another emotion is that of *confidence.* I am not sure that I

7

am right in calling that an emotion, but still in me it is so much akin to it, that I will venture to be wrong if I be so. Now, if when Christ came on this earth God had sent some black creature down from heaven, (if there be such creatures there) to tell us, "Glory to God in the highest, and on earth peace, good will toward men," and if with a frowning brow and a stammering tongue he delivered his message, if I had been there and heard it, I should have scrupled to believe him, for I should have said, "You don't look like the messenger that God would send—stammering fellow as you are—with such glad news as this." But when the angels came there was no doubting the truth of what they said, because it was quite certain that the angel believed it; they told it as if they did, for they told it with singing, with joy and gladness. If some friend, having heard that a legacy was left you, and should come to you with a solemn countenance, and a tongue like a funeral bell, saying, "Do you know so-and-so has left you £10,000?" Why, you would say, "Ah! I dare say," and laugh in his face. But if your brother should suddenly burst into your room, and exclaim, "I say, what do you think? You are a rich man; So-and-so has left you £10,000!" Why you would say, "I think it is very likely to be true, for he looks so happy over it." Well, when these angels came from heaven they told the news just as if they believed it; and though I have often wickedly doubted my Lord's good will, I think I never could have doubted it while I heard those angels singing. No, I should say, "The messengers themselves are proof of the truth, for it seems they have heard it from God's lips; they have no doubt about it, for see how joyously they tell the news." Now, poor soul, thou that art afraid lest God should destroy thee, and thou thinkest that God will never have mercy upon thee, look at the singing angels and doubt if thou darest. Do not go to the synagogue of long-faced hypocrites to hear the minister who preaches with a nasal twang, with misery in his face, whilst he tells you that God has goodwill towards men; I know you won't believe what he says, for he does not preach with joy in his countenance; he is telling you good news with a grunt, and you are not likely to receive it. But go straightway to the plain where Bethlehem shepherds sat by night, and when you hear the angels singing out the gospel, by the grace of God upon you, you cannot help believing that they manifestly feel the preciousness of telling. Blessed Christmas, that brings such creatures as angels to confirm our faith in God's goodwill to men!

III. I must now bring before you the third point. There are some PROPHETIC UTTERANCES contained in these words. The angels sang "Glory to God in the highest, on earth peace, good will toward men." But I look around, and what see I in the wide, wide world? I do not see God honoured. I see the heathen bowing down before their idols; I mark the Romanist casting himself before the rotten rags of his relics, and the ugly figures of his images. I look about me, and I see tyranny lording it over the bodies and souls of men; I see God forgotten; I see a worldly race pursuing mammon; I see a bloody race pursuing Moloch; I see ambition riding like Nimrod over the land, God forgotten, his name dishonoured. And was this all the angels sang about? Is this all that made them sing "Glory to God in the highest?" Ah! no. There are brighter days approaching. They sang, "Peace on earth." But I hear still the clarion of war; and the cannon's horrid roar: not yet have they turned the sword into a ploughshare, and the spear into a pruning-hook! War still reigns. Is this all that the angels sang about? And whilst I see wars to the ends of the earth, am I to believe that this was all the angels expected? Ah! no, brethren; the angels' song is big with prophecy; it travaileth in birth with glories. A few more years, and he that lives them out shall see why angels sang; a few more years, and he that will come shall come, and will not tarry. Christ the Lord will come again, and when he cometh he shall cast the idols from their thrones; he shall dash down every fashion of heresy and every shape of idolatry; he shall reign from pole to pole with illimitable sway: he shall reign, when like a scroll, yon blue heavens have passed away. No strife shall vex Messiah's reign, no blood shall then be shed; they'll hang the useless helmet high, and study war no more. The hour is approaching when the temple of Janus shall be shut for ever, and when cruel Mars shall be hooted from the earth. The day is coming when the lion shall eat straw like the ox, when the leopard shall lie down with the kid; when the weaned child shall put his hand upon the cockatrice den and play with the asp. The hour approacheth; the first streaks of the sunlight have made glad the age in which we live. Lo, he comes, with trumpets and with clouds of glory; he shall come for whom we look with joyous expectation, whose coming shall be glory to his redeemed, and confusion to his enemies. Ah! brethren, when the angels sang this there was an echo through the long aisles of a glorious future. That echo was—

> " Hallelujah! Christ the Lord
> God Omnipotent shall reign."

Ay, and doubtless the angels heard by faith the fulness of the song,

> " Hark! the song of jubilee
> Loud as mighty thunders' roar,
> Or the fulness of the sea,
> When it breaks upon the shore."

" Christ the Lord Omnipotent reigneth."

IV. Now, I have one more lesson for you, and I have done. That lesson is PRECEPTIVE. I wish everybody that keeps Christmas this year, would keep it as the angels kept it. There are many persons who, when they talk about keeping Christmas, mean by that the cutting of the bands of their religion for one day in the year, as if Christ were the Lord of misrule, as if the birth of Christ should be celebrated like the orgies of Bacchus. There are some very religious people, that on Christmas would never forget to go to church in the morning; they believe Christmas to be nearly as holy as Sunday, for they reverence the tradition of the elders. Yet their way of spending the rest of the day is very remarkable; for if they see their way straight up stairs to their bed at night, it must be by accident. They would not consider they had kept Christmas in a proper manner, if they did not verge on gluttony and drunkenness. They are many who think Christmas cannot possibly be kept, except there be a great shout of merriment and mirth in the house, and added to that the boisterousness of sin. Now, my brethren, although we, as successors of the Puritans, will not keep the day in any religious sense whatever, attaching nothing more to it than to any other day: believing that every day may be a Christmas for ought we know, and wishing to make every day Christmas, if we can, yet we must try to set an example to others how to behave on that day; and especially since the angels gave glory to God: let us do the same.

Once more the angels said, "Peace to men:" let us labour if we can to make peace next Christmas day. Now, old gentleman, you won't take your son in: he has offended you. Fetch him at Christmas. "Peace on earth;" you know: that is a Christmas Carol. Make peace in your family.

Now, brother, you have made a vow that you will never speak to your brother again. Go after him and say, " Oh, my dear fellow, let not this day's sun go down upon our wrath." Fetch him in, and give him your hand. Now, Mr. Tradesman, you have an opponent in trade, and you have said some very hard words about him lately. If you do not make the matter up to-day, or to-morrow, or as soon as you can, yet do it on that day. That is the way to keep Christmas, peace on earth and glory to God. And oh, if thou hast anything on thy conscience, any-thing that prevents thy having peace of mind, keep thy Christmas in thy chamber, praying to God to give thee peace; for it is peace on earth, mind, peace in thyself peace with thyself, peace with thy fellow men, peace with thy God. And do not think thou hast well celebrated that day till thou canst say, " O God,

> With the world, myself, and thee
> I ere I sleep at peace will be.' "

And when the Lord Jesus has become your peace, remember, there is another thing, *good will* towards men. Do not try to keep Christmas without keeping good will towards men. You are a gentleman, and have servants. Well, try and set their chimneys on fire with a large piece of good, substantial beef for them. If you are men of wealth, you have poor in your neighbourhood. Find something wherewith to clothe the naked, and feed the hungry, and make glad the mourner. Remember, it is good will towards men. Try, if you can, to show them goodwill at this special season; and if you will do that, the poor will say with me, that indeed they wish there were six Christmases in the year.

Let each one of us go from this place determined, that if we are angry all the year round, this next week shall be an exception; that if we have snarled at everybody last year, this Christmas time we will strive to be kindly affectionate to others; and if we have lived all this year at enmity with God, I pray that by his Spirit he may this week give us peace with him; and then, indeed, my brother, it will be the merriest Christmas we ever had in all our lives. You are going home to your father and mother, young men; many of you are going from your shops to your homes. You remember what I preached on last Christmas time. Go home to thy friends, and tell them what the Lord hath done for thy soul, and that will make a blessed round of stories at the Christmas fire. If you will each of you tell your parents how the Lord met with you in the house of prayer; how, when you left home, you were a gay, wild blade, but have now come back to love your mother's God, and read your father's Bible. Oh, what a happy Christmas that will make! What more shall I say? May God give you peace with yourselves; may he give you good will towards all your friends, your enemies, and your neighbours; and may he give you grace to give glory to God in the highest. I will say no more, except at the close of this sermon to wish every one of you, when the day shall come, the happiest Christmas you ever had in your lives.

> " Now with angels round the throne,
> Cherubim and seraphim,
> And the church, which still is one,
> Let us swell the solemn hymn;
> Glory to the great I AM !
> Glory to the Victim Lamb.
>
> Blessing, honour, glory, might,
> And dominion infinite,
> To the Father of our Lord,
> To the Spirit and the Word;
> As it was all worlds before,
> Is, and shall be evermore "

A Christmas Question

" For unto us a child is born, unto us a Son is given."—Isaiah ix. 6.

UPON other occasions I have explained the main part of this verse—" the government shall be upon his shoulders, his name shall be called Wonderful, Counsellor, the Mighty God." If God shall spare me, on some future occasion I hope to take the other titles, "The Everlasting Father, the Prince of Peace." But now this morning the portion which will engage our attention is this, " Unto us a child is born, unto us a Son is given." The sentence is a double one, but it has in it no tautology. The careful reader will soon discover a distinction; and it is not a distinction without a difference. " Unto us a *child* is *born*, unto us a *Son* is *given*." As Jesus Christ is a child in his human nature, he is born, begotten of the Holy Ghost, born of the Virgin Mary. He is as truly born, as certainly a child, as any other man that ever lived upon the face of the earth. He is thus in his humanity a child born. But as Jesus Christ is God's Son, he is not born, but given, begotten of his Father from before all worlds, begotten—not made, being of the same substance with the Father. The doctrine of the eternal affiliation of Christ is to be received as an undoubted truth of our holy religion. But as to any explanation of it, no man should venture thereon, for it remaineth among the deep things of God—one of those solemn mysteries indeed, into which the angels dare not look, nor do they desire to pry into it—a mystery which we must not attempt to fathom, for it is utterly beyond the grasp of any finite being. As well might a gnat seek to drink in the ocean, as a finite creature to comprehend the Eternal God. A God whom we could understand would be no God. If we could grasp him he could not be infinite: if we could understand him, then were he not divine. Jesus Christ then, I say, as a Son, is not born to us, but given. He is a boon bestowed on us, " For God so loved the world, that he *sent* his only begotten *Son* into the world." He was not born in this world as God's Son, but he was *sent*, or was given, so that you clearly perceive that the distinction is a suggestive one, and conveys much good truth to us. " Unto us *a child* is *born*, unto us a *Son* is *given*."

This morning, however, the principal object of my discourse, and, indeed, the sole one, is to bring out the force of those two little words, " *unto us.*" For you will perceive that here the full force of the passage lies. " For UNTO US a child is born, UNTO US a Son is given." The divisions of my discourse are very simple ones. First, *is it so?* Secondly, *if it is so, what then?* Thirdly, *if it is not so, what then?*

11

I. In the first place, Is IT so? Is it true that *unto us* a child is born, *unto us* a Son is given? It is a fact that a child is born. Upon that I use no argument. We receive it as a fact, more fully established than any other fact in history, that the Son of God became man, was born at Bethlehem, wrapped in swaddling clothes, and laid in a manger. It is a fact, too, that a Son is given. About that we have no question. The infidel may dispute, but we, professing to be believers in Scripture, receive it as an undeniable truth, that God has given his only begotten Son to be the Saviour of men. But THE matter of question is this. Is this child born to us? Is he given to us? This is the matter of anxious enquiry. Have we a personal interest in the child that was born at Bethlehem? Do we know that he is our Saviour?—that he has brought glad tidings to us?—that to us he belongs? and that we belong to him? I say this is matter of very grave and solemn investigation. It is a very observable fact, that the very best of men are sometimes troubled with questions with regard to their own interest in Christ, while men who never are troubled at all about the matter are very frequently presumptuous deceivers, who have no part in this matter. I have often observed that some of the people about whom I felt most sure, were the very persons who were the least sure of themselves. It reminds me of the history of a godly man named Simon Brown, a minister in the olden times in the City of London. He became so extremely sad in heart, so depressed in spirit, that at last he conceived the idea that his soul was annihilated. It was all in vain to talk to the good man, you could not persuade him that he had a soul; but all the time he was preaching, and praying, and working, more like a man that had two souls than none. When he preached, his eyes poured forth plenteous floods of tears, and when he prayed, there was a divine fervour and heavenly prevalence in every petition. Now so it is with many Christians. They seem to be the very picture of godliness; their life is admirable, and their conversation heavenly, but yet they are always crying,—

> " 'Tis a point I long to know,
>   Oft it causes anxious thought,
> Do I love the Lord or no?
>   Am I his or am I not? "

So does it happen, that the best of men will question while the worst of men will presume. Ay, I have seen the men about whose eternal destiny I had serious questioning, whose inconsistencies in life were palpable and glaring, who have prated concerning their sure portion in Israel, and their infallible hope, as though they believed others to be as easily duped as themselves. Now, what reason shall we give for this foolhardiness? Learn it from this illustration: You see a number of men riding along a narrow road upon the edge of the sea. It is a very perilous path, for the way is rugged and a tremendous precipice bounds the pathway on the left. Let but the horse's foot slip once, and they dash downwards to destruction. See how cautiously the riders journey, at what carefully the horses place their feet. But do you observe yon rider, at what a rate he dashes along, as if he were riding a steeple-chase with Satan? You hold up your hands in an agony of fear, trembling lest every moment his horse's foot should slip, and he should be dashed down; and you say, why so careless a rider? The man is a blind rider on a blind horse. They cannot see where they are. He thinks he is on a sure road, and therefore it is that he rides so fast. Or to vary the picture; sometimes when persons are asleep, they take to walking, and they will climb where others will not think of venturing. Giddy heights that would turn our brain seem safe enough to them. So there be many spiritual sleep-walkers in our midst, who think that they are awake. But they are not. Their very presumption in venturing to the high places of self-confidence, proves that they are somnambulists; not awake, but men who walk and talk in their sleep. It is, then, I say, really a matter of serious questioning with all men who would be right at last, as to whether this child is born to us, and this Son given to us?

I shall now help you to answer the question.

1. If this child who now lies before the eyes of your faith, wrapped in swaddling clothes in Bethlehem's manger, is born *to you*, my hearer, then *you are born again!* For this child is not born to you unless you are born to this child. All who have an interest in Christ are, in the fulness of time, by grace converted, quickened, and renewed. All the redeemed are not yet converted, but they will be. Before the hour of death arrives their nature shall be changed, their sins shall be washed

away, and they shall pass from death unto life. If any man tells me that Christ is his Redeemer, although he has never experienced regeneration, that man utters what he does not know; his religion is vain, and his hope is a delusion. Only men who are born again can claim the babe in Bethlehem as being theirs. "But," saith one, "how am I to know whether I am born again or not?" Answer this question also by another: Has there been a change effected by divine grace *within you?* Are your loves the very opposite of what they were? Do you now hate the vain things you once admired, and do you seek after that precious pearl which you at one time despised? Is your heart thoroughly renewed in its object? Can you say that the bent of your desire is changed? that your face is Zionward, and your feet set upon the path of grace? that whereas your heart once longed for deep draughts of sin, it now longs to be holy? and whereas you once loved the pleasures of the world, they have now become as draff and dross to you, for you only love the pleasures of heavenly things, and are longing to enjoy more of them on earth, that you may be prepared to enjoy a fulness of them hereafter? Are you renewed within? For mark, my hearer, the new birth does not consist in washing the outside of the cup and platter, but in cleansing the inner man. It is all in vain to put up the stone upon the sepulchre, wash it extremely white, and garnish it with the flowers of the season; the sepulchre itself must be cleansed. The dead man's bones that lie in that charnel-house of the human heart must be cleansed away. Nay, they must be made to live. The heart must no longer be a tomb of death, but a temple of life. Is it so with you, my hearer? For recollect, you may be very different in the outward, but if you are not changed in the inward, this child is not born to you.

But I put another question. Although the main matter of regeneration lies within, yet it manifests itself without. Say, then, has there been a change in you in the exterior? Do you think that others who look at you would be compelled to say, this man is not what he used to be? Do not your companions observe a change? Have they not laughed at you for what they think to be your hypocrisy, your puritanism, your sternness? Do you think now that if an angel should follow you into your secret life, should track you to your closet and see you on your knees, that he would detect something in you which he could never have seen before? For, mark, my dear hearer, there must be a change in the outward life, or else there is no change within. In vain you bring me to the tree, and say that the tree's nature is changed. If I still see it bringing forth wild grapes, it is a wild vine still. And if I mark upon you the apples of Sodom and the grapes of Gomorrah, you are still a tree accursed and doomed, notwithstanding all your fancied experience. The proof of the Christian is in the living. To other men, the proof of our conversion is not what you feel, but what you do. To yourself your feelings may be good enough evidence, but to the minister and others who judge of you, the outward walk is the main guide. At the same time, let me observe that a man's outward life may be very much like that of a Christian, and yet there may be no religion in him at all. Have you ever seen two jugglers in the street with swords, pretending to fight with one another. See how they cut, and slash, and hack at one another, till you are half afraid there will soon be murder done. They seem to be so very much in earnest that you are half in the mind to call in the police to part them. See with what violence that one has aimed a terrific blow at the other one's head, which his comrade dexterously warded off by keeping a well-timed guard. Just watch them a minute, and you will see that all these cuts and thrusts come in a pre-arranged order. There is no heart in the fighting after all. They do not fight so roughly as they would if they were real enemies. So, sometimes I have seen a man pretending to be very angry against sin. But watch him a little while, and you will see it is only a fencer's trick. He does not give his cuts out of order, there is no earnestness in his blows; it is all pretence, it is only mimic stage-play. The fencers, after they have ended their performance, shake hands with one another, and divide the coppers which the gaping throng have given them; and so does this man do, he shakes hands with the devil in private, and the two deceivers share the spoil. The hypocrite and the devil are very good friends after all, and they mutually rejoice over their profits: the devil leering because he has won the soul of the professor, and the hypocrite laughing because he has won his pelf. Take care, then, that your outward life is not a mere stage-play, but that your antagonism to sin is real and intense; and that you strike right and left, as though you meant to slay the monster, and cast its limbs to the winds of heaven.

13

I will just put another question. If thou hast been born again, there is another matter by which to try thee. Not only is thy inward self altered, and thy outward self too, but the very root and principle of thy life must become totally new. When we are in sin we live to self, but when we are renewed we live to God. While we are unregenerate, our principle is to seek our own pleasure, our own advancement; but that man is not truly born again who does not live with a far different aim from this. Change a man's principles, and you change his feelings, you change his actions. Now, grace changes the principles of man. It lays the axe at the root of the tree. It does not saw away at some big limb, it does not try to alter the sap; but it gives a new root, and plants us in fresh soil. The man's inmost self, the deep rocks of his principles upon which the topsoil of his actions rest, the soul of his manhood is thoroughly changed, and he is a new creature in Christ. "But," says one, "I see no reason why I should be born again." Ah, poor creature, it is because thou hast never seen thyself. Didst thou ever see a man in the looking-glass of the Word of God—what a strange monster he is. Do you know, a man by nature has his heart where his feet ought to be:—that is to say, his heart is set upon the earth, whereas he ought to be treading it beneath his feet; and stranger mystery still, his heels are where his heart should be:—that is to say, he is kicking against the God of heaven when he ought to be setting his affections on things above. Man by nature when he sees clearest, only looks down, can only see that which is beneath him, he cannot see the things which are above; and strange to say the sunlight of heaven blinds him; light from heaven he looks not for. He asks for his light in darkness. The earth is to him his heaven, and he sees suns in its muddy pools and stars in its filth. He is, in fact, a man turned upside down. The fall has so ruined our nature, that the most monstrous thing on the face of the earth is a fallen man. The ancients used to paint griffins, gryphons, dragons, chimeras, and all kinds of hideous things; but if a skilful hand could paint *man* accurately, none of us would look at the picture, for it is a sight that none ever saw except the lost in hell; and that is one part of their intolerable pain, that they are compelled always to look upon themselves. Now, then, see you not that ye must be born again, and unless ye are so this child is not born *to you.*

2. But I go forward. If this child is born to you, you are a *child*, and the question arises, are you so? Man grows from childhood up to manhood naturally; in grace men grow from manhood down to childhood; and the nearer we come to true childhood, the nearer we come to the image of Christ. For was not Christ called "a child," even after he had ascended up to heaven? "Thy holy child Jesus." Brethren and sisters, can you say that you have been made into children? Do you take God's Word just as it stands, simply because your heavenly Father says so? Are you content to believe mysteries without demanding to have them explained? Are you ready to sit in the infant class, and be a little one? Are you willing to hang upon the breast of the church, and suck in the unadulterated milk of the Word—never questioning for a moment what your divine Lord reveals, but believing it on his own authority, whether it seemed to be above reason, or beneath reason, or even contrary to reason? Now, "except ye be converted and become as little children," this child is not born to you; except like a child you are humble, teachable, obedient, pleased with your Father's will and willing to assign all to him, there is grave matter of question whether this child is born *to you.* But what a pleasing sight it is to see a man converted and made into a little child. Many times has my heart leaped for joy, when I have seen a giant infidel who used to reason against Christ, who had not a word in his dictionary bad enough for Christ's people, come by divine grace to believe the gospel. That man sits down and weeps, feels the full power of salvation, and from that time drops all his questionings, becomes the very reverse of what he was. He thinks himself meaner than the meanest believer. He is content to do the meanest work for the church of Christ, and takes his station—not with Locke or Newton, as a mighty Christian philosopher—but with Mary as a simple learner, sitting at Jesus' feet, to hear and learn of him. If ye are not children, then this child is not born to you.

3. And now let us take the second sentence and put a question or two upon that. Is this son given to us? I pause a minute to beg your personal attention. I am trying, if I may, so to preach that I may make you all question yourselves. I pray you let not one of you exempt himself from the ordeal, but let each one ask himself, is it true that unto me a Son is given? Now, if this Son is given *to you, you are a son yourself.* "For unto as many as received him to them gave he power to become

the sons of God." "Christ became a Son that in all things he might be made like unto his brethren." The Son of God is not mine to enjoy, to love, to delight in, unless I am a son of God too. Now, my hearer, have you a *fear* of God before your eyes—a filial fear, a fear which a child has lest it should grieve its parent? Say, have you a child's *love* to God? Do you *trust* to him as your father, your provider, and your friend? Have you in your breast "The spirit of adoption, whereby we cry, Abba, Father?" Are there times with you when on your knees you can say, "My Father and my God." Does the Spirit bear witness with your spirit that you are born of God? and while this witness is borne, does your heart fly up to your Father and to your God, in ecstacy of delight to clasp him who long ago hath clasped you in the covenant of his love, in the arms of his effectual grace? Now, mark my hearer, if thou dost not sometimes enjoy the spirit of adoption, if thou art not a son or daughter of Zion, then deceive not thyself, this Son is not given to thee.

4. And, then, to put it in another shape. If unto us a Son is given, then *we are given to the Son.* Now, what say you to this question also? Are you given up to Christ? Do you feel that you have nothing on earth to live for but to glorify him? Can you say in your heart, " Great God, if I be not deceived I am wholly thine?" Are you ready to-day to write over again your consecration vow? Canst thou say, "Take me! All that I am and all I have, shall be for ever thine. I would give up all my goods, all my powers, all my time, and all my hours; and thine I would be—wholly thine." " Ye are not your own: ye are bought with a price." And if this Son of God be given to you, you will have consecrated yourself wholly to him; and you will feel that his honour is your life's object, that his glory is the one great desire of your panting spirit. Now is it so, my hearer? Ask thyself the question. I pray thee, and do not deceive thyself in the answer.

I will just repeat the four different proofs again. If unto me a child is born, then I have been born again; and, moreover, I am now in consequence of that new birth, a child. If, again, a Son has been given to me, then I am a son; and again I am given to that Son who is given to me. I have tried to put these tests in the way that the text would suggest them. I pray you carry them home with you. If you do not recollect the words, yet do recollect to search yourselves, and see, my hearers, whether you can say, " Unto me this Son is given." For, indeed, if Christ is not my Christ, he is of little worth to me. If I cannot say he loved me and gave himself *for me,* of what avail is all the merit of his righteousness, or all the pleni-tude of his atonement? Bread in the shop is well enough, but if I am hungry and cannot get it, I starve although granaries be full. Water in the river is well enough, but if I am in a desert and cannot reach the stream, if I can hear it in the distance and am yet lying down to die of thirst, the murmuring of the rill, or the flowing of the river, helps to tantalize me, while I die in dark despair. Better for you, my hearers to have perished as Hottentots, to have gone down to your graves as dwellers in some benighted land, than to live where the name of Christ is continually hymned, and where his glory is extolled, and yet to go down to your tombs without an in-terest in him, unblessed by his gospel, unwashed in his blood, unclothed of his robe of righteousness. God help you, that you may be blessed in him, and may sing sweetly, " Unto us a child is born, unto us a Son is given."

II. This brings me to my second head, upon which I shall be brief. **Is it so?** **If it is so, what then?** *If it is so, why am I doubtful to-day?* Why is my spirit questioning? Why do I not realize the fact? My hearer, if the Son be given to thee, how is it that thou art this day asking whether thou art Christ's or not? Why dost thou not labour to make thy calling and election sure? Why tarriest thou in the plains of doubt? Get thee up, get thee up to the high mountains of confidence, and never rest till thou canst say without a fear that thou art mistaken, " I know that my Redeemer liveth. I am persuaded that he is able to keep that which I have committed to him." I may have a large number of persons here to whom it is a matter of uncertainty as to whether Christ is theirs or not. Oh, my dear hearers, rest not content unless you know assuredly that Christ is yours, and that you are Christ's. Suppose you should see in to-morrow's newspaper, (although, by the way, if you believed anything you saw there you would probably be mis-taken) but suppose you should see a notification that some rich man had left you an immense estate. Suppose, as you read it, you were well aware that the person mentioned was a relative of yours, and that it was likely to be true. It may be you have prepared to-morrow for a family meeting, and you are expecting brother

John and sister Mary and their little ones to dine with you. But I very much question whether you would not be away from the head of the table to go and ascertain whether the fact were really so. "Oh," you would say, "I am sure I should enjoy my Christmas dinner all the better if I were quite sure about this matter;" and all day, if you did not go, you would be on the tip-toe of expectation; you would be, as it were, sitting upon pins and needles until you knew whether it were the fact or not. Now there is a proclamation gone forth to-day, and it is a true one, too, that Jesus Christ has come into the world to save sinners. The question with you is whether he has saved you, and whether you have an interest in him. I beseech you, give no sleep to your eyes, and no slumber to your eyelids, till you have read your "title clear to mansions in the skies." What, man! shall your eternal destiny be a matter of uncertainty to you? What! is heaven or hell involved in this matter, and will you rest until you know which of these shall be your everlasting portion? Are you content while it is a question whether God loves you, or whether he is angry with you? Can you be easy while you remain in doubt as to whether you are condemned in sin, or justified by faith which is in Christ Jesus? Get thee up, man; I beseech thee by the living God, and by thine own soul's safety, get thee up and read the records. Search and look, and try and test thyself, to see whether it be so or not. For if it be so, why should not we know it? If the Son is given to me, why should not I be sure of it? If the child is born to me, why should I not know it for a certainty, that I may even now live in the enjoyment of my privilege—a privilege, the value of which I shall never know to the full, till I arrive in glory?

Again, if it be so, another question. *Why are we sad?* I am looking upon faces just now that appear the very reverse of gloomy, but mayhap the smile covers an aching heart. Brother and sister, why are we sad this morning, if unto us a child is born, if unto us a Son is given? Hark, hark to the cry! It is "Harvest home! Harvest home!" See the maidens as they dance, and the young men as they make merry. And why is this mirth? Because they are storing the precious fruits of the earth, they are gathering together unto their barns wheat which will soon be consumed. And what, brothers and sisters, have we the bread which endureth to eternal life and are we unhappy? Does the worldling rejoice when his corn is increased, and do we not rejoice when, "Unto us a child is born, and unto us a Son is given?" Hark, yonder! What means the firing of the Tower guns? Why all this ringing of bells in the church steeples, as if all London were mad with joy? There is a prince born; therefore there is this salute, and therefore are the bells ringing. Ah, Christians, ring the bells of your hearts, fire the salute of your most joyous songs, " For unto us a child is born, unto us a Son is given." Dance, O my heart, and ring out peals of gladness! Ye drops of blood within my veins, dance every one of you! Oh! all my nerves become harp strings, and let gratitude touch you with angelic fingers! And thou, my tongue, shout—shout to his praise, who hath said to thee—" Unto thee a child is born, unto thee a Son is given." Wipe that tear away! Come, stop that sighing! Hush yon murmuring. What matters your poverty? " Unto you a child is born." What matters your sickness? " Unto you a Son is given." What matters your sin? For this child shall take the sin away, and this Son shall wash and make you fit for heaven. I say, if it be so,

> " Lift up the heart, lift up the voice,
> Rejoice aloud! ye saints rejoice!"

But, once more, if it be so, what then? *Why are our hearts so cold?* and why is it that we do so little for him who has done so much for us? Jesus, art thou mine! Am I saved? How is it that I love thee so little? Why is it that when I preach I am not more in earnest, and when I pray I am not more intensely fervent? How is it that we give so little to Christ who gave himself for us? How is it that we serve him so sadly who served us so perfectly? He consecrated himself wholly; how is it that our consecration is marred and partial? We are continually sacrificing to self and not to him?

O beloved brethren, yield yourselves up this morning. What have you got in the world? "Oh," saith one, " I have nothing; I am poor and penniless, and all but houseless." Give thyself to Christ. You have heard the story of the pupils to a Greek philosopher. On a certain day it was the custom to give to the philosopher a present. One came and gave him gold. Another could not bring him gold but brought him silver. One brought him a robe, and another some delicacy for food. But one of them came up, and said, " Oh, Solon, I am poor, I have nothing to give to thee, but yet I will give thee something better than all these have given; I give thee myself." Now, if you have gold and silver, if you have aught of this world's goods, give in your measure to Christ; but take care, above all, that you give yourself to him, and let your cry be from this day forth,

> " Do not I love thee dearest Lord?
> Oh search my heart and see,
> And turn each cursed idol out
> That dares to rival thee.
>
> Do not I love thee from my soul?
> Then let me nothing love:
> Dead be my heart to every joy,
> When Jesus cannot move."

III. Well, now I have all but done, but give your solemn, very solemn attention, while I come to my last head:—IF IT IS NOT SO, WHAT THEN ? Dear hearer, I cannot tell where thou art—but wherever thou mayst be in this hall, the eyes of my heart are looking for thee, that when they have seen thee, they may weep over thee. Ah! miserable wretch, without a hope, without Christ, without God. Unto thee there is no Christmas mirth; for thee no child is born; to thee no Son is given. Sad is the story of the poor men and women, who during the week before last fell down dead in our streets through cruel hunger and bitter cold. But far more pitiable is thy lot, far more terrible shall be thy condition in the day when thou shalt cry for a drop of water to cool thy burning tongue, and it shall be denied thee; when thou shalt seek for death, for grim cold death—seek for him as for a friend, and yet thou shalt not find him. For the fire of hell shall not consume thee, nor its terrors devour thee. Thou shalt long to die, yet shalt thou linger in eternal death—dying every hour, yet never receiving the much coveted boon of death. What shall I say to thee this morning? Oh! Master, help me to speak a word in season, now. I beseech thee, my hearer, if Christ is not thine this morning, may God the Spirit help thee to do what I now command thee to do. First of all, confess thy sins; not into my ear, nor into the ear of any living man. Go to thy chamber and confess that thou art vile. Tell him thou art a wretch undone without his sovereign grace. But do not think there is any merit in confession. There is none. All your confession cannot merit forgiveness, though God has promised to pardon the man who confesses his sin and forsakes it. Imagine that some creditor had a debtor who owed him a thousand pounds. He calls upon him, and says, "I demand my money." But, says the other, "I owe you nothing." That man will be arrested and thrown into prison. However, his creditor says, "I wish to deal mercifully with you; make a frank confession, and I will forgive you all the debt." " Well," says the man, "I do acknowledge that I owe you two hundred pounds." "No," says he, "that will not do." "Well, sir, I confess I owe you five hundred pounds;" and by degrees he comes to confess that he owes the thousand. Is there any merit in that confession? No; but yet you could see that no creditor would think of forgiving a debt which was not acknowledged. It is the least that you can do, to acknowledge your sin; and though there be no merit in the confession, yet true to his promise, God will give you pardon through Christ. That is one piece of advice. I pray you take it. Do not throw it to the winds; do not leave it as soon as you get out of Exeter Hall. Take it with you, and may this day become a confession-day with many of you. But next, when you have made a confession, I beseech you renounce yourself. You have been resting perhaps in some hope that you would make yourself better, and so save yourself. Give up that delusive fancy. You have seen the silk-worm: it will spin, and spin, and spin, and then it will die where it has spun itself a shroud. And your good works are but a spinning for yourself a robe for your dead soul. You can do nothing by your best prayers, your best tears, or your best works, to merit eternal life. Why, the Christian who is converted to God, will tell you that he cannot live a holy life by himself. If the ship in the sea cannot steer itself aright, do you think the wood that lies in the carpenter's yard can put itself together, and make itself into a ship, and then go out to sea and sail to America? Yet, this is just what you imagine. The Christian who is God's workmanship can do nothing, and yet you

17

think you can do something. Now, give up *self.* God help you to strike a black mark through every idea of what you can do.

Then, lastly, and I pray God help you here my dear hearers, when thou hast confessed thy sin and given up all hope of self-salvation, go to the place where Jesus died in agony. Go then in meditation to Calvary. There he hangs. It is the middle cross of these three. Methinks I see him now. I see his poor face emaciated, and his visage more marred than that of any man. I see the beady drops of blood still standing round his pierced temples—marks of that rugged thorn-crown. Ah, I see his body naked—naked to his shame. We may tell all his bones. See there his hands rent with the rough iron, and his feet torn with the nails. The nails have rent through his flesh. There is now not only the hole through which the nail was driven, but the weight of his body has sunken upon his feet, and see the iron is tearing through his flesh. And now the weight of his body hangs upon his arms, and the nails there are rending through the tender nerves. Hark! earth is startled! He cries, "Eli, Eli, lama sabachthani?" Oh, sinner, was ever shriek like that? God hath forsaken him. His God has ceased to be gracious to him. His soul is exceedingly sorrowful, even unto death. But hark, again, he cries, "I thirst!" Give him water! give him water! Ye holy women let him drink. But no, his murderers torture him. They thrust into his mouth the vinegar mingled with gall—the bitter with the sharp, the vinegar and the gall. At last, hear him, sinner, for here is your hope. I see him bow his awful head. The King of heaven dies. The God who made the earth has become a man, and the man is about to expire. Hear him! He cries, "It is finished!" and he gives up the ghost. The atonement is finished, the price is paid, the bloody ransom counted down, the sacrifice is accepted. "It is finished!" Sinner, believe in Christ. Cast thyself on him. Sink or swim, take him to be thy all in all. Throw now thy trembling arms around that bleeding body. Sit now at the feet of that cross, and feel the dropping of the precious blood. And as you go out each one of you say in your hearts,

> " A guilty, weak, and helpless worm,
> On Christ's kind arms I fall,
> He is my strength and righteousness,
> My Jesus, and my all."

God grant you grace to do so for Jesus Christ's sake. May the grace of our Lord Jesus Christ, and the love of God, and the fellowship of the Holy Ghost, be with you all, for ever and ever. Amen and Amen.

No Room for Christ in the Inn

"And she brought forth her firstborn son, and wrapped him in swaddling clothes, and laid him in a manger ; because there was no room for them in the inn."—Luke ii. 7.

IT was needful that it should be distinctly proven, beyond all dispute, that our Lord sprang out of Judah. It was necessary, also, that he should be born in Bethlehem-Ephratah, according to the word of the Lord which he spake by his servant Micah. But how could a public recognition of the lineage of an obscure carpenter and an unknown maiden be procured? What interest could the keepers of registers be supposed to take in two such humble persons? As for the second matter, Mary lived at Nazareth in Galilee, and there seemed every probability that the birth would take place there; indeed, the period of her delivery was so near that, unless absolutely compelled, she would not be likely to undertake a long and tedious journey to the southern province of Judea. How are these two matters to be arranged? Can one turn of the wheel effect two purposes? It can be done! It shall be done! The official stamp of the Roman empire shall be affixed to the pedigree of the coming Son of David, and Bethlehem shall behold his nativity. A little tyrant, Herod, by some show of independent spirit, offends the greater tyrant, Augustus. Augustus informs him that he shall no longer treat him as a friend, but as a vassal; and albeit Herod makes the most abject submission, and his friends at the Roman court intercede for him, yet Augustus, to show his displeasure, orders a census to be taken of all the Jewish people, in readiness for a contemplated taxation, which, however, was not carried out till some ten years after. Even the winds and waves are not more fickle than a tyrant's will; but the Ruler of tempests knoweth how to rule the perverse spirits of princes. The Lord our God has a bit for the wildest war horse, and a hook for the most terrible leviathan. Autocratical Cæsars are but puppets moved with invisible strings, mere drudges to the King of kings. Augustus must be made offended with Herod; he is constrained to tax the people; it is imperative that a census be taken; nay, it is of necessity that inconvenient, harsh, and tyrannical regulations should be published, and every person must repair to the town to which he was reputed to belong; thus, Mary is brought to Bethlehem, Jesus Christ is born as appointed, and, moreover, he is recognised officially as being descended from David by the fact that his mother came to Bethlehem as being of that lineage, remained there, and returned to Galilee without having her claims questioned, although the jealousy of all the women of the clan would have been aroused had an intruder ventured to claim a place among the few females to whom the birth of Messias was now by express prophecies confined. Remark here the wisdom of a God of providence, and believe that all things are ordered well.

When all persons of the house of David were thus driven to Bethlehem, the scanty accommodation of the little town would soon be exhausted. Doubtless friends entertained their friends till their houses were all full, but Joseph had no such willing kinsmen in the town. There was the caravanserai, which was provided in every village, where free accommodation was given to travellers; this, too, was full, for coming from a distance, and compelled to travel slowly, the humble couple had arrived late in the day. The rooms within the great brick square were already occupied with families; there remained no better lodging, even for a woman in travail, than one of the meaner spaces appropriated to beasts of burden. The stall of the ass was the only place where the child could be born. By hanging a curtain at its front, and perhaps tethering the animal on the outer side to block the paassge, the needed seclusion could be obtained, and here, in the stable, was the King of Glory born, and in the manger was he laid.

My business this morning is to lead your meditations to the stable at Bethlehem, that you may see this great sight—the Saviour in the manger, and think over the reason for this lowly couch—" because there was no room for them in the inn."

I. I shall commence by remarking that THERE WERE OTHER REASONS WHY CHRIST SHOULD BE LAID IN THE MANGER.

1. I think it was intended thus *to show forth his humiliation.* He came, according to prophecy, to be "despised and rejected of men, a man of sorrows and acquainted with grief;" he was to be "without form or comeliness," "a root out of a dry ground." Would it have been fitting that the man who was to die naked on the cross should be robed in purple at his birth? Would it not have been inappropriate that the Redeemer who was to be buried in a borrowed tomb should be born anywhere but in the humblest shed, and housed anywhere but in the most ignoble manner? The manger and the cross standing at the two extremities of the Saviour's earthly life seem most fit and congruous the one to the other. He is to wear through life a peasant's garb; he is to associate with fishermen; the lowly are to be his disciples; the cold mountains are often to be his only bed; he is to say, "Foxes have holes, and the birds of the air have nests, but the Son of Man hath not where to lay his head;" nothing, therefore, could be more fitting than that in his season of humiliation, when he laid aside all his glory, and took upon himself the form of a servant, and condescended even to the meanest estate, he should be laid in a manger.

2. By being in a manger *he was declared to be the king of the poor.* They, doubtless, were at once able to recognise his relationship to them, from the position in which they found him. I believe it excited feelings of the tenderest brotherly kindness in the minds of the shepherds, when

the angel said—"This shall be a sign unto you; you shall find the child wrapped in swaddling-clothes and lying in a manger." In the eyes of the poor, imperial robes excite no affection, but a man in their own garb attracts their confidence. With what pertinacity will working-men cleave to a leader of their own order, believing in him because he knows their toils, sympathizes in their sorrows, and feels an interest in all their concerns. Great commanders have readily won the hearts of their soldiers by sharing their hardships and roughing it as if they belonged to the ranks. The King of Men who was born in Bethlehem, was not exempted in his infancy from the common calamities of the poor, nay, his lot was even worse than theirs. I think I hear the shepherds comment on the manger-birth, "Ah!" said one to his fellow, "then he will not be like Herod the tyrant; he will remember the manger and feel for the poor; poor helpless infant, I feel a love for him even now, what miserable accommodation this cold world yields its Saviour; it is not a Cæsar that is born to-day; he will never trample down our fields with his armies, or slaughter our flocks for his courtiers, he will be the poor man's friend, the people's monarch; according to the words of our shepherd-king, he shall judge the poor of the people; he shall save the children of the needy." Surely the shepherds, and such as they—the poor of the earth, perceived at once that here was the plebeian king; noble in descent, but still as the Lord hath called him, "one chosen out of the people." Great Prince of Peace! the manger was thy royal cradle! Therein wast thou presented to all nations as Prince of our race, before whose presence there is neither barbarian, Scythian, bond nor free ; but thou art Lord of all. Kings, your gold and silver would have been lavished on him if ye had known the Lord of Glory, but inasmuch as ye knew him not he was declared with demonstration to be a leader and a witness to the people. The things which are not, under him shall bring to nought the things that are, and the things that are despised which God hath chosen, shall under his leadership break in pieces the might, and pride, and majesty of human grandeur.

3. Further, in thus being laid in a manger, he did, as it were, *give an invitation to the most humble to come to him.* We might tremble to approach a throne, but we cannot fear to approach a manger. Had we seen the Master at first riding in state through the streets of Jerusalem with garments laid in the way, and the palm-branches strewed, and the people crying, "Hosanna!" we might have thought, though even the thought would have been wrong, that he was not approachable. Even there, riding upon a colt the foal of an ass, he was so meek and lowly, that the young children clustered about him with their boyish "Hosanna!" Never could there be a being more approachable than Christ. No rough guards pushed poor petitioners away; no array of officious friends were allowed to keep off the importunate widow or the man who clamoured that his son might be made whole ; the hem of his garment was always trailing where sick folk could reach it, and he himself had a hand always ready to touch the disease, an ear to catch the faintest accents of misery, a soul going forth everywhere in rays of mercy, even as the light of the sun streams on every side beyond that orb itself. By being laid in a manger he proved himself a priest taken from among men, one who has suffered like his brethren, and therefore

can be touched with a feeling of our infirmities. Of him it was said "He doth eat and drink with publicans and sinners;" "this man receiveth sinners and eateth with them." Even as an infant, by being laid in a manger, he was set forth as the sinner's friend. Come to him, ye that are weary and heavy-laden! Come to him, ye that are broken in spirit, ye who are bowed down in soul! Come to him, ye that despise yourselves and are despised of others! Come to him, publican and harlot! Come to him, thief and drunkard! In the manger there he lies, unguarded from your touch and unshielded from your gaze. Bow the knee, and kiss the Son of God; accept him as your Saviour, for he puts himself into that manger that you may approach him. The throne of Solomon might awe you, but the manger of the Son of David must invite you.

4. Methinks there was yet another mystery. You remember, brethren, that this place was *free to all;* it was an inn, and please to remember the inn in this case was not like our hotels, where accommodation and provision must be paid for. In the early and simple ages of the world every man considered it an honour to entertain a stranger; afterwards, as travelling became more common, many desired to shift the honour and pleasure upon their neighbours; wherefore should they engross all the dignity of hospitality? Further on still, some one person was appointed in each town and village, and was expected to entertain strangers in the name of the rest; but, as the ages grew less simple, and the pristine glow of brotherly love cooled down, the only provision made was the erection of a huge square block, arranged in rooms for the travellers, and with lower stages for the beasts, and here, with a certain provision of water and in some cases chopped straw for the cattle, the traveller must make himself as comfortable as he could. He had not to purchase admittance to the caravanserai, for it was free to all, and the stable especially so. Now, beloved, our Lord Jesus Christ was born in the stable of the inn to show how free he his to all comers. The Gospel is preached to every creature and shuts out none. We may say of the invitations of Holy Scripture,

"None are excluded hence but those	Though Jesus' grace can save the prince,
Who do themselves exclude;	The poor may take their share;
Welcome the learned and polite,	No mortal has a just pretence
The ignorant and rude.	To perish in despair."

Class exclusions are unknown here, and the prerogatives of caste are not acknowledged. No forms of etiquette are required in entering a stable; it cannot be an offence to enter the stable of a public cara-vanserai. So, if you desire to come to Christ you may come to him just as you are; you may come *now.* Whosoever among you hath the desire in his heart to trust Christ is free to do it. Jesus is free to you; he will receive you; he will welcome you with gladness, and to show this, I think, the young child was cradled in a manger. We know that sinners often imagine that they are shut out. Oftentimes the convicted conscience will write bitter things against itself and deny its part and lot in mercy's stores. Brother, if *God* hath not shut thee out, do not shut thyself out. Until thou canst find it written in the Book that thou mayest not trust Christ; till thou canst quote a positive passage in which it is written that he is not able to save thee, I pray thee take that other word wherein it is written—" He is able to save unto the attermost them that come unto God by him." Venture on that promise: come to Christ in the strength and faith of it, and thou shalt find him free to all comers.

5. We have not yet exhausted the reasons why the Son of Man was laid in a manger. It was at the manger that *the beasts were fed;* and does the Saviour lie where weary beasts receive their provender, and shall there not be a mystery here? Alas, there are some men who have become so brutal through sin, so utterly depraved by their lusts, that to their own consciences every thing manlike has departed, but even to such the remedies of Jesus, the Great Physician, will apply. We are constantly reading in our papers of men who are called incorrigible, and it is fashionable just now to demand ferociously, that these men should be treated with unmingled severity. Some few years ago all the world went mad with a spurious humanity, crying out that gentleness would reform the brutal thief whom harsh punishments would harden hopelessly; now the current has turned, and everybody is demanding the abandonment of the present system. I am no advocate for treating criminals daintily; let their sin bring them a fair share of smart; but if by any means they can be reformed, pray let the means be tried. The day will come when the paroxysm of this garrotting fever is over, we shall blush to think that we were frightened by silly fears into a dangerous interference with a great and good work which hitherto has been successfully carried on. It is a fact that under the present system, which (abating some faults that it may be well to cure) is an admirable one, crime is growing less frequent, and the class of gross offenders has been materially lessened. Whereas in 1844 18,490 convicts were transported, in 1860 the corresponding number was 11,533, and that notwithstanding the increase of the population. The ticket-of-leave system, when the public would employ the convicts and so give them a chance of gaining a new character, worked so well that little more than one per cent. in a year were re-convicted, and even now only five per cent. per annum are found returning to crime and to prison. Well, now, if the five per cent. receive no good, or even become worse, ought we not to consider the other ninety-five, and pause awhile before we give loose to our vengeance and exchange a Christian system of hopeful mercy for the old barbarous rule of unmitigated severity. Beware, fellow-citizens, beware of restoring the old idea that men can sin beyond hope of reformation, or you will generate criminals worse than those which now trouble us. The laws of Draco must ever be failures, but fear not for the ultimate triumph of plans which a Christian spirit has suggested. I have wandered from the subject,—I thought I might save some from the crime of opposing true philanthropy on account of a sudden panic; but I will return at once to the manger and the babe. I believe our Lord was laid in the manger where the beasts were fed, to show *that even beast-like men may come to him and live.* No creature can be so degraded that Christ cannot lift it up. Fall it may, and seem to fall most certainly to hell, but the long and strong arm of Christ can reach it even in its most desperate degradation; he can bring it up from apparently hopeless ruin. If there be one who has strolled in here this morning whom society abhors, and who abhors himself, my Master in the stable with the beasts presents himself as able to save the vilest

of the vile, and to accept the worst of the worst even now. Believe on him and he will make thee a new creature.

6. But as Christ was laid where beasts were fed, you will please to recollect that after he was gone *beasts fed there again.* It was only his presence which could glorify the manger, and here we learn that if Christ were taken away *the world would go back to its former heathen darkness.* Civilisation itself would die out, at least that part of it which really civilises man, if the religion of Jesus could be extinguished. If Christ were taken away from the human heart, the most holy would become debased again, and those who claim kinship with angels would soon prove that they have relationship to devils. The manger, I say, would be a manger for beasts still, if the Lord of Glory were withdrawn, and we should go back to our sins and our lusts if Christ should once take away his grace and leave us to ourselves. For these reasons which I have mentioned, methinks, Christ was laid in a manger.

II. But still the text says that he was laid in a manger because there was no room for him in the inn, and this leads us to the second remark, THAT THERE WERE OTHER PLACES BESIDES THE INN WHICH HAD NO ROOM FOR CHRIST.

The palaces of emperors and the halls of kings afforded the royal stranger no refuge? Alas! my brethren, seldom is there room for Christ in palaces! How could the kings of earth receive the Lord? He is the Prince of Peace, and they delight in war! He breaks their bows and cuts their spears in sunder; he burneth their war-chariots in the fire. How could kings accept the humble Saviour? They love grandeur and pomp, and he is all simplicity and meekness. He is a carpenter's son, and the fisherman's companion. How can princes find room for the new-born monarch? Why he teaches us to do to others as we would that they should do to us, and this is a thing which kings would find very hard to reconcile with the knavish tricks of politics and the grasping designs of ambition. O great ones of the earth, I am but little astonished that amid your glories, and pleasures, and wars, and councils, ye forget the Anointed, and cast out the Lord of All. There is no room for Christ with the kings. Look throughout the kingdoms of the earth now, and with here and there an exception it is still true—"The kings of the earth stand up, and the rulers take counsel together, against the Lord and against his Anointed." In heaven we shall see here and there a monarch; but ah! how few; indeed a child might write them. "Not many great men after the flesh, not many mighty are chosen." State-chambers, cabinets, throne-rooms, and royal palaces, are about as little frequented by Christ as the jungles and swamps of India by the cautious traveller. He frequents cottages far more often than regal residences, for there is no room for Jesus Christ in regal halls.

"When the Eternal bows the skies	He bids his awful chariot roll
To visit earthly things,	Far downward from the skies,
With scorn divine he turns his eyes	To visit every humble soul
From towers of haughty kings.	With pleasure in his eyes."

But there were *senators, there were forums of political discussion, there were the places where the representatives of the people make the laws,* was there no room for Christ there? Alas! my brethren, none, and to this day there is very little room for Christ in parliaments. How seldom is religion recognised by politicians! Of course a State-religion, if it will consent to be a poor, tame, powerless thing, a lion with its teeth all drawn, its mane all shaven off, and its claws all trimmed—yes, that may be recognised; but the true Christ and they that follow him and dare to obey his laws in an evil generation, what room is there for such? Christ and his gospel—oh! this is sectarianism, and is scarcely worthy of the notice of contempt. Who pleads for Jesus in the senate? Is not his religion, under the name of sectarianism, the great terror of all parties? Who quotes his golden rule as a direction for prime ministers, or preaches Christ-like forgiveness as a rule for national policy? One or two will give him 'a good word, but if it be put to the vote whether the Lord Jesus should be obeyed or no, it will be many a day before the *ayes* have it. Parties, policies, place-hunters, and pleasure-seekers exclude the Representative of Heaven from a place among representatives of Earth.

Might there not be found some room for Christ *in what is called good society?* Were there not in Bethlehem some people that were very respectable, who kept themselves aloof from the common multitude; persons of reputation and standing—could not they find room for Christ? Ah! dear friends, it is too much the case that there is no room for Him in what is called good society. There is room for all the silly little forms by which men choose to trammel themselves; room for the vain niceties of etiquette; room for frivolous conversation; room for the adoration of the body; there is room for the setting up of this and that as the idol of the hour, but there is too little room for Christ, and it is far from fashionable to follow the Lord fully. The advent of Christ would be the last thing which gay society would desire; the very mention of his name by the lips of love would cause a strange sensation. Should you begin to talk about the things of Christ in many a circle, you would be tabooed at once. "I will never ask that man to my house again," so-and-so would say—"if he must bring his religion with him." Folly and finery, rank and honour, jewels and glitter, frivolity and fashion, all report that there is no room for Jesus in their abodes.

But is there not room for him *on the exchange?* Cannot he be taken to the marts of commerce? Here are the shop-keepers of a shop-keeping nation—is there not room for Christ here? Ah! dear friends, how little of the spirit, and life, and doctrine of Christ can be found here! The trader finds it inconvenient to be too scrupulous; the merchant often discovers that if he is to make a fortune he must break his conscience. How many there are—well, I will not say they tell lies directly, but still, still, still—I had better say it plainly—they do lie indirectly with a vengeance. Who does not know as he rides along that there must be many liars abroad? for almost every house you see is "The cheapest house in London," which can hardly be; full sure they cannot all be cheapest! What sharp practise some indulge in! What puffery and falsehood! What cunning and sleight of hand! What woes would my Master pronounce on some of you if he looked into your shop-windows, or stood behind your counters. Bankruptcies, swindlings, frauds are so abundant that in hosts of cases there is no room for Jesus in the mart or the shop.

Then there are *the schools of the philosophers*, surely they will entertain him. The wise men will find in him incarnate wisdom; he, who as a youth is to become the teacher of doctors, who will sit down and ask them questions and receive their answers, surely he will find room at once among the Grecian sages, and men of sense and wit will honour him. "Room for him, Socrates and Plato! Stoics and Epicurians give ye way; and you, ye teachers of Israel, vacate your seats; if there is no room for this child without your going, go; we must have him in the schools of philosophy if we put you all forth." No, dear friends, but it is not so; there is very little room for Christ in colleges and universities, very little room for him in the seats of learning. How often learning helps men to raise objections to Christ! Too often learning is the forge where the nails are made for Christ's crucifixion; too often human wit has become the artificer who has pointed the spear and made the shaft with which his heart should be pierced. We must say it, that philosophy, falsely so called, (for true philosophy, if it were handled aright, must ever be Christ's friend) philosophy, falsely so called, hath done mischief to Christ, but seldom hath it served his cause. A few with splendid talents, a few of the erudite and profound have bowed like children at the feet of the Babe of Bethlehem, and have been honoured in bowing there, but too many, conscious of their knowledge, stiff and stern in their conceit of wisdom, have said,—"Who is Christ, that we should acknowledge him?" They found no room for him in the schools.

But there was surely one place where he could go—it was *the Sanhedrim*, where the elders sit. Or could he not be housed in the priestly chamber where the priests assemble with the Levites. Was there not room for him in the temple or the synagogue? No, he found no shelter there; it was there, his whole life long, that he found his most ferocious enemies. Not the common multitude, but the priests were the instigators of his death; the priests moved the people to say "Not this man, but Barabbas." The priests paid out their shekels to bribe the popular voice, and then Christ was hounded to his death. Surely there ought to have been room for him in the Church of his own people; but there was not. Too often in the priestly church, when once it becomes recognised and mounts to dignity, there is no room for Christ. I allude not now to any one denomination, but take the whole sweep of Christendom, and it is strange that when the Lord comes to his own his own receives him not. The most accursed enemies of true religion have been the men who pretended to be its advocates. It is little marvel when bishops undermine the popular faith in revelation; this is neither their first nor last offence. Who burned the martyrs, and made Smithfield a field of blood, a burning fiery furnace, a great altar for the Most High God? Why, those who professed to be anointed of the Lord, whose shaven crowns had received episcopal benediction. Who put John Bunyan in prison? Who chased such men as Owen and the Puritans from their pulpits? Who harried the Covenanters upon the mountains? Who, Sirs, but the professed messengers of heaven and priests of God? Who have hunted the baptized saints in every land, and hunt them still in many a Continental state? The priests ever; the priests ever; there is no room for Christ with the prophets of Baal, the servants of Babylon. The false hirelings that are not Christ's shepherds, and love not his sheep, have ever been the most ferocious enemies of our God and of his Christ. There is no room for him where his name is chanted in solemn hymns and his image lifted up amid smoke of incense. Go where ye will, and there is no space for the Prince of peace but with the humble and contrite spirits which by grace he prepares to yield him shelter.

III. But now for our third remark, THE INN ITSELF HAD NO ROOM FOR HIM; and this was the main reason why he must be laid in a manger.

What can we find in modern times which stands in the place of the inn? Well, there is *public sentiment free to all.* In this free land, men speak of what they like, and there is a public opinion upon every subject; and you know there is free toleration in this country to everything—permit me to say, toleration to everything but Christ. You will discover that the persecuting-spirit is now as much abroad as ever. There are still men at whom it is most fashionable to sneer. We never scoff at Christians now-a-days; we do not sneer at that respectable title, lest we should lose our own honour; we do not now-a-days, talk against the followers of Jesus under that name. No; but we have found out a way of doing it more safely. There is a pretty word of modern invention—a very pretty word—the word " *Sectarian.*" Do you know what it means? A sectarian means a true Christian; a man who can afford to keep a conscience, and does not mind suffering for it; a man who, whatever he finds to be in that old Book, believes it, and acts upon it, and is zealous for it. I believe that the men aimed at under the term, " sectarians," are the true followers of Christ, and that the sneers and jeers, and all the nonsense that you are always reading and hearing, is really aimed at the Christian, the true Christian, only he is disguised and nick-named by the word sectarian. I would give not a farthing for your religion, nay, not even the turn of a rusty nail, unless you will sometimes win that title. If God's Word be true, every atom of it, then we should act upon it; and whatsoever the Lord commandeth, we should diligently keep and obey, remembering that our Master tells us if we break one of the least of his commandments, and teach men so, we shall be least in his kingdom. We ought to be very jealous, very precise, very anxious, that even in the minutiæ of our Saviour's laws, we may obey, having our eyes up to him as the eyes of servants are to their mistresses. But if you do this, you will find you are not tolerated, and you will get the cold shoulder in society. A zealous Christian will find as truly a cross to carry now-a-days, as in the days of Simon the Cyrenian. If you will hold your tongue, if you will leave sinners to perish, if you will never endeavour to propagate your faith, if you will silence all witnessing for truth, if, in fact, you will renounce all the attributes of a Christian, if you will cease to be what a Christian must be, then the world will say, "Ah! that is right; this is the religion we like." But if you will believe, believe firmly, and if you let your belief actuate your life, and if your belief is so precious that you feel compelled to spread it, then at once you will find that there is no room for Christ even in the inn of public sentiment, where everything else is received. Be an infidel, and none will therefore treat you contemptuously; but be a Christian, and many will despise you. "There was no room for him in the inn."

How little room is there for Christ, too, *in general conversation,* which is also like an inn. We talk about many things; a man may now-a-days talk of any subject he pleases; no one can stop him and say, "There is a spy catching your words; he will report you to some central authority." Speech is very free in this land; but, ah! how

27

little room is there for Christ in general talk! Even on Sunday afternoon how little room there is for Christ in some professed Christian's houses. They will talk about ministers, tell queer anecdotes about them—perhaps invent a few, or, at least, garnish the old ones, and add to them, and make them a little more brilliant; they will talk about the Sunday school, or the various agencies in connection with the Church, but how little they say about Christ! And if some one should in conversation make this remark, "Could we not speak upon the Godhead and manhood, the finished work and righteousness, the ascension, or the second advent of our Lord Jesus Christ," why we should see many, who even profess to be followers of Christ, who would hold up their heads and say, "Why, dear, that man is quite a fanatic, or else he would not think of introducing such a subject as that into general conversation." No, there is no room for him in the inn ; to this day he can find but little access there.

I address many who are working-men. You are employed among a great many artisans day after day; do you not find, brethren—I know you do—that there is very little room for Christ *in the workshop?* There is room there for everything else ; there is room for swearing ; there is room for drunkenness ; there is room for lewd conversation ; there is room for politics, slanders, or infidelities ; but there is no room for Christ. Too many of our working men think religion would be an incumbrance, a chain, a miserable prison to them. They can frequent the theatre, or listen in a lecture-hall, but the house of God is too dreary for them. I wish I were not compelled to say so, but truly in our factories, workshops, and foundries, there is no room for Christ. The world is elbowing and pushing for more room, till there is scarce a corner left where the Babe of Bethlehem can be laid.

As for the inns of modern times—who would think of finding Christ there ? Putting out of our catalogue those hotels and roadside houses which are needed for the accommodation of travellers, what greater curse have we than our taverns and pot-houses ? What wider gates of hell ? Who would ever resort to such places as we have flaring with gas light at the corners of all our streets to find Christ there? As well might we expect to find him in the bottomless pit! We should be just as likely to look for angels in hell, as to look for Christ in a gin palace ! He who is separate from sinners, finds no fit society in the reeking temple of Bacchus. There is no room for Jesus in the inn. I think I would rather rot or feed the crows, than earn my daily bread by the pence of fools, the hard-earnings of the poor man, stolen from his ragged children, and his emaciated wife. What do many publicans fatten upon but the flesh, and bones, and blood, and souls of men. He who grows rich on the fruits of vice is a beast preparing for the slaughter. Truly, there is no room for Christ among the drunkards of Ephraim. They who have anything to do with Christ should hear him say—"Come ye out from among them, and be ye separate; touch not the unclean thing, and I will receive you, and be a father unto you, and ye shall be my sons and daughters." There is no room for Christ now-a-days even in the places of public resort.

IV. This brings me to my fourth head, which is the most pertinent,

and the most necessary to dwell upon for a moment. HAVE YOU ROOM
FOR CHRIST? HAVE YOU ROOM FOR CHRIST?

As the palace, and the forum, and the inn, have no room for Christ,
and as the places of public resort have none, have *you* room for Christ?
" Well," says one, " I have room for him, but I am not worthy that he
should come to me." Ah! I did not ask about worthiness; have you
room for him? " Oh," says one, " I have an empty void the world can
never fill!" Ah! I see you have room for him. " Oh! but the room
I have in my heart is so base!" So was the manger. "But it is so
despicable!" So was the manger a thing to be despised. " Ah! but my
heart is so foul!" So, perhaps, the manger may have been. " Oh! but
I feel it is a place not at all fit for Christ!" Nor was the manger a
place fit for him, and yet there was he laid. " Oh! but I have been such
a sinner; I feel as if my heart had been a den of beasts and devils!"
Well, the manger had been a place where beasts had fed. Have you
room for him? Never mind what the past has been; he can forget and
forgive. It mattereth not what even the present state may be if thou
mournest it. If thou hast but room for Christ he will come and be thy
guest. Do not say, I pray you, " I hope *I shall have* room for him;"
the time is come that he shall be born; Mary cannot wait months
and years. Oh! sinner, if thou hast room for him let him be born
in thy soul to-day. " To day if ye will hear his voice harden not your
hearts as in the provocation." " To-day is the accepted time; to-
day is the day of salvation." Room for Jesus! Room for Jesus now!
" Oh!" saith one, " I have room for him, but will he come?" Will
he come indeed! Do you but set the door of your heart open, do
but say, " Jesus, Master, all unworthy and unclean I look to thee;
come, lodge within my heart," and he will come to thee, and he will
cleanse the manger of thy heart, nay, will transform it into a golden
throne, and there he will sit and reign for ever and for ever. Oh!
I have such a free Christ to preach this morning! I would I could
preach him better. I have such a precious loving Jesus to preach, he
is willing to find a home in humble hearts. What! are there no hearts
here this morning that will take him in? Must my eye glance round
these galleries and look at many of you who are still without him, and
are there none who will say, " Come in, come in?" Oh! it shall be a
happy day for you if you shall be enabled to take him in your arms and
receive him as the consolation of Israel! You may then look forward
even to death with joy, and say with Simeon—" Lord, now lettest thou
thy servant depart in peace, according to thy word, for mine eyes have
seen thy salvation." My Master wants room! Room for him! Room
for him! I, his herald, cry aloud, Room for the Saviour! Room!
Here is my royal Master—have you room for him? Here is the
Son of God made flesh—have you room for him? Here is he who can
forgive all sin—have you room for him? Here is he who can take you
up out of the horrible pit and out of the miry clay—have you room for
him? Here is he who when he cometh in will never go out again, but
abide with you for ever to make your heart a heaven of joy and bliss
for you—have you room for him? 'Tis all I ask. Your emptiness,
your nothingness, your want of feeling, your want of goodness, your
want of grace—all these will be but room for him. Have you room for

him? Oh! Spirit of God, lead many to say, "Yes, my heart is ready." Ah! then he will come and dwell with you.

> "Joy to the world the Saviour comes, | Let every heart prepare a throne
> The Saviour promised long; | And every voice a song."

V. I conclude with the remark, that if you have room for Christ, then from this day forth remember THE WORLD HAS NO ROOM FOR YOU; for the text says not only that there was no room for him, but look—"There was no room *for them*,"—no room for Joseph, nor for Mary, any more than for the babe. Who are his father, and mother, and sister, and brother, but those that receive his word and keep it? So, as there was no room for the blessed Virgin, nor for the reputed father, remember henceforth there is no room in this world for any true follower of Christ. There is no room for you to take your *ease*; no, you are to be a soldier of the cross, and you will find no ease in all your life-warfare. There is no room for you to sit down *contented with your own attainments*, for you are a traveller, and you are to forget the things that are behind, and press forward to that which is before; no room for you *to hide your treasure* in, for here the moth and rust doth corrupt; no room for you *to put your confidence*, for "Cursed is he that trusteth in man, and maketh flesh his arm." From this day there will be no room for you in *the world's good opinion*— they will count you to be an offscouring; no room for you in the world's *polite society*—you must go without the camp, bearing his reproach. From this time forth, I say, if you have room for Christ, the world will hardly find room of *sufferance* for you; you must expect now to be laughed at; now you must wear the fool's cap in men's esteem; and your song must be at the very beginning of your pilgrimage.

> "Jesus, I thy cross have taken, | Naked, poor, despised, forsaken,
> All to leave and follow thee; | Thou from hence my all shall be."

There is no room for you in the worldling's love. If you expect that everybody will praise you, and that your good actions will all be applauded, you will quite be mistaken. The world, I say, has no room for the man who has room for Christ. If any man love the world, the love of the Father is not in him. "Woe unto you when all men speak well of you." "Ye are not of the world, even as Christ is not of the world." Thank God, you need not ask the world's hospitality. If it will give you but a stage for action, and lend you for an hour a grave to sleep in, 'tis all you need; you will require no permanent dwelling-place here, since you seek a city that is to come, which hath foundations; whose builder and maker is God. You are hurrying through this world as a stranger through a foreign land, and you rejoice to know that though you are an alien and a foreigner here, yet you are a fellow citizen with the saints, and of the household to God.

What say you, young soldier, will you enlist on such terms as these? Will you give room for Christ when there is to be henceforth no room for you—when you are to be separated for ever, cut off from among the world's kith and kin mayhap—cut off from carnal confidence for ever? Are you willing, notwithstanding all this, to receive the traveller in? The Lord help you to do so, and to him shall be glory for ever and ever. Amen.

Holy Work for Christmas

"And when they had seen it, they made known abroad the saying which was told them concerning this child. And all they that heard it wondered at those things which were told them by the shepherds. But Mary kept all these things, and pondered them in her heart. And the shepherds returned, glorifying and praising God for all the things that they had heard and seen, as it was told unto them."
— Luke ii. 17—20.

EVERY season has its own proper fruit: apples for autumn, holly berries for Christmas. The earth brings forth according to the period of the year, and with man there is a time for every purpose under heaven. At this season, the world is engaged in congratulating itself and in expressing its complimentary wishes for the good of its citizens; let me suggest extra and more solid work for Christians. As we think to-day of the birth of the Saviour, let us aspire after a fresh birth of the Saviour in our hearts; that as he is already "formed in us the hope of glory," we may be "renewed in the spirit of our minds;" that we may go again to the Bethlehem of our spiritual nativity and do our first works, enjoy our first loves, and feast with Jesus as we did in the holy, happy, heavenly days of our espousals. Let us go to Jesus with something of that youthful freshness and excessive delight which was so manifest in us when we looked to him at the first; let him be crowned anew by us, for he is still adorned with the dew of his youth, and remains "the same yesterday, to-day, and for ever." The citizens of Durham, though they dwell not far from the Scotch border, and consequently in the olden times were frequently liable to be attacked, were exempted from the toils of war because there was a cathedral within their walls, and they were set aside to the bishop's service, being called in the olden times by the name of "holy work-folk." Now, we citizens of the New Jerusalem, having the Lord Jesus in our midst, may well excuse ourselves from the ordinary ways of celebrating this season; and considering ourselves to be "holy work-folk," we may keep it after a different sort from other men, in holy contemplation and in blessed service of that gracious God whose unspeakable gift the new-born King is to us.

I selected this text this morning because it seemed to indicate to me four ways of serving God, four methods of executing holy work and exercising Christian thought. Each of the verses sets before us a different way of sacred service. Some, it appears, published abroad the news, told to others what they had seen and heard; some wondered with a holy marvelling and astonishment; one, at least, according to the third of the verses, pondered, meditated, thought upon these things; and others, in the fourth place, glorified God and gave him praise. I know not which of these four did God best service, but I think if we could combine all these mental emotions and outward exercises, we should be sure to praise God after a most godly and acceptable fashion.

I. To begin then, in the first place, we find that some celebrated the Saviour's birth by PUBLISHING ABROAD what they had heard and seen; and truly we may say of them that *they had something* to rehearse in men's ears well worth the telling. That for which prophets and kings had waited long, had at last arrived and arrived to them. They had found out the answer to the perpetual riddle. They might have run through the streets with the ancient philosopher, crying, "Eureka! Eureka!" for their discovery was far superior to his. They had found out no solution to a mechanical problem or metaphysical dilemma, but their discovery was second to none ever made by men in real value, since it has been like the leaves of the tree of life to heal the nations, and a river of water of life to make glad the city of God. They had seen angels; they had heard them sing a song all strange and new. They had seen more than angels,—they had beheld the angel's King, the Angel of the Covenant whom we delight in. They had heard the music of heaven, and when near that manger the ear of their faith had heard the music of earth's hope, a mystic harmony which should ring all down the ages,—the grave sweet melody of hearts attuned to praise the Lord, and the glorious swell of the holy joy of God and man rejoicing in glad accord. They had seen God incarnate,—such a sight that he who gazeth on it must feel his tongue unloosed, unless indeed an unspeakable astonishment should make him dumb. Be silent when their eyes had seen such a vision! Impossible! To the first person they met outside that lowly stable door they began to tell their matchless tale, and they wearied not till nightfall, crying, "Come and worship! Come and worship Christ, the new-born King!" As for us, beloved, have we also not something to relate which demands utterance? If we talk of Jesus, who can blame us? This, indeed, might make the tongue of him that sleeps to move,—the mystery of God incarnate for our sake, bleeding and dying that we might neither bleed nor die, descending that we might ascend, and wrapped in swaddling bands that we might be unwrapped of the grave-clothes of corruption. Here is such a story, so profitable to all hearers that he who repeats it the most often does best, and he who speaks the least hath most reason to accuse himself for sinful silence.

They had something to tell, and *that something had in it the inimitable blending which is the secret sign and royal mark of Divine authorship; a peerless marrying of sublimity and simplicity;* angels singing!—singing to shepherds! Heaven bright with glory! bright at midnight! God! A Babe!! The Infinite! An Infant of a span long!! The Ancient of Days! Born of a woman!! What more simple than the inn, the manger, a carpenter, a carpenter's wife, a child? What more sublime than a "multitude of the heavenly host" waking the midnight with their joyous chorales, and God himself in human flesh made manifest.

A child is but an ordinary sight; but what a marvel to see that Word which was "in the beginning with God, tabernacling among us that we might behold his glory—the glory as of the only begotten of the Father, full of grace and truth?" Brethren, we have a tale to tell, as simple as sublime. What simpler?—"Believe and live." What more sublime?—"God was in Christ reconciling the world unto himself!" A system of salvation so wonderful that angelic minds cannot but adore as they meditate upon it; and yet so simple that the children in the temple may fitly hymn its virtues as they sing, "Hosanna! Blessed is he that cometh in the name of the Lord." What a splendid combining of the sublime and the simple have we in the great atonement offered by the incarnate Saviour! Oh make known to all men this saving truth!

The shepherds need no excuse for making everywhere the announcement of the Saviour's birth, *for what they told they first received from heaven.* Their news was not muttered in their ears by Sybilline oracles, not brought to light by philosophic search, not conceived in poetry nor found as treasure trove among the volumes of the ancient; but it was revealed to them by that notable gospel preacher who led the angelic host, and testified, "Unto you is born this day, in the city of David, a Saviour, which is Christ the Lord." When heaven entrusts a man with a merciful revelation, he is bound to deliver the good tidings to others. What, keep that a secret whose utterance eternal mercy makes to charm the midnight air? To what purpose were angels sent, if the message were not to be spread abroad? According to the teaching of our own beloved Lord we must not be silent, for he bids us "What ye hear in secret that reveal ye in public; and what I tell you in the ear in closets, that proclaim ye upon the house-tops." Beloved, you have heard a voice from heaven—you twice-born men, begotten again unto a lively hope, you have heard the Spirit of God bearing witness of God's truth with you, and teaching you of heavenly things. You then must keep this Christmas by telling to your fellow-men what God's own holy Spirit has seen fit to reveal to you.

But though the shepherds told what they heard from heaven, remember that *they spoke of what they had seen below.* They had, by observation, made those truths most surely their own which had first been spoken to them by revelation. No man can speak of the things of God with any success until the doctrine which he finds in the book he finds also in his heart. We must bring down the mystery and make it plain, by knowing, by the teaching of the Holy Ghost, its practical power on the heart and conscience. My brethren, the gospel which we preach is most surely revealed to us by the Lord; but, moreover, our hearts have tried and proved, have grasped, have felt, have realized its truth and power. If we have not been able to understand its heights and depths, yet we have felt its mystic power upon our heart and spirit. It has revealed sin to us better; it has revealed to us our pardon. It has killed the reigning power of sin, it has given us Christ to reign over us, the Holy Spirit to dwell within our bodies as in a temple. Now *we must* speak. I do not urge any of you to speak of Jesus who merely know the Word as you find it in the Bible, your teaching can have but little power; but I do speak earnestly to you who know its mighty influence upon the heart, who have not only heard of the babe but have seen him in the manger, taken him up in your own arms and received him as being born to you, a Saviour to you, Christos, the anointed for you, Jesus the Saviour from sin for you. Beloved, can you do otherwise than speak of the things which you have seen and heard. God has made you to taste and to handle of this good word of life, and you must not, you dare not hold your peace, but you *must* tell to friends and neighbours what you have felt within.

These were shepherds, *unlettered men.* I will warrant you they could not read in a book; there is no probability that they even knew a single letter. They were shepherds, but they preached right well; and, my brethren, whatever some may think, preaching is not to be confined to those learned gentlemen who have taken their degrees at Oxford or at Cambridge, or at any College or University. It is true that learning need not be an impediment to grace, and may be a fitting weapon in a gracious hand, but often the grace of God has glorified itself by the plain clear way in which unlettered men have understood the gospel and have proclaimed it. I would not mind asking the whole world to find a Master of Arts now living who has brought more souls to Christ Jesus than Richard Weaver. If the whole bench of bishops have done a tenth as much in the way of soul-winning as that one man, it is more than most of us give them credit for. Let us give to our God all the glory, but still let us not deny the fact that this sinner saved, with the brogue of the collier still about him, fresh from the coal pit, tells the story of the cross by God's grace in such a way that Right Reverend Fathers in God might humbly sit at his feet to learn the way to reach the heart and melt the stubborn soul. It is true an uneducated brother is not fitted for all work—he has his own sphere—but he is quite able to tell of what he has seen and heard, and so it strikes me is every man in a measure. If you have seen Jesus and heard his saving voice, if you have received truth as from the Lord, felt its tremendous power as coming from God to you, and if you have experienced its might upon your own spirit, why you can surely tell out what God has written within. If you cannot get beyond that into the deeper mysteries, into the more knotty points, well, well, there are some who can, and so you need not be uneasy; but you can at least reveal the first and foundation truths, and they are by far the most important. If you cannot speak in the pulpit, if as yet your cheek would mantle with a blush, and your tongue would refuse to do her office in the presence of many, there are your children, you are not ashamed to speak before them; there is the little cluster round the hearth on Christmas night, there is the little congregation in the workshop, there is a little audience somewhere to whom you might tell out of Jesu's love to lost ones. Do not get beyond what you know; do not plunge into what you have not experienced, for if you do you will be out of your depth, and then very soon you will be floundering and making confusion worse confounded. Go as far as you know; and since you do know yourself a sinner and Jesus a Saviour, and a great one too, talk about those two matters, and good will come of it. Beloved, each one in his own position, tell what you have heard and seen; publish that abroad among the sons of men.

But *were they authorized?* It is a great thing to be authorized! Unauthorized ministers are most shameful intruders! Unordained men entering the pulpit, who are not in the apostolical succession—very horrible! Very horrible indeed! The Puseyite mind utterly fails to fathom the depth of horror which is contained in the idea of an unauthorized man preaching, and a man out of the apostolical succession daring to teach the way of salvation. To me this horror seems very like a schoolboy's fright at a hobgoblin which his fears had conjured up. I think if I saw a man slip through the ice into a cold grave, and I could rescue him from drowning, it would not be so very horrible to me to be the means of saving him, though I may not be employed by the Royal Humane Society. I imagine if I saw a fire, and heard a poor woman scream at an upper window, and likely to be burned alive, if I should wheel the fire-escape up to the window, and preserve her life, it would not be so very dreadful a matter though I might not belong to the regular Fire Brigade. If a company of brave volunteers should chase an enemy out of their own county, I do not know that it would be anything so shocking, although a whole army of mercenaries might be neglecting their work in obedience to some venerable military rubric which rendered them incapable of effective service. But mark you, the shepherds and others like them are in the apostolical succession, and they are authorized by divine ordinance, for every man who hears the gospel is authorized to tell it to others. Do you want authority? here it is in confirmation strong from Holy Writ: "Let him that heareth say, Come"—that is, let every man who truly hears the gospel bid others come to drink of the water of life. This is all the warrant you require for preaching the gospel according to your ability. It is not every man who has ability to preach the Word; and it is not every man that we should like to hear preach it in the great congregation, for if all were mouth, what a great vacuum the Church would be; yet every Christian in some method should deliver the glad tidings. Our wise God takes care that liberty of prophesying shall not run to riot, for he does not give efficient pastoral and ministerial gifts to very many; yet every man according to his gifts, let him minister. Every one of you though not in the pulpit, yet in the pew, in the workshop, somewhere, anywhere, everywhere, do make known the savour of the Lord Jesus. Be this your authority: "Let him that heareth say, Come." I never thought of asking any authority for crying "Fire," when I saw a house burning; I never dreamed of seeking any authority for doing my best to rescue a poor perishing fellow-man, nor do I mean to seek it now! All the authority you want, any of you, is not the authority which can stream from prelates decorated with lawn sleeves, but the authority which comes direct from the great Head of the Church, who gives authority to every one of those who hear the gospel, to teach every man his fellow, saying, "Know the Lord."

Here, dear brethren, is one way for you to keep a right holy, and in some sense a right merry, Christmas. Imitate these humble men, of whom it is said, "When they had seen it they made known abroad the saying which was told them concerning the child."

II. We set before you, now, another mode of keeping Christmas, by HOLY WONDER, ADMIRATION, AND ADORATION. "And all they that heard it wondered at those things which were told them by the shepherds"

We shall have little to say of those persons who merely wondered, and did nothing more. Many are set a wondering by the Gospel. They are content to hear it, pleased to hear it; if not in itself something new, yet there are new ways of putting it, and they are glad to be refreshed with the variety. The preacher's voice is unto them as the sound of one that giveth a goodly tune upon an instrument. They are glad to listen. They are not sceptics, they do not cavil, they raise no difficulties; they just say to themselves, "It is an excellent gospel, it is a wonderful plan of salvation. Here is most astonishing love, most extraordinary condescension." Sometimes they marvel that these things should be told them by shepherds; they can hardly understand how unlearned and ignorant men should speak of these things, and how such things should ever get into these shepherds' heads, where they can have learned them, how it is that they seem so earnest about them, what kind of operation they must have passed through to be able to speak as they do. But after holding up their hands and opening their mouths for about nine days, the wonder subsides, and they go their way and think no more about it. There are many of you who are set a wondering whenever you see a work of God in your district. You hear of somebody converted who was a very extraordinary sinner, and you say, "It is very wonderful!" There is a revival; you happen to be present at one of the meetings when the Spirit of God is working gloriously: you say, "Well, this is a singular thing! very astonishing!" Even the newspapers can afford a corner at times for very great and extraordinary works of God the Holy Spirit; but there all emotion ends; it is all wondering, and nothing more. Now, I trust it will not be so with any of us; that we shall not think of the Saviour and of the doctrines of the gospel which he came to preach simply with amazement and astonishment, for this will work us but little good. On the other hand, there is another mode of wondering which is akin to adoration, if it be not adoration. I think it would be very difficult to draw a line between holy wonder and real worship, for when the soul is overwhelmed with the majesty of God's glory, though it may not express itself in song, or even utter its voice with bowed head in humble prayer, yet it silently adores. I am inclined to think that the astonishment which sometimes seizes upon the human intellect at the remembrance of God's greatness and goodness is, perhaps, the purest form of adoration which ever rises from mortal men to the throne of the Most High. This kind of wonder I recommend to those of you who from the quietness and solitariness of your lives are scarcely able to imitate the shepherds in telling out the tale to others : you can at least fill up the circle of the worshippers before the throne by wondering at what God has done.

Let me suggest to you that holy wonder at what God has done should be very natural to you. That God should consider his fallen creature, man, and instead of sweeping him away with the besom of destruction should devise a wonderful scheme for his redemption, and that he should himself undertake to be man's Redeemer, and to pay his ransom price, is, indeed, marvellous! Probably it is most marvellous to you in its relation to yourself, that *you* should be redeemed by blood; that God should forsake the thrones and royalties above to suffer ignominiously below for you. If you know yourself you can never see any adequate motive or reason in your own flesh for such a deed as this. "Why such love to me?" you will say. If David sitting in his house could only say, "Who am I, O Lord God, and what is mine house, that thou hast brought me hitherto?" what should you and I say? Had we been the most meritorious of individuals, and had unceasingly kept the Lord's commands, we could not have deserved such a priceless boon as incarnation; but sinners, offenders, who revolted and went from God, further and further, what shall we say of this incarnate God dying for us, but "Herein is love, not that we loved God but that God loved us." Let your soul lose itself in wonder, for wonder, dear friends, is in this way a very practical emotion. Holy wonder will lead you to grateful worship; being astonished at what God has done, you will pour out your soul with astonishment at the foot of the golden throne with the song, " Blessing, and honour, and glory, and majesty, and power, and dominion, and might be unto Him who sitteth on the throne and doeth these great things to me." Filled with this wonder it will cause you a godly watchfulness; you will be afraid to sin against such love as this. Feeling the presence of the mighty God in the gift of his dear Son, you will put off your shoes from off your feet, because the place whereon you stand is holy ground. You will be moved at the same time to a glorious hope. If Jesus has given himself to you, if he has done this marvellous thing on your behalf, you will feel that heaven itself is not too great for your expectation, and that the rivers of pleasure at God's right hand are not too sweet or too deep for you to drink thereof. Who can be astonished at anything when he has once been astonished at the manger and the cross? What is there wonderful left after one has seen the Saviour? The nine wonders of the world! Why, you may put them all into a nutshell—machinery and modern art can excel them all; but this one wonder is not the wonder of earth only, but of heaven and earth, and even hell itself. It is not the wonder of the olden time, but the wonder of all time and the wonder of eternity. They who see human wonders a few times, at last cease to be astonished; the noblest pile that architect ever raised, at last fails to impress the onlooker ; but not so this marvellous temple of incarnate Deity; the more we look the more we are astonished, the more we become accustomed to it, the more have we a sense of its surpassing splendour of love and grace. There is more of God, let us say, to be seen in the manger and the cross, than in the sparkling stars above, the rolling deep below, the towering mountain, the teeming valleys, the abodes of life, or the abyss of death. Let us then spend some choice hours of this festive season in holy wonder, such as will produce gratitude, worship, love, and confidence.

III. A third manner of holy work, namely, HER SACRED HEART PONDERING AND PRESERVING, you will find in the next verse.

One at least, and let us hope there were others, or at any rate let us ourselves be others—one kept all these things and pondered them in her heart. She wondered: she did more—she pondered. You will observe there was an exercise on the part of this blessed woman of the three great parts of her being; her memory—she kept all these things; her affections—she kept them in her heart; her intellect—she pondered them, considered them, weighed them, turned them over; so that memory, affection, and understanding, were all exercised about these things. We delight to see this in Mary, but we are not at all surprised when we recollect that she was in some sense the most concerned of all on earth, for it was of her that Jesus Christ had been born. Those who come nearest to Jesus and enter the most closely into fellowship with him, will be sure to be the most engrossed with him. Certain persons are best esteemed at a distance, but not the Saviour; when you shall have known him to the very full, then shall you love him with the love which passeth knowledge; you shall comprehend the heights, and depths, and lengths, and breadths of his love; and when you shall do so, then your own love shall swell beyond all length and breadth, all height and depth. The birth most concerned Mary, and therefore she was the most impressed with it. Note the way in which her concern was shown; she was a woman, and the grace which shines best in the female is not boldness— that belongs to the masculine mind; but affectionate modesty is a feminine beauty, and hence we do not read so much of her telling abroad as pondering within. No doubt she had her circle, and her word to speak in it; but for the most part she, like another Mary, sat still in the house. She worked, but her work was most directly for *him*, her heart's joy and delight. Like other children, the holy child needed care, which only a mother's hand and heart could exercise; she was therefore engrossed with him. O blessed engrossment! Sweet engagement! Count not that to be unacceptable service which occupies itself rather with Jesus than with his disciples or his wandering sheep. That woman who broke the alabaster box and poured the ointment upon our Jesus himself was blamed by Judas, and even the rest of the disciples thought that the poor had lost a benefit, but "she hath wrought a good work on me" was the Saviour's answer. I desire to bring you to this thought, that if during this season you retiring quiet ones cannot speak to others, or have no desirable opportunity or suitable gift for that work, you may sit still with Jesus and honour him in peace. Mary took the Lord in her arms; oh that you may bear him in yours! She executed works for his person directly; do you imitate her. You can love him, bless him, praise him, study him, ponder him, comprehend his character, study the types that set him forth, and imitate his life; and in this way, though your worship will not blaze forth among the sons of men, and scarcely benefit them as some other forms of work, yet it will both benefit you and be acceptable to your Lord. Beloved, remember what you have heard of Christ, and what he has done for you; make your heart the golden cup to hold the rich recollections of his past loving-kindness; make it a pot of manna to preserve the heavenly bread whereon saints have fed in days gone by. Let your memory treasure up everything about Christ which you have either heard, or felt, or known, and then let your fond affections hold him fast evermore. Love him! Pour out that alabaster box of your heart, and let all the precious ointment of your affection come streaming on his feet. If you cannot do it with joy do it sorrowfully, wash his feet with tears, wipe them with the hairs of your head; but do love him, love the blessed Son of God, your ever tender Friend. Let your intellect be exercised concerning the Lord Jesus. Turn over and over by meditation what you read. Do not be lettermen—do not stop at the surface; dive into the depths. Be not as the swallow which toucheth the brook with her wing, but as the fish which penetrates the lowest wave. Drink deep draughts of love; do not sip and away, but dwell at the well as Isaac did at the well Lahai-roi. Abide with your Lord: let him not be to you as a wayfaring man that tarrieth for a night, but constrain him, saying, "Abide with us, for the day is far spent." Hold him, and do not let him go. The word "ponder," as you know, means to weigh. Make ready the scales of judgment. Oh, but where are the scales that can weigh the Lord Christ? "He taketh up the isles as a very little thing"—who shall take *him* up? "He weigheth the mountains in scales." In what scales shall we weigh *him?* Be it so, if your understanding cannot comprehend, let your affections apprehend; and if your spirit cannot compass the Lord Jesus in the arms of its understanding, let it embrace him in the arms of your affection. Oh, beloved, here is blessed Christmas work for you, if, like Mary, you lay up all these things in your heart and ponder upon them.

IV. The last piece of holy Christmas work is to come. "The shepherds returned," we read in the twentieth verse, "GLORIFYING AND PRAISING GOD for all the things that they had heard and seen, as it was told unto them." Returned to what? *Returned to business* to look after the lambs and sheep again. Then if we desire to glorify God we need not give up our business.

Some people get the notion into their heads that the only way in which they can live for God is by becoming ministers, missionaries, or Bible women. Alas! how many of us would be shut out from any opportunity of magnifying the Most High if this were the case. The shepherds went back to the sheep-pens glorifying and praising God. Beloved, it is not office, it is not earnestness; it is not position, it is grace which will enable us to glorify God. God is most surely glorified in that cobbler's stall where the godly worker as he plies the awl sings of the Saviour's love, ay, glorified far more than in many a prebendal stall where official *religiousness* performs its scanty duties. The name of Jesus is glorified by yonder carter as he drives his horse and blesses his God, or speaks to his fellow labourer by the roadside as much as by yonder divine who, throughout the country like Boanerges, is thundering out the gospel. God is glorified by our abiding in our vocation. Take care you do not fall out of the path of duty by leaving your calling, and take care you do not dishonour your profession while in it; think not much of yourselves, but do not think too little of your callings. There is no trade which is not sanctified by the gospel. If you turn to the Bible, you will find the most menial forms of labour have been in some way or other connected either with the most daring deeds of faith, or else with persons whose lives have been otherwise illustrious; keep to your calling, brother, keep to your calling! Whatever God has made thee, when he calls thee abide in that, unless thou art quite sure, mind that, unless thou art quite sure that he calls thee to something else. The shepherds glorified God though they went to their trade.

They glorified God *though they were shepherds.* As we remarked, they were not men of learning. So far from having an extensive library full of books, it is probable they could not read a word; yet they glorified God. This takes away all excuse for you good people who say, " I am no scholar; I never had any education, I never went even to a Sunday-school." Ah, but if your heart is right, you can glorify God. Never mind, Sarah, do not be cast down because you know so little; learn more if you can, but make good use of what you do know. Never mind, John; it is indeed a pity that you should have had to toil so early, as not to have acquired even the rudiments of knowledge; but do not think that you cannot glorify God. If you would praise God, live a holy life; you can do that by his grace, at any rate, without scholarship. If thou wouldst do good to others, be good thyself; and that is a way which is as open to the most illiterate as it is to the best taught. Be of good courage! Shepherds glorified God, and so may you. Remember there is one thing in which they had a preference over the wise men. The wise men wanted a star to lead them; the shepherds did not. The wise men went wrong even with a star, stumbled into Jerusalem; the shepherds went straight away to Bethlehem. Simple minds sometimes find a glorified Christ where learned heads, much puzzled with their lore, miss him. A good doctor used to say, " Lo, these simpletons have entered into the kingdom, while we learned men have been fumbling for the latch." It is often so; and so, ye simple minds, be ye comforted and glad.

The way in which these shepherds honoured God is worth noticing. They did it by praising him. Let us think more of sacred song than we sometimes do. When the song is bursting in full chorus from the thousands in this house, it is but a noise in the ear of some men; but inasmuch as many true hearts, touched with the love of Jesus, are keeping pace with their tongues, it is not a mere noise in God's esteem, there is a sweet music in it that makes glad his ear. What is the great ultimatum of all Christian effort? When I stood here the other morning preaching the gospel, my mind was fully exercised with the winning of souls, but I seemed while preaching to get beyond that. I thought, Well, that is not the chief end after all—the chief end is to glorify God, and even the saving of sinners is sought by the right-minded as the means to that end. Then it struck me all of a sudden, " If in psalm singing and hymn singing we do really glorify God, we are doing more than in the preaching; because we are not then in the means, we are close upon the great end itself." If we praise God with heart and tongue we glorify him in the surest possible manner, we are really glorifying him then. " Whoso offereth praise glorifieth me," saith the Lord. Sing then, my brethren! Sing not only when you are together but sing alone. Cheer your labour with psalms, and hymns, and spiritual songs. Make glad the family with sacred music. We sing too little, I am sure, yet the revival of religion has always been attended with the revival of Christian psalmody. Luther's translations of the psalms were of as much service as Luther's discussions and controversies; and the hymns of Charles Wesley, and Cennick, and Toplady, and Newton, and Cowper, aided as much in the quickening of spiritual life in England as the preaching of John Wesley and George Whitefield. We want more singing. Sing more and murmur less, sing more and slander less, sing more and cavil less, sing more and mourn less. God grant us to-day, as these shepherds did, to glorify God by praising him.

I have not quite done with them. What was the subject of their praise? It appears that they *praised God for what they had heard.* If we think of it, there is good reason for blessing God every time we hear a gospel sermon. What would souls in hell give if they could hear the gospel once more, and be on terms in which salvation grace might come to them? What would dying men give whose time is all but over if they could once more come to the house of God, and have another warning and another invitation? My brethren, what would you give sometimes when you are shut up by sickness and cannot meet with the great congregation, when your heart and your flesh cry out for the living God? Well, praise God for what you have heard. You have heard the faults of the preacher; let him mourn them. You have heard his Master's message, do you bless God for that? Scarcely will you ever hear a sermon which may not make you sing if you are in a right mind. George Herbert says, "Praying is the end of preaching." So it is, but praising is its end too. Praise God that you hear there is a Saviour! Praise God that you hear that the plan of salvation is very simple! Praise God that you have a Saviour for your own soul! Praise God that you are pardoned, that you are saved! Praise him for what you have heard, but observe, *they also praised God for what they had seen.* Look at the twentieth verse—"heard and seen." There is the sweetest music—what we have experienced, what we have felt within, what we have made our own—the things that we have made touching the King. Mere hearing may make some music, but the soul of song must come from seeing with the eye of faith. And, dear friends, you who have seen with that God-giving eyesight, I pray you, let not your tongues be steeped in sinful silence, but loud to the praise of sovereign grace, wake up your glory and awake psaltery and harp. One point for which they praised God was *the agreement between what they had heard and what they had seen.* Observe the last sentence. "As it was told them." Have you not found the gospel to be in yourselves just what the Bible said it would be? Jesus said he would give you grace —have you not had it? He promised you rest—have you not received it? He said that you should have joy, and comfort, and life through believing in him—have you not had all these? Are not his ways ways of pleasantness, and his paths paths of peace? Surely you can say with the queen of Sheba, "The half has not been told me." I have found Christ more sweet than his servants could set him forth as being. I looked upon the likeness as they painted it, but it was a mere daub as compared with himself—the King in his beauty. I have heard of the goodly land, but oh! it floweth with milk and honey more richly and sweetly than men were ever able to tell me when in their best trim for speech. Surely, what we have seen keeps pace with what we have heard. Let us then glorify and praise God for what he has done.

This word to those who are not yet converted, and I have done. I do not think you can begin at the seventeenth verse, but I wish you would begin at the eighteenth. You cannot begin at the seventeenth— you cannot tell to others what you have not felt; do not try it. Neither teach in the Sunday-school, nor attempt to preach if you are not converted. Unto the wicked God saith, "What hast thou to do to declare my statutes?" But I would to God you would begin with the eighteenth verse—wondering! Wondering that you are spared—wondering that you are out of hell—wondering that still doth his good Spirit strive with the chief of sinners. Wonder that this morning the gospel should have a word for you after all your rejections of it and sins against God. I should like you to begin there, because then I should have good hope that you would go on to the next verse and change the first letter, and so go from wondering to pondering. Oh sinner, I wish you would ponder the doctrines of the cross. Think of thy sin, God's wrath, judgment, hell, thy Saviour's blood, God's love, forgiveness, acceptance, heaven—think on these things. Go from wondering to pondering. And then I would to God thou couldst go on to the next verse, from pondering to glorifying. Take Christ, look to him, trust him. Then sing "I am forgiven," and go thy way a believing sinner, and therefore a sinner saved, washed in the blood, and clean. Then go back after that to the seventeenth verse, and begin to tell to others.

But as for you Christians who are saved, I want you to begin this very afternoon at the seventeenth.

> "Then will I tell to sinners round
> What a dear Saviour I have found:
> I'll point to thy redeeming blood,
> And say—'Behold the way to God!'"

Then when the day is over get up to your chambers and wonder, admire and adore; spend half an hour also like Mary in pondering and treasuring up the day's work and the day's hearing in your hearts, and then close all with that which never must close—go on to-night, to-morrow, and all the days of your life, glorifying and praising God for all the things that you have seen and heard. May the Master bless you for Jesus Christ's sake. Amen.

God Incarnate, the End of Fear

" And the angel said unto them, Fear not."—Luke ii. 10.

No sooner did the angel of the Lord appear to the shepherds, and the glory of the Lord shine round about them, than they were sore afraid. It had come to this, that man was afraid of his God, and when God sent down his loving messengers with tidings of great joy, men were filled with as much fright as though the angel of death had appeared with uplifted sword. The silence of night and its dreary gloom caused no fear in the shepherds' hearts, but the joyful herald of the skies, robed in mildest glories of grace, made them sore afraid. We must not condemn the shepherds on this account as though they were peculiarly timid or ignorant, for they were only acting as every other person in that age would have done under the same circumstances. Not because they were simple shepherds were they amazed with fear, but it is probable that if they had been well-instructed prophets they would have displayed the same feeling; for there are many instances recorded in Scripture, in which the foremost men of their time trembled and felt a horror of great darkness when special manifestations of God were vouchsafed to them. In fact, a slavish fear of God was so common, that *a tradition* had grown out of it, which was all but universally received as nothing less than truth. It was generally believed that every supernatural manifestation was to be regarded as a token of speedy death. " We shall surely die because we have seen God" was not only Manoah's conclusion, but that of most men of his period. Few indeed were those happy minds who, like Manoah's wife, could reason in a more cheerful style, " If the Lord had meant to destroy us he would not have shewed us such things as these." It became *the settled conviction* of all men, whether wise or simple, whether good or bad, that a manifestation of God was not so much to be rejoiced in as to be dreaded; even as Jacob said, " How dreadful is this place! it is none other but the house of God." Doubtless the spirit which originated this tradition was much fostered by the *legal dispensation*, which is better fitted for trembling servants than for rejoicing sons. It was of the bondwoman, and it gendered into bondage. The solemn night in which its greatest institution was ordained was a night of trembling, death was there in the slaughter of the lamb; blood was there sprinkled on a conspicuous part of the house; fire was there to roast the lamb, all the emblems of judgment were there to strike the mind with awe. It was at the dread hour of midnight when the solemn family conclave was assembled, the door being shut; the guests themselves standing in an uneasy attitude, and awestricken, for their hearts could hear the wings of the destroying angel as he passed by the house. Afterwards, when Israel came into the wilderness, and the law was proclaimed, do we not read that the people stood afar off, and that bounds were set about the mount, and if so much as a beast touched the mountain it must be stoned, or thrust through with a dart? It was a day of fear and trembling when God spake unto them out of the fire. Not with the melting notes of harp, psaltery, or dulcimer, did God's law come to his people's ears; no soft wings of angels brought the message, and no sunny smiles of heaven sweetened it to the mind; but with sound of trumpet and thunder, out of the midst of blazing lightnings, with Sinai altogether on a smoke, the law was given. The law's voice was, "Come not nigh hither!" The spirit of Sinai is fear and trembling. The legal ceremonies were such as rather to inspire fear than to beget trust. The worshipper at the temple saw bloodshed from the first of the year to the end of the year; the morning was ushered in with the blood-shedding of the lamb, and the evening shades could not gather without blood again being spilt upon the altar. God was in the midst of the camp, but the pillar of cloud and fire was his unapproachable pavilion. The emblem of his glory was concealed behind the curtain of blue and scarlet and fine twined linen; behind which only one foot might pass, and that but once in the year. Men spake of the God of Israel with bated breath, and with voices hushed and solemn. They had not learned to say, "Our Father which art in heaven." They had not received the spirit of adoption, and were not able to say Abba; they smarted under the spirit of bondage, which made them sore afraid when by any peculiar glory the Lord displayed his presence among them. At the bottom of all this slavish dread lay *sin*. We never find Adam afraid of God, nor of any manifestation of Deity while he was in Paradise an obedient creature, but no sooner had he touched the fatal fruit than he found that he was naked, and hid himself. When he heard the voice of the Lord God walking in the garden in the cool of the day, Adam was afraid and hid himself from the presence of the Lord God amongst the trees of the garden. Sin makes miserable cowards of us all. See the man who once could hold delightful converse with his Maker, now dreading to hear his Maker's voice and skulking in the grove like a felon, who knows his guilt, and is afraid to meet the officers of justice.

Beloved, in order to remove this dread nightmare of slavish fear from the breast of humanity, where its horrible influence represses all the noblest aspirations of the soul, our Lord Jesus Christ came in the flesh. This is one of the works of the devil which he was manifested to destroy. Angels came to proclaim the good news of the advent of the incarnate God, and the very first note of their song was a foretaste of the sweet result of his coming to all those who shall receive him. The angel said, "Fear not," as though the times of fear were over, and the days of hope and joy had arrived. "Fear not." These words were not meant for

44

those trembling shepherds only, but were intended for you and for me, yea all nations to whom the glad tidings shall come. "Fear not." Let God no longer be the object of your slavish dread! Stand not at a distance from him any more. The Word is made flesh. God has descended to tabernacle among men, that there may be no hedge of fire, no yawning gulf between God and man.

Into this subject I wish to go this morning as God may help me. I am sensible of the value of the theme, and am very conscious that I cannot do it justice. I would earnestly ask God the Holy Spirit to make you drink of the golden cup of the incarnation of Christ such draughts as I have enjoyed in my quiet meditations. I can scarce desire more delight for my dearest friends. There is no antidote for fear more excellent than the subject of that midnight song, the first and best of Christmas chorales, which from its first word to its last note chimes out the sweet message, which begins with, "Fear not."

> "It is my sweetest comfort, Lord,
> And will for ever be,
> To muse upon the gracious truth
> Of thy humanity.

> "Oh joy! there sitteth in our flesh,
> Upon a throne of light,
> One of a human mother born,
> In perfect Godhead bright!

> "Though earth's foundations should be moved,
> Down to their lowest deep;
> Though all the trembling universe
> Into destruction sweep;

> "For ever God, for ever man,
> My Jesus shall endure;
> And fix'd on Him, my hope remains
> Eternally secure."

Dear friends, I shall first detain your attention with a few remarks upon *the fear* of which I have already spoken; then, secondly, we shall invite your earnest attention to *the remedy* which the angels came to proclaim; and then, thirdly, as we may have time, we shall endeavour to *make an application of this remedy to various cases.*

I. Turning to THE FEAR of the text, it may be well to discriminate. There is a kind of fear towards God from which we must not wish to be free. There is that lawful, necessary, admirable, excellent fear which is always due from the creature to the Creator, from the subject to the king, ay, and from the child toward the parent. That holy, filial fear of God, which makes us dread sin, and constrains us to be obedient to his command, is to be cultivated; "we had fathers of our flesh, and we gave them reverence, shall we not be in subjection to the Father of spirits and live?" This is the "fear of the Lord which is the beginning of wisdom." To have a holy awe of our most holy, just, righteous, and tender Parent is a privilege, not a bondage. Godly fear is not the "fear which hath torment;" perfect love doth not cast out, but dwells with it in joyful harmony. The angels perfectly love God, and yet with holy fear they veil their faces with their wings as they approach him; and when we shall in glory behold the face of God, and shall be filled with all his fulness, we shall not cease humbly and reverently to adore the infinite Majesty. Holy fear is a work of the Holy Ghost, and woe unto the man who does not possess it; let him boast as he may, his "feeding himself without fear" is a mark of his hypocrisy.

The fear which is to be avoided is *slavish fear;* the fear which perfect love casts out, as Sarah cast out the bondwoman and her son. That trembling which keeps us at a distance from God, which makes us think of him as a Spirit with whom we can have no communion; as a being who has no care for us except to punish us, and for whom consequently we have no care except to escape if possible from his terrible presence. This fear sometimes arises in men's hearts from their *thoughts dwelling exclusively upon the divine greatness.* Is it possible to peer long into the vast abyss of Infinity and not to fear? Can the mind yield itself up to the thought of the Eternal, Self-existent, Infinite One without being filled, first with awe and then with dread? What am I? An aphis creeping upon a rosebud is a more considerable creature in relation to the universe of beings than I can be in comparison with God. What am I? A grain of dust, that does not turn the scale of the most delicate balance is a greater thing to man than a man is to Jehovah. At best we are less than nothing and vanity. But there is more to abase us than this. We have had the impertinence to be disobedient to the will of this great One; and now the goodness and greatness of his nature are as a current against which sinful humanity struggles in vain, for the irresistible torrent must run its course, and overwhelm every opponent. What does the great God seem to us out of Christ but a stupendous rock, threatening to crush us, or a fathomless sea, hastening to swallow us up? The contemplation of the divine greatness may of itself fill man with horror, and cast him into unutterable misery! Dwell long upon such themes, and like Job, you will tremble before Jehovah, who shaketh the earth out of her place, and the pillars thereof tremble.

Each one of the sterner attributes of God will cause the like fear. Think of his power by which he rolls the stars along, and lay thine hand upon thy mouth. Think of his wisdom by which he numbers the clouds, and settles the ordinances of heaven. Meditate upon any one of these attributes, but especially upon his justice, and upon that devouring fire which burns unceasingly against sin, and it is no wonder if the soul becomes full of fear. Meanwhile let *a sense of sin* with its great whip of wire, flagellate the conscience, and man will dread the bare idea of God. For this is the burden of the voice of conscience to guilty man, "If thou wert an obedient creature, this God were still terrible to thee, for the heavens are not pure in his sight, and he charged his angels with folly. What art thou that thou shouldst be just with God, or have any claims upon him; for thou hast offended, thou hast lifted the hand of thy rebellion against the infinite majesty of omnipotence—what can become of thee? what can be thy portion but to be set up for ever as a monument of his righteous wrath?"

Now such a fear as that being very easily created in the thoughtful mind, and being indeed, as it seems to me, the natural heritage of man, as the result of sin is most doleful and injurious. For wherever there is a slavish dread of the Divine Being, *it alienates man most thoroughly from his God.* We are by our evil nature enemies to God, and the

46

imagination that God is cruel, harsh, and terrible, adds fuel to the fire of our enmity. Those whom we slavishly dread we cannot love. You could not make your child show forth love to you if its little heart was full of fear ; if it dreaded to hear your footstep, and was alarmed at the sound of your voice, it could not love you. You might obey some huge ogre because you were afraid of him, but to love him would be impossible. It is one of the master-pieces of Satan to deceive man by presenting to his mind a hateful picture of God. He knows that men cannot love that which terrifies them, and therefore he paints the God of grace as a hard, unforgiving being who will not receive the penitent and have pity upon the sorrowful. God is love ! Surely if men had but grace enough to see the beauty of that portrait of God— that miniature sketched with a single line, " God is love ! " they would willingly serve such a God. When the Holy Ghost enables the mind to perceive the character of God, the heart cannot refuse to love him. Base, fallen, depraved as men are, when they are illuminated from on high so as to judge rightly of God, their hearts melt under the genial beams of divine love, and they love God because he has first loved them. But here is the master-piece of Satan, that he will not let the understanding perceive the excellence of God's character, and then the heart cannot love that which the understanding does not perceive to be loveable.

In addition to alienating the heart from God, this fear *creates a prejudice against God's gospel of grace.* There are persons in this place this morning who believe that if they were religious they would be miserable. It is the settled conviction of half London that to trust in Jesus and to be obedient to God, which is the essence of all true religion, would be wretchedness itself. " Oh," says the worldly man, " I should have to give up my pleasure if I were to become a Christian." Now, this is one of the most wicked slanders that ever was invented, and yet it has current belief everywhere. It is the popular theology that to be an enemy to God is happiness, but to be the friend of God is misery. What an opinion men must have of God, when they believe that to love him is to be wretched! Oh, could they comprehend, could they but know how good God is, instead of imagining that his service would be slavery, they would understand that to be his friends is to occupy the highest and happiest position which created beings can occupy.

This fear in some men *puts them out of all heart of ever being saved.* Thinking God to be an ungenerous being, they keep at a distance from him, and if there be some sweet attractions now and then in a sermon, some gentle meltings of conscience, the good desire never matures into the practical resolve. They do not say, " I will arise and go unto my Father," because they do not know him as a Father, they only know him as a consuming fire. A man does not say, " I will arise and go unto a consuming fire." Nay, but, like Jonah, he would fain pay his fare, regardless of the expense, and go to Tarshish to flee from the presence of the Lord. This it is that makes calamity of being a man at all to most men, that they cannot get away from God, since they imagine that if they could but escape from his presence they would then wander into bliss ; but being doomed to be where God is, then they conceive that for them wretchedness and misery alone remain. The soft warnings of mercy and the thunderings of justice are alike powerless upon men so long as their hearts are seared and rendered callous by an unholy dread of God.

This wicked dread of God frequently *drives men to extremities of sin.* The man says, "There is no hope for me; I have made one fatal mistake in being God's enemy, and I am irretrievably ruined. There is no hope that I shall ever be restored to happiness or peace. Then what will I do? I will cast the reins upon the neck of my passions, I will defy fate and take my chance. I will get such happiness as may be found in sin. If I cannot be reconciled to heaven I will be a good servant of hell." Hence men have been known to hasten from one crime to another with a malicious inventiveness of rebellion against God, as if they could never be satisfied nor contented till they had heaped up more and more rebellions against the majesty of God whom in their hearts they dreaded with a burning Satanic dread mingled with hate. If they could but comprehend that he is still willing to receive the rebellious, that his bowels yearn towards sinners; if they could but once believe that he is love and willeth not the death of a sinner but had rather that he should turn unto him and live, surely the course of their lives must be changed; but the god of this world blindeth them, and maligns the Lord until they count it folly to submit to him.

Dear friends, this evil which works a thousand ills, operates in ways of evil quite innumerable. *It dishonours God.* Oh, it is infamous, it is villainous to make out our God, who is light and in whom is no darkness at all, to be an object of horrible fear. It is infernal; I may say no less; it is devilish to the highest degree to paint him as a demon, who is Jehovah, the God of Love. Oh, the impertinence of the prince of darkness, and the madness of man to consent thereunto, that God should be depicted as being unwilling to forgive, unkind, untender, hard, cruel; whereas he is love; supremely and above all things, love. He is just, but alll the more truly loving because he is just. He is true, and therefore sure to punish sin, yet even punishing sin because it were not good to let sin go unpunished. This is base ingratitude on the part of a much-receiving creature that he should malign his benefactor.

The evil which is thus done to God recoils upon man, for this *fear hath torment.* No more tormenting misery in the world than to think of God as being our implacable foe. You Christians who have lost for a while the spirit of adoption, you who have wandered to a distance from God, nothing can be more tormenting to you than the fear that the Lord has cast you away and will not again receive you. You backsliders, nothing can hold you back from your heavenly Father like a dread of him. If you can but really know that he is not to be dreaded with slavish fear, you will come to him as your child does to you, and you will say, "My Father, I have offended—pity me! My Father, I am vexed and grieved for my sin—forgive me, receive me again to thine arms, and help me by thy mighty grace that henceforth I may walk in thy commandments, and be obedient to thy will." My dear friends, you who know anything about spiritual life, do not you feel that when you have sweet thoughts of God breathed into you from above, and have his special love to you shed abroad in your hearts, it is then that you are holiest! Have you not perceived that the only way in which you can grow in that which is morally and spiritually lovely, is by having your gracious God high in your esteem, and feeling his precious love firing your hearts?

That they may be like little children is the very thing which God desires for his elect ones. It is this which his Spirit works in his chosen; it is to this that we must come if we are to be meet to be partakers of the inheritance of the saints in light. Slavish fear is so opposed to the child-like spirit that it is as the poison of asps to it. Dread and fear bring out everything in us that is of the man rather than of the child, for it stirs us up to resist the object of our fear. An assured confidence in the goodness of God casts out fear and brings forth everything that is child-like in us. Have you never seen a child trust to some big rough man, and melt him down by its trustfulness? It trusted where there was no ground for trust apparently, and made ground for itself. That same child simply and implicitly trusting in a good and generous father is a noble picture, and if I, a poor, weak, feeble child, conscious that I am such, knowing that I am all folly and weakness, can just believe in my good, great God, through Jesus Christ, and come and trust myself with him, and leave him to do as he likes with me, believing that he will not be unkind, and cannot be unwise; if I can wholly repose in his love and be obedient to his will, why then I shall have reached the highest point that the creature can reach; the Holy Ghost will then have wrought his finished work in me, and I shall be fit for heaven. Beloved, it is because fear opposes this, and prevents this, that I would say with the angel, "Fear not."

II. I fear I weary you while I speak upon this somewhat dolorous theme, and therefore with as much brevity as the abundance of the matter may permit, let us notice in the second place, THE CURE FOR THIS FEAR, which the angel came to proclaim. It lies in this:—"Unto you is born this day in the city of David, a Saviour, which is Christ the Lord."

> " Till God in human flesh I see,
> My thoughts no comfort find;
> The holy, just and sacred Three,
> Are terrors to my mind.
>
> " But if Immanuel's face appear,
> My hope, my joy begins ;
> His name forbids my slavish fear,
> His grace removes my sins."

That is the remedy—God with us—God made flesh. Let us try and show this from the angel's song.

According to the text they were not to fear, first of all, because *the angel had come to bring them good news.* How does it run? It says, " I bring you good tidings of great joy." But what was this gospel? Further on we are told that the gospel was the fact that Christ was born. So, then, it is good news to men that Christ is born, that God has come down and taken manhood into union with himself. Verily this is glad tidings. He who made the heavens slumbers in a manger. What then? Why then God is not of necessity an enemy to man, because here is God actually taking manhood into alliance with Deity.

There cannot be permanent, inveterate, rooted enmity between the two natures, or otherwise the divine nature could not have taken the human into hypostatical union with itself. Is there not comfort in that? Thou art a poor, erring, feeble man, and that which makes thee afraid of the Lord is this fear that there is an enmity between God and man; but there need not be such enmity, for thy Maker has actually taken manhood into union with himself.

Dost thou not see another thought? The Eternal seems to be so far away from us. He is infinite, and we are such little creatures. There appears to be a great gulf fixed between man and God, even on the ground of creatureship. But observe, he who is God has also become man. We never heard that God took the nature of angels into union with himself; we may therefore say that between Godhead and angelhood there must be an infinite distance still; but here the Lord has actually taken manhood into union with himself; there is therefore no longer a great gulf fixed, on the contrary, here is a marvellous union; Godhead has entered into marriage bonds with manhood. O my soul, thou dost not stand now like a poor lone orphan wailing across the deep sea after thy Father who has gone far away and cannot hear thee ; thou dost not now sob and sigh like an infant left naked and helpless, its Maker having gone too far away to regard its wants or listen to its cries. No, thy Maker has become like thyself. Is that too strong a word to use? He without whom was not anything made that was made is that same Word who tabernacled among us and was made flesh, made flesh in such a way that he was tempted in all points like as we are, yet without sin. O manhood, was there ever such news as this for thee! Poor manhood, thou weak worm of the dust, far lower than the angels, lift up thy head, and be not afraid! Poor manhood, born in weakness, living in toil, covered with sweat, and dying at last to be eaten by the worms, be not thou abashed even in the presence of seraphs, for next to God is man, and not even an archangel can come in between; nay, not next to God, there is scarcely that to be said, for Jesus who is God is man also; Jesus Christ, eternally God, was born, and lived and died as we also do. That is the first word of comfort to expel our fear.

The second point that takes away fear is that this man who was also God was actually *born*. Observe the angel's word, "Unto you is *born*."

Our Lord Jesus Christ is in some senses more man than Adam. Adam was not born ; Adam never had to struggle through the risks and weaknesses of infancy ; he knew not the littlenesses of childhood—he was full grown at once. Father Adam could not sympathize with me as a babe and a child. But how man-like is Jesus! he is cradled with us in the manger ; he does not begin with us in mid-life, as Adam, but he accompanies us in the pains and feebleness and infirmities of infancy, and he continues with us even to the grave. Beloved, this is such sweet comfort. He that is God this day was once an infant : so that if my cares are little and even trivial and comparatively infantile, I may go to him, for he was once a child. Though the great ones of the earth may sneer at the child of poverty, and say, "You are too mean, and your trouble is too slight for pity;" I recollect with humble joy, that the King of heaven did hang upon a woman's breast, and was wrapped in swaddling bands, and therefore I tell him all my griefs.

How wonderful that he should have been an infant, and yet should be God over all, blessed for ever! I am not afraid of God now ; this blessed link between me and God, the holy child Jesus, has taken all fear away.

Observe, the angel told them somewhat of his *office*, as well as of his birth. "Unto you is born this day *a Saviour*." The very object for which he was born and came into this world was that he might deliver us from sin. What, then, was it that made us afraid? Were we not afraid of God because we felt that we were lost through sin? Well then, here is joy upon joy. Here is not only the Lord come among us as a man, but made man in order to save man from that which separated him from God. I feel as if I could burst out into a weeping for some here who have been spending their living riotously and gone far away from God their Father by their evil ways. I know they are afraid to come back. They think that the Lord will not receive them, that there is no mercy for such sinners as they have been. Oh, but think of it—Jesus Christ has come to seek and to save that which was lost. He was born to save. If he does not save he was born in vain, for the object of his birth was salvation. If he shall not be a Saviour, then the mission of God to earth has missed its end, for its design was that lost sinners might be saved. Lost one, lost one, if there were news that an angel had come to save thee there might be some cheer in it ; but there are better tidings still. God has come; the Infinite, the Almighty, has stooped from the highest heaven that he may pick thee up, a poor undone and worthless worm. Is there not comfort here ? Does not the incarnate Saviour take away the horrible dread which hangs over men like a black pall ?

Note that the angel did not forget to describe *the person* of this Saviour—"A Saviour which is *Christ*." There is his manhood. As man he was anointed. "*The Lord*." There is his Godhead. Yes, this is the solid truth upon which we plant our foot. Jesus of Nazareth is God; he who was conceived in the womb of the virgin and born in Bethlehem's manger is now, and always was, God over all, blessed for ever. There is no gospel if he be not God. It is no news to me to tell me that a great prophet is born. There have been great prophets before; but the world has never been redeemed from evil by mere testimony to the truth, and never will be. Tell me that God is born, that God himself has espoused our nature, and taken it into union with himself, then the bells of my heart ring merry peals, for now may I come to God since God has come to me.

You will observe, dear friends, however, that the pith of what the angel said lay in this. "*Unto you*." You will never get true comfort from the incarnate Saviour till you perceive your personal interest in him. Christ as man was a representative man. There never were but two thoroughly representative men; the first is Adam: Adam obedient the whole race stands, Adam disobedient the whole race falls. "In Adam all die." Now, the man Jesus is the second great representative man. He does not represent the whole human race, he represents as many as his Father gave him; he represents a chosen company. Now, whatever Christ did, if you belong to those who are in him he did for you. So that Christ circumcised or Christ crucified, Christ dead or

Christ living, Christ buried or Christ risen, you are a partaker of all that he did and all that he is, for you are reckoned as one with him. See then, the joy and comfort of the incarnation of Christ. Does Jesus, as man, take manhood up to heaven? He has taken me up there. Father Adam fell, and I fell for I was in him. The Lord Jesus Christ rises, and I rise if I am in him. See, beloved, when Jesus Christ was nailed to the cross all his elect were nailed there, and they suffered and died in him. When he was put into the grave the whole of his people lay slumbering there in him, for they were in the loins of Jesus as Levi was in the loins of Abraham; and when he rose they rose and received the foretaste of their own future resurrection, because he lives they shall live also; and now that he has gone up on high to claim the throne, he has claimed the throne for every soul that is in him. Oh, this is joy indeed! Then how can I be afraid of God, for this day, by faith, I, a poor undeserving sinner, having put my trust in Jesus, am bold to say that I sit upon the throne of God. Think not that we have said too much, for in the person of Christ every believer is raised up together, and made to sit together in heavenly places in Christ Jesus. Because as Jesus is there, representatively, we are each one of us there in him.

I wish that I had power to bring out this precious doctrine of the incarnation as I could desire, but the more one muses upon it, the more happy one becomes. Let us view it as an all-important truth, that Jesus, the Son of God, has really come in the flesh. It is so important a truth, that we have three witnesses appointed to keep it before us upon earth. We have been insisting many times in this place upon the spirituality of Christian worship. We have shown that the outward in religion, by itself, availeth nothing; it is the inward spirit that is the great thing. I must confess that I have sometimes said in myself, I hope not rebelliously, " What is this Baptism for, and what is this Communion of the Lord's Supper for?" These two outward ordinances, whatever may be their excellent uses, have been the two things around which more errors have clustered than around anything else; and I have heard it said, by friends inclined to follow more fully the teachings of the Quakers, " Why not put aside the outward and visible altogether? Let it be the Spirit Baptism, and not the water; let there be no bread and wine, but let there be fellowship with Christ without the outward sign." I must confess, though I dare not go with it, because I hope to be held fast by the plain testimony of Scripture, yet my heart has somewhat gone with the temptation, and I have half said, "Men always will pervert these two ordinances, would not it be as well to have done with them?" While I have been exercised upon the point, conscious that the ordinances must be right, and must be held, I have rested upon that text, " There are three that bear witness in earth, the Spirit, the water, and the blood." And what do they bear witness to? They bear witness to the mission of Jesus as the Christ, in other words to the real incarnation of God. They bear witness to the materialism of Christ. Have you ever noticed that when people have given up the two outward ordinances, they have usually betrayed a tendency to give up the literal fact that "God was made flesh"? The literal fact that Christ was really a man has generally been doubted or thrown into the background when the two outward ordinances have been given up, and I believe that these two symbolical ordinances, which are a link between the spiritual and the material, are set up on purpose to show that Christ Jesus, though most gloriously a spirit, was also a man clothed in a body of real flesh and blood like our own; so that he could be touched and handled even as he said, "Handle me and see; a spirit hath not flesh and bones as ye see me have." When I think of the Holy Spirit who bears witness that Christ was really a man, I thank him for that witness; then I turn to the water, and when I read that Christ was publicly baptized in Jordan, I perceive that he could not have been a phantom; he could not have been a mere spectral appearance, for he was immersed in water; he must have been a solid substantial man. The preservation of the ordinance of baptism is a witness to the reality of the incarnate God. Then comes the blood, he could not have shed blood on Calvary if he had been a spectre. There could have been no blood streaming down from his side when the spear pierced him if he had been only a ghostly apparition; he must have been solid flesh and blood like ourselves; and as often as we come to his table, and we take the cup and hear it said, "This cup is the new covenant in my blood," there is a third witness on earth to the fact that Jesus did appear in very flesh and blood among men. So that the Spirit, the water, and the blood, are the three standing testimonies in the church of God, that Christ was God, and that he was also really, solidly, and substantially man. I shall delight in the ordinances all the more because of this. Those two ordinances serve to make us recollect that Christ was really flesh and blood, and that religion has something to do with this flesh and blood of ours. This very body is to rise again from the tomb; Jesus came to deliver this poor flesh from corruption ; and so, while we must ever keep the spiritual uppermost, we are prevented from casting away the material body as though that were of the devil. Christ purified as well the realm of matter as the realm of spirit ; and in both he reigns triumphant. There is much comfort here.

III. Lastly, we can only occupy a few seconds in APPLYING THE CURE TO VARIOUS CASES.

Child of God, you say, "I dare not come to God to-day, I feel so weak." Fear not, for he that is born in Bethlehem said, "A bruised reed I will not break, and the smoking flax I will not quench." "I shall never get to heaven," says another; "I shall never see God's face with acceptance; I am so tempted." "Fear not," for ye have not an high priest which cannot be touched with a feeling of your infirmities, for he was tempted in all points like as ye are." "But I am so lonely in the world," says another, "no man cares for me." There is one man at any rate who does so care; a true man like yourself. He is your brother still, and does not forget the lonely spirit.

But I hear a sinner say, "I am afraid to go to God this morning and confess that I am a sinner." Well, do not go to God but go to Christ. Surely you would not be afraid of him. Think of God *in* Christ, not out of Christ. If you could but know Jesus you would go to him at once; you would not be afraid to tell him your sins, for you would know that he would say, "Go, and sin no more." "I cannot pray," says one, " I feel afraid to pray." What, afraid to pray when it is a man who listens to you! You might dread the face of God, but when God in human flesh you see why be alarmed? Go, poor sinner, go to Jesus. " I feel," says one, " unfit to come." You may be unfit to come to God, but you cannot be unfit to come to Jesus. There is a fitness necessary to stand in the holy hill of the Lord, but there is no fitness needed in coming to the Lord Jesus. Come as you are, guilty, and lost, and ruined. Come just as you are, and he will receive you. " Oh," says another, " I cannot trust." I can understand your not being able to trust the great invisible God, but cannot you trust that dying, bleeding Son of Man who is also the Son of God? " " But I cannot hope," says another, " that he would even look on me:" and yet he used to look on such as you are. He received publicans and sinners and ate with them, and even harlots were not driven from his presence. Oh, since God has thus taken man into union with himself be not afraid! If I speak to one who by reason of sin has wandered so far away from God that he is even afraid to think of God's name, yet inasmuch as Jesus Christ is called " the sinner's Friend," I pray thee think of *him*, poor soul, as *thy* friend. And, oh! may the Spirit of God open thy blind eyes to see that there is no cause for thy keeping away from God, except thine own mistaken thoughts of him! May you believe that he is able and willing to save to the uttermost! May you understand his good and gracious character, his readiness to pass by transgression, iniquity, and sin! And may the sweet influences of grace constrain you to come to him this very morning! God grant that Jesus Christ may be formed in you, the hope of glory; and then you may well sing, "Glory to God in the highest; on earth peace, and goodwill toward men." Amen.

The Sages, the Star, and the Saviour

"Where is he that is born King of the Jews? for we have seen his star in the east, and are come to worship him."—Matthew ii. 2.

THE incarnation of the Son of God was one of the greatest events in the history of the universe. Its actual occurrence was not, however, known to all mankind, but was specially revealed to the shepherds of Bethlehem and to certain wise men of the east. To shepherds—the illiterate, men little versed in human learning—the angels in choral song made known the birth of the Saviour, Christ the Lord, and they hastened to Bethlehem to see the great sight; while the Scribes, the writers of the law and expounders of it, knew nothing concerning the long-promised birth of the Messias. No angelic bands entered the assembly of the Sanhedrim and proclaimed that the Christ was born; and when the chief priests and Pharisees were met together, though they gathered around copies of the law to consider where Christ should be born, yet it was not known to them that he was actually come, nor do they seem to have taken more than a passing interest in the matter, though they might have known that then was the time spoken of by the prophets when the great Messiah should come. How mysterious are the dispensations of grace; the base things are chosen and the eminent are passed by! The advent of the Redeemer is revealed to the shepherds who kept their flocks of sheep by night, but not to the shepherds whose benighted sheep were left to stray. Admire therein the sovereignty of God.

The glad tidings were made known also to wise men, magi, students of the stars and of old prophetic books from the far-off east. It would not be possible to tell how far off their native country lay; it may have been so distant that the journey occupied nearly the whole of the two years of which they spake concerning the appearance of the star. Travelling was slow in those days, surrounded with difficulties and many dangers. They may have come from Persia, or India, or Tartary, or even from the mysterious land of Sinim, now known to us as China. If so, strange and uncouth must have been the speech of those who worshipped around the young Child at Bethlehem, yet needed he no interpreter to understand and accept their adoration. Why was the birth of the King of the Jews made known to these foreigners, and not to those nearer home? Why did the Lord select those who were so many hundreds of miles away, while the children of the kingdom, in whose very midst the Saviour was brought forth, were yet strangely ignorant of his presence? See here again another instance of the sovereignty of God. Both in shepherds and in Eastern magi gathering around the young Child, I see God dispensing his favours as he wills; and, as I see it, I exclaim, " I thank thee, O Father, Lord of heaven and earth, because thou hast hid these things from the wise and prudent, and hast revealed them unto babes. Even so, Father; for so it seemed good in thy sight." Herein we see again another instance of God's sovereign will; for as of old there were many widows in Israel in the days of Elias the prophet, but unto none of them was Elias sent, save unto the woman of Sarepta; so many there were who were called wise men among the Jews, but unto none of them did the star appear; but it shone on Gentile eyes, and led a chosen company from the ends of the earth to bow at Emmanuel's feet.

Sovereignty in these cases clothed itself in the robes of mercy. It was great mercy that regarded the low estate of the shepherds, and it was far-reaching mercy which gathered from lands which lay in darkness a company of men made wise unto salvation. Mercy wearing her resplendent jewels was present with divine sovereignty in the lowly abode of Bethlehem. Is it not a delightful thought, that around the cradle of the Saviour, as well as around his throne in the highest heaven, these two attributes meet? He makes known himself—and herein is mercy; but it is to those whom he has chosen—and herein he shows that he will have mercy on whom he will have mercy, and he will have compassion on whom he will have compassion.

We will now endeavour to learn a practical lesson from the story of the wise men who came from the east to worship Christ. We may, if God the Holy Spirit shall teach us, gather such instruction as may lead us also to become worshippers of the Saviour, and joyful believers in him.

Notice, first, *their enquiry;* may many of us become enquirers upon the same matter—" Where is he that is born King of the Jews ?" Notice, secondly, *their encouragement*—" We have seen his star." Because they had seen his star they felt bold to ask, " Where is he?" And then, thirdly, *their example*—" We have come to worship him."

I. THEIR ENQUIRY—" Where is he ?"

Many things are evident in this question. It is clear that when the wise men thus enquired, there was in their minds *interest awakened.* The King of the Jews was born, but Herod did not ask, " Where is he?" until his jealousy was excited, and then he asked the question in a malicious spirit. Christ was born at Bethlehem, near to Jerusalem; yet throughout all the streets of the holy city there were no enquirers, " Where is he?" He was to be the glory of Israel, and yet in Israel there were few indeed who, like these wise men, asked the question, " Where is he ?" My dear hearers, I will believe that there are some here this morning whom God intends to bless, and it will be a very hopeful sign that he intends to do so, if there be an interest awakened in your mind concerning the work and person of the incarnate God. Those who anxiously desire to know of him, are but a slender company. Alas! when we preach most earnestly of him, and tell of his sorrows as the atonement for human sin, we are compelled to lament most bitterly the carelessness of mankind, and enquire mournfully—

> " Is it nothing to you, all ye that pass by;
> Is it nothing to you that Jesus should die?"

He is despised and rejected of men, men see in him no beauty that they should desire him; but there are a chosen number who enquire diligently, and who come to receive him; to these he gives power to become the sons of God. A happy circumstance it is, therefore, when there is interest evinced. Interest is not always evinced in the things of Christ, even by our regular hearers. It gets to be a mere mechanical habit to attend public worship; you become accustomed to sit through such a part of the service, to stand and sing at such another time, and to listen to the preacher with an apparent attention during the discourse; but to be really interested, to long to know what it is all about, to know especially whether you have a part in it, whether Jesus came from heaven to save you, whether for you he was born of the virgin, to make such personal enquiries with deep anxiety, is far from being a general practice : would God that all who have ears to hear would hear in truth. Wherever the word is heard with solemn interest, it is a very encouraging sign. It was said of old, " They shall ask the way to Zion with their faces thitherward." When a man listens with deep attention to the word of God, searches God's book, and engages in thoughtful meditation with the view of understanding the gospel, we have much hope of him. When he feels that there is something weighty and important, something worth the knowing, in the gospel of Jesus, then are we encouraged to hope good things of him.

But in the case of the wise men we see not only interest evinced, but *belief avowed.* They said, " Where is he that is born King of the Jews?" They were, therefore, fully convinced that he was the King of the Jews, and had lately been born. As a preacher I feel it to be a great mercy that I have to deal generally with persons who have some degree of belief concerning the things of God. Would to God we had more missions to those who have no sort of faith and no knowledge of Christ; and may the day come when everywhere Jesus Christ shall be known. But here at home with the most of you we have something to begin with. You do believe somewhat concerning Jesus of Nazareth, who was born King of the Jews. Set much store by that which you have already believed. I count it no small advantage to a young man to believe his Bible true. There are some who have a hard fight to reach so far as that, for infidel training has warped their minds. It is not, of course, an advantage which will save you, for many go down to hell believing the Scriptures to be true, and thus they accumulate guilt upon themselves from that very fact; but it is a fine vantage ground to occupy, to be assured that you have God's word before you, and not to be troubled with questions about its inspiration and authenticity. O that you may go from that point of faith to another, and become a hearty believer in Jesus. These wise men were so far advanced that they had some leverage for a further lift of faith, for they believed that Christ was born, and born a King. Many who are not saved, yet know that Jesus is the Son of God. We have not to argue with you this morning to bring you out of Socinianism— no, you believe Jesus to be the divine Saviour; nor have we to reason against doubts and scepticisms concerning the atonement, for these do not perplex you. This is a great mercy. You certainly stand in the position of highly favoured persons. I only trust you may have grace given you to avail yourselves of the favourable position in which God has placed you. Value what you have already received. When a man's eyes have long been closed in darkness, if the oculist gives him but a little light he is very thankful for it, he is hopeful that the eye is not destroyed, that perhaps by another operation further scales may be removed, and the full light may yet stream in upon the darkened eyeball. So, dear friend, be thankful for any light. O soul, so soon to pass into another world, so sure to be lost except thou have the light divine, so certain to be cast into the outer darkness, where there is weeping and wailing and gnashing of teeth, be thankful for a spark of heavenly light; prize it, treasure it, be anxious about it that it may come to something more, and who knows but yet the Lord will bless thee with the fulness of his truth? When the great bridge across the Niagara was made, the difficulty was to pass the first rope across the broad stream. I have read that it was accomplished by flying a kite, and allowing it to fall on the opposite bank. The kite carried across a piece of string, then to the string was tied a line, and to the line a rope, and to the rope a stronger rope, and by-and-by Niagara was spanned, and the bridge was finished. Even thus by degrees God works. It is a fair sight to see in human hearts a little interest concerning things divine, a little desire after Christ, a feeble wish to know who he is and what he is, and whether he is available to the sinner's case. This hunger will lead to a craving after more, and that craving will be followed by another, till at last the soul shall find her Lord and be satisfied in him. In the wise men's case therefore we have, as I trust we have in some here, interest evinced, and a measure of belief avowed.

Furthermore, in the case of the wise men, we see *ignorance admitted.* Wise men are never above asking questions, because they are wise men; so the magi asked, "Where is he?" Persons who have taken the name and degree of wise men, and are so esteemed, sometimes think it beneath them to confess any degree of ignorance, but the really wise think not so; they are too well instructed to be ignorant of their own ignorance. Many men might have been wise if they had but been aware that they were fools. The knowledge of our ignorance is the doorstep of the temple of knowledge. Some think they know, and therefore never know.

Had they known that they were blind, they would soon have been made to see, but because they say, "We see," therefore their blindness remains upon them. Beloved hearer, dost thou want to find a Saviour? Wouldst thou fain have all thy sins blotted out? Wouldst thou be reconciled to God through Jesus Christ? Then blush not to enquire, admit that thou dost not know. How shouldst thou know if heaven teach thee not? How should any man attain the knowledge of divine things, unless it be given him from above? We must all be taught of the Spirit of God, or be fools for ever. To know that we need to be taught of the Holy Ghost is one of the first lessons that the Holy Ghost himself teaches us. Admit that thou needest a guide, and diligently enquire for one. Cry to God to lead thee, and he will be thine instructor. Be not high-minded and self-sufficient. Ask for heavenly light, and thou shalt receive it. Is it not better to ask God to teach thee, than to trust to thine own unaided reason? Bow, then, the knee, confess thine aptness to err, and say, "What I know not, teach thou me."

Notice, however, that the wise men were not content with admitting their ignorance, but in their case there was *information entreated*. I cannot tell where they began to ask. They thought it likeliest that Jesus would be known at the metropolitan city. Was he not the King of the Jews? where would he be so certain to be known as at the Capital? They went, therefore, to Jerusalem. Perhaps they asked the guards at the gate, "Where is he that is born King of the Jews?" and the guards laughed them to scorn, and replied, "We know no king but Herod." Then they met a loiterer in the streets, and to him they said, "Where is he that is born King of the Jews?" and he answered, "What care I for such crazy questions? I am looking for a drinking companion." They asked a trader, but he sneered, and said, "Never mind kings, what will you buy, or what have you to sell?" Where is he that is born King of the Jews?" said they to a Sadducee, and he replied, "Be not such fools as to talk in that fashion, or if you do, pray call on my religious friend the Pharisee." They passed a woman in the streets, and asked, "Where is he that is born King of the Jews?" but she said, "My child is sick at home, I have enough to do to think of my poor babe; I care not who is born, or who may die beside." When they went to the very highest quarters, they obtained but poor information, but they were not content till they had learned all that could be known. They did not know at first where the new-born King was, but they used every means to find him, and asked information on all hands. It is delightful to see the holy eagerness of a soul which God has quickened; it cries, "I must be saved; I know something of the way of salvation, I am grateful for that, but I do not know all I want to know, and I cannot rest satisfied till I do. If beneath the canopy of heaven a Saviour is to be found, I will have him; if that book can teach me how to be saved, I will turn its pages day and night; if any book within my reach may help me, I will spare no midnight oil if I may but in the reading thereof find out Christ my Saviour. If there be one whose preaching has been blessed to the souls of others, I will hang on his lips, if perhaps the word may be blessed to me, for Christ I must have: it is not I may or I may not have him, but I *must* have him; my hunger is great for this bread of heaven, my thirst insatiable for this water of life; tell me, Christians, tell me, wise men, tell me, good men, tell me any of you who can tell, where is he that is born King of the Jews? for Christ I must have, and I long to have him now."

Notice further, that in reference to these wise men from the east, there was for their search after Christ *a motive declared.* "Where is he," said they, "that we may go and worship him?" Ah! soul, and if thou wouldst find Christ, let it be thy motive that thou mayst be saved by him, and that then henceforth and for ever thou mayst live to his glory. When it comes to this, that you do not hear the gospel merely as a habit, but because you long to obtain its salvation, it will not be long before you will find it. When a man can say, "I am going up to the house of God this morning, and O may God meet with me there," he will not long go there in vain. When a hearer can declare, "As soon as I take my seat in the congregation, my one thought is, "Lord, bless my soul this day?" he cannot for long be disappointed. Usually in going up to God's house we get what we go for. Some come because it is the custom, some to meet a friend, some they scarce know why; but when you know what you come for, the Lord who gave you the desire will gratify it. I was pleased with the word of a dear sister this morning when I came in at the back gate; she said to me, "My dear sir, my soul is very hungry this morning. May the Lord give you bread for me." I believe that food convenient will be given. When a sinner is very hungry after Christ, Christ is very near to him. The worst of it is, many of you do not come to find Jesus, it is not him you are seeking for; if you were seeking him, he would soon appear to you. A young woman was asked during a revival, "How is it you have not found Christ?" "Sir," said she, "I think it is because I have not sought him." It is so. None shall be able to say at the last, "I sought him, but I found him not." In all cases at the last, if Jesus Christ be not found, it must be because he has not been devoutly, earnestly, importunately sought, for his promise is, "Seek, and ye shall find." These wise men are to us a model in many things, and in this among the rest—that their motive was clear to themselves, and they avowed it to others. May all of us seek Jesus that we may worship him.

All through there was about the wise men an intense earnestness, which we would delight to see in any who as yet have not believed in

Jesus. They were evidently not triflers. They came a long way, they underwent many fatigues, they spoke about finding the new-born King in a practical, common-sense way; they were not put off with this rebuff or that; they desired to find him, and find him they would. It is most blessed to see the work of the Spirit in men's hearts impelling them to long for the Saviour to be their Lord and King; and so to long for him that they mean to have him, and will leave no stone unturned, by the Holy Spirit's help, but what they will be able to say, "We have found him, of whom Moses in the law, and the prophets, did write, and he is become our salvation."

Am I at this moment speaking to anybody in particular? I trust I am. Some years ago there was a young man, who, upon much such a morning as this—cold, snowy, dark—entered a house of prayer, as you have done to-day. I thought as I came here, this morning, of that young man. I said to myself, "This morning is so very forbidding that I shall have a very small congregation, but perhaps among them there will be one like that young man." To be plain with you, it comforted me to think that the morning when God blessed my soul, the preacher had a very small congregation, and it was cold and bitter, and therefore I said to myself this morning, "Why should not I go up merrily to my task, and preach if there should only be a dozen there?" for Jesus may intend to reveal himself to some one as he did to me, and that some one may be a soul-winner, and the means of the salvation of tens of thousands in years to come. I wonder if that will occur to that young man yonder, for I trust he has the enquiry of the wise men upon his lips. I trust he will not quench those desires which now burn within him, but rather may the spark be fanned to a flame, and may this day witness his decision for Jesus. Oh, has the Lord looked on that young woman, or on that dear child, or on yonder aged man? "I know not who it may be, but I shall indeed bless God this morning, if the cry may be heard from many a lip, "Sir, what must I do to be saved? Where is he that is born King of the Jews?"

II. Having spoken of their enquiry, I shall now notice THEIR EN-COURAGEMENT. Something encouraged these wise men to seek Jesus. It was this, "We have seen his star."

Now, the most of you seekers after Christ have a great encouragement in the fact that you have heard his gospel; you live in a land where you have the Scriptures, where the ordinances of God's house are freely dispensed. These are, as it were, Jesus Christ's star; they are meant to lead you to himself. Here, observe, that to see his star was *a great favour*. It was not given to all the dwellers in the east or west to see his star. These men, therefore, were highly privileged. It is not given to all mankind to hear the gospel, Jesus is not preached in all our streets; his cross is not lifted high even in every place that is dedicated to his worship. You are highly favoured, O my friend, if you have seen the star, the gospel, which points to Jesus.

To see the star involved these wise men in *great responsibility.* For, suppose they had seen his star and had not set out to worship him, they would have been far more guilty than others, who, not having received such an indication from heaven, would not have been able to set it at nought. Oh, think of the responsibility of some of you, who in your childhood heard of a Saviour, for whom a mother has wept many tears ; you know the truth, in the theory of it at any rate ; you have the responsibility of having seen his star.

The wise men *did not regard the favour of seeing the star as a matter to be rested in.* They did not say, " We have seen his star, and that is enough." Many say, " Well, we attend a place of worship regularly, is not that enough ? " There are those who say, "We were baptised, baptism brought regeneration with it ; we come to the sacrament, and do we not get grace through it ? " Poor souls ! the star which leads to Christ they mistake for Christ himself, and worship the star instead of the Lord. O may none of you ever be so foolish as to rest in outward ordinances ! God will say to you, if you depend upon sacraments or upon public worship, " Bring no more vain oblations ; incense is an abomination unto me. Who hath required this at your hands, to tread my courts ? " What careth God for outward forms and ceremonies ? When I see men putting on white gowns, and scarfs and bands, and singing their prayers, and bowing and scraping, I wonder what sort of god it is they worship. Surely he must have more affinity with the gods of the heathen than with the great Jehovah who has made the heavens and the earth. Mark ye well the exceeding glory of Jehovah's works on sea and land ; behold the heavens and their countless hosts of stars, hark to the howling of the winds and the rush of the hurricane, think of him who maketh the clouds his chariot, and rideth on the wings of the wind, and then consider whether this infinite God is like unto that being to whom it is a matter of grave consequence whether a cup of wine is lifted in worship as high as a man's hair or only as high as his nose ! O foolish generation, to think that Jehovah is contained in your temples made with hands, and that he cares for your vestments, your processions, your postures, and your genuflexions. Ye fight over your ritual, even to its jots and tittles do ye consider it. Surely ye know not the glorious Jehovah, if ye conceive that these things yield any pleasure to him. Nay, beloved, we desire to worship the Most High in all simplicity and earnestness of spirit, and never to stop in the outward form, lest we be foolish enough to think that to see the star is sufficient, and therefore fail to find the incarnate God.

Note well, that these wise men *did not find satisfaction in what they had themselves done to reach the child.* As we have observed, they may have come hundreds of miles, but they did not mention it; they did not sit down and say, "Well, we have journeyed across deserts, over hills, and across rivers, it is enough." No, they must find the new-born King, nothing else would satisfy them. Do not say, dear hearer, "I have been praying now for months, I have been searching the Scriptures for weeks, to find the Saviour." I am glad you have done so, but do not rest in it; you must get Christ, or else you perish after all your exertion and your trouble. Jesus you want, nothing more than Jesus, but nothing less than Jesus. Nor must you be satisfied with travelling in the way the star would lead you, you must reach HIM. Do not stop short of eternal life. Lay hold on it, not merely seek it and long for it, but lay hold on eternal life, and do not be content until it is an ascertained fact with you that Jesus Christ is yours.

I should like you to notice how these wise men were not satisfied with merely getting to Jerusalem. They might have said, " Ah ! now we are in the land where the Child is born, we will be thankful and sit down." No, but "Where is he ? " He is born at Bethlehem. Well, they get to Bethlehem, but we do not find that when they reached that village they said, " This is a favoured spot, we will sit down here." Not at all, they wanted to know where the house was. They reached the house, and the star got over it. It was a fair sight to see the cottage with the star above it, and to think that the new-born King was there, but that did not satisfy them. No, they went right into the house; they rested not till they saw the Child himself, and had worshipped him. I pray that you and I may always be so led by the Spirit of God that we may never put up with anything short of a real grasping of Christ, a believing sight of Christ as a Saviour, as our Saviour, as our Saviour even now. If there be one danger above another that the young seeker should strive against, it is the danger of stopping short of a hearty faith in Jesus Christ. While thy heart is tender like wax, take care that no seal but the seal of Christ be set on thee. Now that thou art uneasy and out of comfort, make this thy vow, " I will not be comforted till Jesus comfort me." It would be better for thee never to be awakened than to be lulled to sleep by Satan—for a sleep that follows upon a partial conviction is generally a deeper slumber than any other that falls upon the sons of men. My soul, I charge thee get to the blood of Christ, and be washed in it ; get to the life of Christ, and let that life be in thee, that thou be indeed God's child ; put not up with suppositions, be not satisfied with appearances and perhapses ; rest nowhere till thou hast said—God having given thee the faith to say it, " He loved me and gave himself for me, he is all my salvation and all my desire. See, then, how these wise men were not made by the sight of the star to keep away from Christ, but they were encouraged by it to come to Christ, and do you be encouraged, dear seeker, this morning to come to Jesus by the fact that you are blessed with the gospel. You have an invitation given you to come to Jesus, you have the motions of God's Spirit upon your conscience, awakening you; O come, come and welcome, and let this strange winter's day be a day of brightness and of gladness to a many a seeking soul.

I have turned my thoughts on this last head into verse, and I will repeat the lines—

> O where is Christ my King?
> I languish for the sight,
> Fain would I fall to worshipping,
> For he's my soul's delight.

> Himself, himself alone,
> I seek no less, no more,
> Or on his cross, or on his throne,
> I'd equally adore.

> The sages saw his star,
> But rested not content,
> The way was rough, the distance far,
> Yet on that way they went.

> And now my thoughts discern
> The sign that Christ is nigh,
> With love unquenchable I burn,
> T' enjoy his company.

> No star nor heavenly sign
> My soul's desire can fill,
> For him, my Lord, my King divine,
> My soul is thirsting still.

III. And now we shall conclude, by considering THE EXAMPLE of these wise men. They came to Jesus, and in so doing, they did three things: they saw, they worshipped, they gave. Those are three things which every believer here may do this morning over again, and which every seeker should do for the first time.

First, *they saw* the young Child. I do not think they merely said, "There he is," and so ended the matter, but they stood still and looked. Perhaps for some minutes they did not speak. About his very face I do not doubt there was a supernatural beauty. Whether there was a beauty to everyone's eye I know not, but to theirs there was assuredly a superhuman attraction. The incarnate God ! They gazed with all their eyes. They looked, and looked, and looked again. They glanced at his mother, but they fixed their eyes on him. "They saw the young Child." So, too, this morning let us think of Jesus with fixed and continuous thought. He is God, he is man, he is the substitute for sinners ; he is willing to receive all who trust him. He will save, and save this morning, every one of us who will rely upon him. Think of him. If you are at home this afternoon, spend the time in thinking upon him. Bring him before your mind's eye, consider and admire him. Is it not a wonder that God should enter into union with man and come to this world as an infant ? He who made heaven and earth hangs on a woman's breast for us ! For our redemption the Word was made flesh. This truth will breed the brightest hope within your soul. If you follow that babe's wondrous life till it ends at the cross, I trust you may there be able to give such a look at him that, like as Moses lifted up the serpent in the wilderness, and they that looked were healed, so you looking may be healed of all your spiritual diseases. Though it is many a year since I first looked to him, I desire to look to Jesus again. The incarnate God ! My eyes swim with tears to think that he who might have crushed me into hell for ever, becomes a young child for my sake ? See him, all of you, and seeing worship.

What did the wise men next ? They *worshipped* him. We cannot properly worship a Christ whom we do not know. " To the unknown God " is poor worship. But, oh, when you think of Jesus Christ, whose goings forth were of old from everlasting, the eternally-begotten Son of the Father, and then see him coming here to be a man of the substance of his mother, and know and understand why he came and what he did when he came, then you fall down and worship him.

> " Son of God, to thee we bow,
> Thou art Lord, and only thou ;
> Thou the woman's promised seed ;
> Thou who didst for sinners bleed."

We worship Jesus. Our faith sees him go from the manger to the cross, and from the cross right up to the throne, and there where Jehovah dwells, amidst the insufferable glory of the divine presence stands the man, the very man who slept at Bethlehem in the manger ; there he reigns as Lord of lords. Our souls worship him again. Thou art our Prophet, every word thou sayest, Jesu, we believe and desire to follow : thou art our Priest, thy sacrifice hath made us clean, we are washed in thy blood ; thou art our King, command, we will obey, lead on, and we will follow : We worship thee. We should spend much time in worshipping the Christ, and he should ever have the highest place in our reverence.

After worshipping, the wise men presented *their gifts.* One broke open his casket of gold, and laid it at the feet of the new-born King. Another presented frankincense—one of the precious products of the country from which they came ; and others laid myrrh at the Redeemer's feet ; all these they gave to prove the truth of their worship. They gave substantial offerings with no niggard hand. And now, after you have worshipped Christ in your soul, and seen him with the eye of faith, it will not need that I should say to you, give him yourself, give him your heart, give him your substance. Why, you will not be able to help doing it. He who really loves the Saviour in his heart, cannot help devoting to him his life, his strength, his all. With some people, when they give Christ anything, or do anything for him, it is dreadfully forced work. They say, "The love of Christ ought to constrain us." I do not know that there is any such text as that in the Bible, however. I do remember one text that runs thus—"The love of Christ constraineth us." If it does not constrain us, it is because it is not in us. It is not merely a thing which ought to be, it must be. If any man love Christ, he will very soon be finding out ways and means of proving his love by his sacrifices. Go home, Mary, and fetch the alabaster box, and pour the ointment on his head, and if any say, "Wherefore is this waste?" thou wilt have a good reply, thou hast had much forgiven thee, and therefore thou lovest much. If thou hast gold, give it; if thou hast frankincense, give it; if thou hast myrrh, give it to Jesus; and if thou hast none of these things, give him thy love, all thy love, and that will be gold and spices all in one; give him thy tongue, speak of him; give him thy hands, work for him; give him thy whole self. I know thou wilt, for he loved thee, and gave himself for thee. The Lord bless you, and may this Christmas Sabbath morning be a very memorable day to many out of the crowd assembled here. I am surprised to see so vast a number present, and I can only hope the blessing will be in proportion, for Jesus' sake. Amen.

Joy Born at Bethlehem

"And the angel said unto them, Fear not: for, behold, I bring you good tidings of great joy, which shall be to all people. For unto you is born this day in the city of David a Saviour, which is Christ the Lord. And this shall be a sign unto you; Ye shall find the babe wrapped in swaddling clothes, lying in a manger."—Luke ii. 10, 11, 12.

WE have no superstitious regard for times and seasons. Certainly we do not believe in the present ecclesiastical arrangement called *Christmas:* first, because we do not believe in the *mass* at all, but abhor it, whether it be said or sung in Latin or in English; and, secondly, because we find no Scriptural warrant whatever for observing any day as the birth-day of the Saviour ; and, consequently, its observance is a superstition, because not of divine authority. Superstition has fixed most positively the day of our Saviour's birth, although there is no possibility of dis-covering when it occurred. Fabricius gives a catalogue of 136 different learned opinions upon the matter; and various divines invent weighty arguments for advocating a date in every month in the year. It was not till the middle of the third century that any part of the church celebrated the nativity of our Lord ; and it was not till very long after the Western church had set the example, that the Eastern adopted it. Because the day is not known, therefore superstition has fixed it; while, since the day of the death of our Saviour might be determined with much certainty, therefore superstition shifts the date of its observance every year. Where is the method in the madness of the superstitious ? Probably the fact is that the holy days were arranged to fit in with heathen festivals. We venture to assert, that if there be any day in the year, of which we may be pretty sure that it was not the day on which the Saviour was born, it is the twenty-fifth of December. Nevertheless, since, the current of men's thoughts is led this way just now, and I see no evil in the current itself, I shall launch the bark of our discourse upon that stream, and make use of the fact, which I shall neither justify nor condemn, by endeavouring to lead your thoughts in the same direction. Since it is lawful, and even laudable, to meditate upon the incarnation of the Lord upon any day in the year, it cannot be in the power of other men's superstitions to render such a meditation improper for to-day. Regarding not the day, let us, nevertheless, give God thanks for the gift of his dear Son.

In our text we have before us the sermon of the first evangelist under the gospel dispensation. The preacher was an angel, and it was meet it should be so, for the grandest and last of all evangels will be proclaimed by an angel when he shall sound the trumpet of the resurrection, and the children of the regeneration shall rise into the fulness of their joy. The key-note of this angelic gospel is *joy*—"I bring unto you good tidings of great joy." Nature fears in the presence of God—the shepherds were sore afraid. The law itself served to deepen this natural feeling of dismay; seeing men were sinful, and the law came into the world to reveal sin, its tendency was to make men fear and tremble under any and every divine revelation. The Jews unanimously believed that if any man beheld supernatural appearances, he would be sure to die, so that what nature dictated, the law and the general beliefs of those under it also abetted. But the first word of the gospel ended all this, for the angelic evangelist said, " Fear not, behold I bring you good tidings." Henceforth, it is to be no dreadful thing for man to approach his Maker ; redeemed man is not to fear when God unveils the splendour of his majesty, since he appears no more a judge upon his throne of terror, but a Father unbending in sacred familiarity before his own beloved children.

The joy which this first gospel preacher spoke of was no mean one, for he said, "I bring you good tidings"—that alone were joy : and not good tidings of joy only, but " good tidings of *great* joy." Every word is emphatic, as if to show that the gospel is above all things intended to promote, and will most abundantly create the greatest possible joy in the human heart wherever it is received. Man is like a harp unstrung, and the music of his soul's living strings is discordant, his whole nature wails with sorrow ; but the son of David, that mighty harper, has come to restore the harmony of humanity, and where his gracious fingers move among the strings, the touch of the fingers of an incarnate God brings forth music sweet as that of the spheres, and melody rich as a seraph's canticle. Would God that all men felt that divine hand.

In trying to open up this angelic discourse this morning, we shall note three things: *the joy which is spoken of ;* next, *the persons to whom this joy comes ;* and then, thirdly, *the sign*, which is to us a sign as well as to these shepherds—a sign of the birth and source of joy.

I. First, then, THE JOY, which is mentioned in our text—whence comes it, and what is it ?

We have already said it is a "*great* joy "—" good tidings of great joy." Earth's joy is small, her mirth is trivial, but heaven has sent us joy immeasurable, fit for immortal minds. Inasmuch as no note of time is appended, and no intimation is given that the message will ever be reversed, we may say that it is a *lasting* joy, a joy which will ring all down the ages, the echoes of which shall be heard until the trumpet brings the resurrection ; aye, and onward for ever and for ever. For when God sent forth the angel in his brightness to say, " I bring you good tidings of great joy, which shall be to all people," he did as much as say, "From this time forth it shall be joy to the sons of men ; there shall be peace to the human race, and goodwill towards men for ever and for ever, as long as there is glory to God in the highest." O blessed thought ! the Star of Bethlehem shall never set. Jesus, the fairest among ten thousand, the most lovely among the beautiful, is a joy for ever.

Since this joy is expressly associated with the glory of God, by the words, "Glory to God in the highest," we may be quite clear that it is a *pure and holy* joy. No other would an angel have proclaimed, and, indeed, no other joy is joy. The wine pressed from the grapes of Sodom may sparkle and foam, but it is bitterness in the end, and the dregs thereof are death ; only that which comes from the clusters of Eschol is the true wine of the kingdom, making glad the heart of God and man. Holy joy is the joy of heaven, and that, be ye sure, is the very cream of joy. The joy of sin is a fire-fountain, having its source in the burning soil of hell, maddening and consuming those who drink its fire-water ; of such delights we desire not to drink. It were to be worse than damned to be happy in sin, since it is the beginning of grace to be wretched in sin, and the consummation of grace to be wholly escaped from sin, and to shudder even at the thought of it. It is hell to live in sin and misery, it is a deep lower still when men could fashion a joy in sin. God save us from unholy peace and from unholy joy ! The joy announced by the angel of the nativity is as pure as it is lasting, as holy as it is great. Let us then always believe concerning the Christian religion that it has its joy within itself, and holds its feasts within its own pure precincts, a feast whose viands all grow on holy ground. There are those who, to-morrow, will pretend to exhibit joy in the remembrance of our Saviour's birth, but they will not seek their pleasure in the Saviour : they will need many additions to the feast before they can be satisfied. Joy in Immanuel would be a poor sort of mirth to them. In this country, too often, if one were unaware of the name, one might believe the Christmas festival to be a feast of Bacchus, or of Ceres, certainly not a commemoration of the Divine birth. Yet is there cause enough for holy joy in the Lord himself, and reasons for ecstacy in his birth among men. It is to be feared that most men imagine that in Christ there is only seriousness and solemnity, and to them consequently weariness, gloom, and discontent ; therefore, they look out of and beyond what Christ allows, to snatch from the tables of Satan the delicacies with which to adorn the banquet held in honour of a Saviour. Let it not be so among you. The joy which the gospel brings is not borrowed but blooms in its own garden. We may truly say in the language of one of our sweetest hymns—

> "I need not go abroad for joy,
> I have a feast *at home*,
> My sighs are turned into songs,
> My heart has ceased to roam.
>
> Down from above the Blessed Dove
> Has come into my breast,
> To witness his eternal love,
> And give my spirit rest."

Let our joy be living water from those sacred wells which the Lord himself has digged; may his joy abide in us, that our joy may be full. Of Christ's joy we cannot have too much ; no fear of running to excess when his love is the wine we drink. Oh to be plunged in this pure stream of spiritual delights !

But why is it that the coming of Christ into the world is the occasion of joy ? The answer is as follows :—First, because *it is evermore a joyous fact that God should be in alliance with man*, especially when the alliance is so near that God should in very deed take our manhood into union with his godhead ; so that God and man should constitute one divine, mysterious person. Sin had separated between God and man ; but the incarnation bridges the separation : it is a prelude to the atoning sacrifice, but it is a prelude full of the richest hope. From henceforth, when God looks upon man, he will remember that his own Son is a man. From this day forth, when he beholds the sinner, if his wrath should burn, he will remember that his own Son, as man, stood in the sinner's place, and bore the sinner's doom. As in the case of war, the feud is ended when the opposing parties intermarry, so there is no more war between God and man, because God has taken man into intimate union with himself. Herein, then, there was cause for joy.

But there was more than that, for the shepherds were aware that *there had been promises made of old* which had been the hope and comfort of believers in all ages, and these *were now to be fulfilled.* There was that ancient promise made on the threshold of Eden to the first sinners of our race, that the seed of the woman should bruise the serpent's head ; another promise made to the Father of the faithful that in his seed should all the nations of the earth be blessed, and promises uttered by the mouths of prophets and of saints since the world began. Now, the announcement of the angel of the Lord to the shepherds was a declaration that the covenant was fulfilled, that now in the fulness of time God would redeem his word, and the Messiah, who was to be Israel's glory and the world's hope, was now really come. Be glad ye heavens, and be joyful O earth, for the Lord hath done it, and in mercy hath he visited his people. The Lord hath not suffered his word to fail, but hath fulfilled unto his people his promises. The time to favour Zion, yea the set time, is come. Now that the sceptre is departed from Judah, behold the Shiloh comes, the Messenger of the covenant suddenly appears in his temple !

But the angel's song had in it yet fuller reason for joy ; for our Lord who was born in Bethlehem came as *a Saviour.* " Unto you is born this day a Saviour." God had come to earth before, but not as a Saviour. Remember that terrible coming when there went three angels into Sodom at night-fall, for the Lord said, " I will go now and see whether it be altogether according to the cry thereof." He had come as a spy to witness human sin, and as an avenger to lift his hand to heaven, and bid the red fire descend and burn up the accursed cities of the plain. Horror to the world when God thus descends. If Sinai smokes when the law is proclaimed, the earth itself shall melt when the breaches of the law are punished. But now not as an angel of vengeance, but as a man in mercy God has come ; not to spy out our sin, but to remove it : not to punish guilt, but to forgive it. The Lord might have come with thunderbolts in both his hands, he might have come like Elias to call fire from heaven ; but no, his hands are full of gifts of love, and his presence is the guarantee of grace. The babe born in the manger might have been another prophet of tears, or another son of thunder, but he was not so : he came in gentleness, his glory and his thunder alike laid aside.

> " 'Twas mercy filled the throne,
>   And wrath stood silent by,
>   When Christ on the kind errand came
>   To sinners doomed to die."

Rejoice, ye who feel that ye are lost; your Saviour comes to seek and save you. Be of good cheer ye who are in prison, for he comes to set you free. Ye who are famished and ready to die, rejoice that he has consecrated for you a Bethlehem, a house of bread, and he has come to be the bread of life to your souls. Rejoice, O sinners, every-where for the restorer of the castaways, the Saviour of the fallen is born. Join in the joy, ye saints, for he is the preserver of the saved ones, delivering them from innumerable perils, and he is the sure prefecter of such as he preserves. Jesus is no partial Saviour, beginning a work and not concluding it ; but, restoring and upholding, he also prefects and presents the saved ones without spot or wrinkle, or any such thing before his Father's throne. Rejoice aloud all ye people, let your hills and valleys ring with joy, for a Saviour who is mighty to save is born among you.

Nor was this all the holy mirth, for the next word has also in it a fulness of joy :—" a Saviour, who is *Christ*," or the Anointed. Our Lord was not an amateur Saviour who came down from heaven upon an unauthorised mission ; but he was chosen, ordained, and anointed of God ; he could truly say, " the Spirit of the Lord is upon me, because the Lord hath anointed me." Here is great comfort for all such as need a Saviour; it is to them no mean consolation that God has himself authorised Christ to save. There can be no fear of a jar between the mediator and the judge, no peril of a nonacceptance of our Saviour's work ; because God has commissioned Christ to do what he has done, and in saving sinners he is only executing his Father's own will. Christ is here called " *the* anointed." All his people are anointed, and there were priests after the order of Aaron who were anointed, but he is *the* anointed, " anointed with the oil of gladness above his fellows ;" so plenteously anointed that, like the unction upon Aaron's head, the sacred anointing of the Head of the church distils in copious streams, till we who are like the skirts of his garments are made sweet with the rich perfume. He is " the anointed " in a threefold sense : as prophet to preach the gospel with power; as priest to offer sacrifice ; as king to rule and reign. In each of these he is preeminent ; he is such a teacher, priest, and ruler as was never seen before. In him was a rare conjunction of glorious offices, for never did prophet, priest, and king meet in one person before among the sons of men, nor shall it ever be so again. Triple is the anointing of him who is a priest after the order of Melchisedec, a prophet like unto Moses, and a king of whose dominion there is no end. In the name of Christ, the Holy Ghost is glor'fied, by being seen as anointing the incarnate God. Truly, dear brethren, if we did but understand all this, and receive it into our hearts, our souls would leap for joy on this Sabbath day, to think that there is born unto us a Saviour who is anointed of the Lord.

One more note, and this the loudest, let us sound it well and hear it well—" which is Christ *the Lord.*" Now the word Lord, or *Kurios,* here used is tantamouut to Jehovah. We cannot doubt that, because it is the same word used twice in the ninth verse, and in the ninth verse none can question that it means Jehovah. Hear it, " And, lo, the angel of the *Lord* came upon them, and the glory of the *Lord* shone round about them."   And if this be not enough, read the 23rd verse, " As it is written in the law of the *Lord,* every male that openeth the womb shall be called holy to the *Lord.*" Now the word Lord here assuredly refers to Jehovah, the one God, and so it must do here. Our Saviour is Christ, God, Jehovah. No testimony to his divinity could be plainer; it is indisputable. And what joy there is in this; for suppose an angel had been our Saviour, he would not have been able to bear the load of my sin or yours ; or if anything less than God had been set up as the ground of our salvation, it might have been found too frail a foundation. But if he who undertakes to save is none other than the Infinite and the Almighty, then the load of our guilt can be carried upon such shoulders, the stupendous labour of our salvation can be achieved by such a worker, and that with ease : for all things are possible with God, and he is able to save to the uttermost them that come unto God by him. Ye sons of men perceive ye here the subject of your joy. The God who made you, and against whom you have offended, has come down from heaven and taken upon himself your nature that he might save you. He has come in the fulness of his glory and the infinity of his mercy that he might redeem you. Do you not welcome this news ? What ! will not your hearts be thankful for this ? Does this matchless love awaken no gratitude ? Were it not for this divine Saviour, your life here would have been wretchedness, and your future existence would have been endless woe. Oh, I pray you adore the incarnate God, and trust in him. Then will you bless the Lord for delivering you from the wrath to come, and as you lay hold of Jesus and find salvation in his name, you will tune your songs to his praise, and exult with sacred joy. So much concerning this joy.

II.   Follow me while I briefly speak of THE PEOPLE to whom this joy comes.   Observe how the angel begins, " Behold, I bring *you* good tidings of great joy, for *uuto you* is born this day."   So, then, the joy began with the first who heard it, the shepherds.   " *To you,*" saith he; " for unto you is born." Beloved hearer, shall the joy begin with you to-day ?—for it little avails you that Christ was born, or that Christ died, unless unto *you* a child is born, and for you Jesus bled.   A personal interest is the main point. " But I am poor," saith one.   So were the shepherds. O ye poor, to you this mysterious child is born. " The poor have the gospel preached unto them." " He shall judge the poor and needy, and break in pieces the oppressor." But I am obscure and unknown," saith one. So were the watchers on the midnight plain. Who knew the men who endured hard toil, and kept their flocks by night ? But you, unknown of men, are known to God : shall it not be said, that "unto you a child is born? The Lord regardeth not the greatness of men, but hath respect unto the lowly. But you are illiterate, you say, you cannot understand much. Be it so, but unto the shephords Christ was born, and their simplicity did not hinder their receiving him, but even helped them to it. Be it so with yourself: receive gladly the simple truth as it is in Jesus. The Lord hath exalted one chosen out of the people. No aristocratic Christ have I to preach to you, but the Saviour of the people, the friend of publicans and sinners. Jesus is the true "poor man's friend;" he is "a covenant for the people," given to be "a leader and commander to the people." To you is Jesus given. O that each heart might truly say, to me is Jesus born ; for if I truly believe in Jesus, unto me Christ is born, and I may be as sure of it as if an angel announced it, since the Scripture tells me that if I believe in Jesus He is mine.

After the angel had said "to you," he went on to say, "it shall be *to all people*." But our translation is not accurate, the Greek is, "it shall be to all *the* people." This refers most assuredly to the Jewish nation ; there can be no question about that; if any one looks at the original, he will not find so large and wide an expression as that given by our translators. It should be rendered "to all *the* people." And here let us speak a word for the Jews. How long and how sinfully has the Christian church despised the most honorable amongst the nations ! How barbarously has Israel been handled by the so-called church ! I felt my spirit burn indignantly within me in Rome when I stood in the Jew's quarter, and heard of the cruel indignities which Popery has heaped upon the Jews, even until recently. At this hour there stands in the Jew's quarter a church built right in front of the entrance to it, and into this the unhappy Jews were driven forcibly on certain occasions. To this church they were compelled to subscribe—subscribe, mark you, as worshippers of the one invisible God, to the support of a system which is as leprous with idolatry as were the Canaanites whom the Lord abhorred. Paganism is not more degrading than Romanism. Over the door of this church is placed, in their own tongue in the Hebrew, these words :—"All day long have I stretched out my hands to a disobedient and gainsaying generation ;" how, by such an insult as that, could they hope to convert the Jew. The Jew saw everywhere idols which his soul abhorred, and he loathed the name of Christ, because he associated it with idol worship, and I do not wonder that he did. I praise the Jew that he could not give up his own simple theism, and the worship of the true God, for such a base, degrading superstition as that which Rome presented to him. Instead of thinking it a wonder of unbelief that the Jew is not a Christian, I honour him for his faith and his courageous resistance of a fascinating heathenism. If Romanism be Christianity I am not, neither could I be, a Christian. It were a more manly thing to be a simple believer in one God, or even an honest doubter upon all religion, than worship such crowds of gods and goddesses as Popery has set up, and to bow, as she does, before rotten bones and dead men's winding sheets. Let the true Christian church think lovingly of the Jew, and with respectful earnestness tell him the true gospel ; let her sweep away superstition, and set before him the one gracious God in the Trinity of his divine Unity ; and the day shall yet come when the Jews, who were the first apostles to the Gentiles, the first missionaries to us who were afar off, shall be gathered in again. Until that shall be, the fulness of the church's glory can never come. Matchless benefits to the world are bound up with the restoration of Israel; their gathering in shall be as life from the dead. Jesus the Saviour is the joy of all nations, but let not the chosen race be denied their peculiar share of whatever promise holy writ has recorded with a special view to them. The woes which their sins brought upon them have fallen thick and heavily; and even so let the richest blessings distil upon them.

Although our translation is not literally correct, it, nevertheless, expresses a great truth, taught plainly in the context ; and, therefore, we will advance another step. The coming of Christ is a joy to *all people.* It is so, for the fourteenth verse says : " On earth peace," which is a wide and even unlimited expression. It adds, " Good will towards " — not Jews, but " men " — all men. The word is the generic name of the entire race, and there is no doubt that the coming of Christ does bring joy to all sorts of people. It brings a measure of joy even to those who are not Christians. Christ does not bless them in the highest and truest sense, but the influence of his teaching imparts benefits of an inferior sort, such as they are capable of receiving; for wherever the gospel is proclaimed, it is no small blessing to all the population. Note this fact: there is no land beneath the sun where there is an open Bible and a preached gospel, where a tyrant long can hold his place. It matters not who he be, whether pope or king; let the pulpit be used properly for the preaching of Christ crucified, let the Bible be opened to be read by all men, and no tyrant can long rule in peace. England owes her freedom to the Bible ; and France will never possess liberty, lasting and well-established, till she comes to reverence the gospel, which too long she has rejected. There is joy to all mankind where Christ comes. The religion of Jesus makes men think, and to make men think is always dangerous to a despot's power. The religion of Jesus Christ sets a man free from superstition ; when he believes in Jesus, what cares he for Papal excommunications, or whether priests give or withhold their absolution ? The man no longer cringes and bows down ; he is no more willing, like a beast, to be led by the nose; but, learning to think for himself, and becoming a man, he disdains the childish fears which once held him in slavery. Hence, where Jesus comes, even if men do not receive him as the Saviour, and so miss the fullest joy, yet they get a measure of benefit; and I pray God that everywhere his gospel may be so proclaimed, and that so many may be actuated by the spirit of it, that it may be better for all mankind. If men receive Christ, there will be no more oppression : the true Christian does to others as he would that they should do to him, and there is no more contention of classes, nor grinding of the faces of the poor. Slavery must go down where Christianity rules, and mark you, if Romanism be once destroyed, and pure Christianity shall govern all nations, war itself must come to an end ; for if there be anything which this book denounces and counts the hugest of all crimes, it is the crime of war. Put up thy sword into thy sheath, for hath not he said, "Thou shalt not kill," and he meant not that it was a sin to kill one but a glory to kill a million, but he meant that bloodshed on the smallest or largest scale was sinful. Let Christ govern, and men shall break the bow and cut the spear in sunder, and burn the chariot in the fire. It is joy to all nations that Christ is born, the Prince of Peace, the King who rules in righteousness.

But, beloved, the greatest joy is to those who know Christ *as a Saviour*. Here the song rises to a higher and sublimer note. Unto us indeed a child is born, if we can say that he is our "Saviour who is Christ the Lord." Let me ask each of you a few personal questions. Are your sins forgiven you for his name's sake? Is the head of the serpent bruised in your soul? Does the seed of the woman reign in sanctifying power over your nature? Oh then, you have the joy that is to all the people in the truest form of it; and, dear brother, dear sister, the further you submit yourself to Christ the Lord, the more completely you know him, and are like him, the fuller will your happiness become. Surface joy is to those who live where the Saviour is preached; but the great deeps, the great fathomless deeps of solemn joy which glisten and sparkle with delight, are for such as know the Saviour, obey the anointed one, and have communion with the Lord himself. He is the most joyful man who is the most Christly man. I wish that some Christians were more truly Christians : they are Christians and something else; it were much better if they were altogether Christians. Perhaps you know the legend, or perhaps true history of the awakening of St. Augustine. He dreamed that he died, and went to the gates of heaven, and the keeper of the gates said to him, "Who are you?" And he answered, "*Christianus sum*," I am a Christian. But the porter replied, "No, you are not a Christian, you are a Ciceronian, for your thoughts and studies were most of all directed to the works of Cicero and the classics, and you neglected the teaching of Jesus. We judge men here by that which most engrossed their thoughts, and you are judged not to be a Christian but a Ciceronian." When Augustine awoke, he put aside the classics which he had studied, and the eloquence at which he had aimed, and he said, "I will be a Christian and a theologian;" and from that time he devoted his thoughts to the word of God, and his pen and his tongue to the instruction of others in the truth. Oh I would not have it said of any of you, "Well, he may be somewhat Christian, but he is far more a keen money-getting tradesman." I would not have it said, "Well, he may be a believer in Christ, but he is a good deal more a politician." Perhaps he is a Christian, but he is most at home when he is talking about science, farming, engineering, horses, mining, navigation, or pleasure-taking. No, no, you will never know the fulness of the joy which Jesus brings to the soul, unless under the power of the Holy Spirit you take the Lord your Master to be your All in all, and make him the fountain of your intensest delight. "He is my Saviour, my Christ, my Lord," be this your loudest boast. Then will you know the joy which the angel's song predicts for men.

III. But I must pass on. The last thing in the text is THE SIGN. The shepherds did not ask for a sign, but one was graciously given. Sometimes it is sinful for us to require as an evidence what God's tenderness may nevertheless see fit to give as an aid to faith. Wilful unbelief shall have no sign, but weak faith shall have compassionate aid. The sign that the joy of the world had come was this,—they were to go to the manger to find the Christ in it, and he was to be the sign. Every circumstance is therefore instructive. The babe was found " wrapped in swaddling clothes." Now, observe, as you look at this infant, that there is not the remotest appearance of *temporal power* here. Mark the two little puny arms of a little babe that must be carried if it go. Alas, the nations of the earth look for joy in military power. By what means can we make a nation of soldiers? The Prussian method is admirable; we must have thousands upon thousands of armed men and big cannon and iron-clad vessels to kill and destroy by wholesale. Is it not a nation's pride to be gigantic in arms? What pride flushes the patriot's cheek when he remembers that his nation can murder faster than any other people. Ah, foolish generation, ye are groping in the flames of hell to find your heaven, raking amid blood and bones for the foul thing which ye call glory. A nation's joy can never lie in the misery of others. Killing is not the path to prosperity; huge armaments are a curse to the nation itself as well as to its neighbours. The joy of a nation is a golden sand over which no stream of blood has ever rippled. It is only found in that river, the streams whereof make glad the city of God. The weakness of submissive gentleness is true power. Jesus founds his eternal empire not on force but on love. Here, O ye people, see your hope; the mild pacific prince, whose glory is his self-sacrifice, is our true benefactor.

But look again, and you shall observe *no pomp* to dazzle you. Is the child wrapped in purple and fine linen? Ah, no. Sleeps he in a cradle of gold? The manger alone is his shelter. No crown is upon the babe's head, neither does a coronet surround the mother's brow. A simple maiden of Galilee, and a little child in ordinary swaddling bands, it is all you see.

> " Bask not in courtly bower,
> Or sunbright hall of power,
> Pass Babel quick, and seek the holy land.
> From robes of Tyrian dye,
> Turn with undazzled eye
> To Bethlehem's glade, and by the manger stand."

Alas, the nations are dazzled with a vain show. The pomp of empires, the pageants of kings are their delight. How can they admire those gaudy courts, in which too often glorious apparel, decorations, and rank stand in the stead of virtue, chastity, and truth. When will the people cease to be children? Must they for ever crave for martial music which stimulates to violence, and delight in a lavish expenditure which burdens them with taxation? These make not a nation great or joyous. Bah! how has the bubble burst across yon narrow sea. A bubble empire has collapsed. Ten thousand bayonets and millions of gold proved but a sandy foundation for a Babel throne. Vain are the men who look for joy in pomp; it lies in truth and righteousness, in peace and salvation, of which yonder new-born prince in the garments of a peasant child is the true symbol.

Neither was there *wealth* to be seen at Bethlehem. Here in this quiet island, the bulk of men are comfortably seeking to acquire their thousands by commerce and manufactures. We are the sensible people who follow the main chance, and are not to be deluded by ideas of glory ; we are making all the money we can, and wondering that other nations waste so much in fight. The main prop and pillar of England's joy is to be found, as some tell us, in the Three per Cents., in the possession of colonies, in the progress of machinery, in steadily increasing our capital. Is not Mammon a smiling deity? But, here, in the cradle of the world's hope at Bethlehem, I see far more of poverty than wealth; I perceive no glitter of gold, or spangle of silver. I perceive only a poor babe, so poor, so very poor, that he is in a manger laid ; and his mother is a mechanic's wife, a woman who wears neither silk nor gem. Not in your gold, O Britons, will ever lie your joy, but in the gospel enjoyed by all classes, the gospel freely preached and joyfully received. Jesus, by raising us to spiritual wealth, redeems us from the chains of Mammon, and in that liberty gives us joy.

And here, too, I see *no superstition*. I know the artist paints angels in the skies, and surrounds the scene with a mysterious light, of which tradition's tongue of falsehood has said that it made midnight as bright as noon. This is fiction merely; there was nothing more there than the stable, the straw the oxen ate, and perhaps the beasts themselves, and the child in the plainest, simplest manner, wrapped as other children are ; the cherubs were invisible and of haloes there were none. Around this birth of joy was no sign of superstition : that demon dared not intrude its tricks and posturings into the sublime spectacle : it would have been there as much out of place as a harlequin in the holy of holies. A simple gospel, a plain gospel, as plain as that babe wrapped in the commonest garments, is this day the only hope for men. Be ye wise and believe in Jesus, and abhor all the lies of Rome, and inventions of those who ape her detestable abominations.

Nor does the joy of the world lie in *philosophy*. You could not have made a schoolmen's puzzle of Bethlehem if you had tried to do so; it was just a child in the manger and a Jewish woman looking on and nursing it, and a carpenter standing by. There was no metaphysical difficulty there, of which men could say, "A doctor of divinity is needed to explain it, and an assembly of divines must expound it." It is true the wise men came there, but it was only to adore and offer gifts; would that all the wise had been as wise as they. Alas, human subtlety has disputed over the manger, and logic has darkened counsel with its words. But this is one of man's many inventions ; God's work was sublimely simple. Here was "The Word made flesh" to dwell among us, a mystery for faith, but not a football for argument. Mysterious, yet the greatest simplicity that was ever spoken to human ears, and seen by mortal eyes. And such is the gospel, in the preaching of which our apostle said, "we use great plainness of speech." Away, away, away with your learned sermons, and your fine talk, and your pretentious philosophies; these never created a jot of happiness in this world. Fine-spun theories are fair to gaze on, and to bewilder fools, but they are of no use to practical men, they comfort not the sons of toil, nor cheer the daughters of sorrow. The man of common sense, who feels the daily rub and tear of this poor world, needs richer consolation than your novel theologies, or neologies, can give him. In a simple Christ, and in a simple faith in that Christ, there is a peace deep and lasting; in a plain, poor man's gospel there is a joy and a bliss unspeakable, of which thousands can speak, and speak with confidence, too, for they declare what they do know, and testify what they have seen.

I say, then, to you who would know the only true peace and lasting joy, come ye to the babe of Bethlehem, in after days the Man of Sorrows, the substitutionary sacrifice for sinners. Come, ye little children, ye boys and girls, come ye; for he also was a boy. "The holy child Jesus" is the children's Saviour, and saith still, "Suffer the little children to come unto me, and forbid them not. Come hither, ye maidens, ye who are still in the morning of your beauty, and, like Mary, rejoice in God your Saviour. The virgin bore him on her bosom, so come ye and bear him in your hearts, saying, "Unto us a child is born, unto us a son is given." And you, ye men in the plenitude of your strength, remember how Joseph cared for him, and watched with reverent solicitude his tender years; be you to his cause as a Father and a helper; sanctify your strength to his service. And ye women advanced in years, ye matrons and widows, come like Anna and bless the Lord that you have seen the salvation of Israel, and ye hoar heads, who like Simeon are ready to depart, come ye and take the Saviour in your arms, adoring him as your Saviour and your all. Ye shepherds, ye simple hearted, ye who toil for your daily bread, come and adore the Saviour; and stand not back ye wise men, ye who know by experience and who by meditation peer into deep truth, come ye, and like the sages of the East bow low before his presence, and make it your honour to pay honour to Christ the Lord. For my own part, the incarnate God is all my hope and trust. I have seen the world's religion at the fountain head, and my heart has sickened within me; I come back to preach, by God's help, yet more earnestly the gospel, the simple gospel of the Son of Man. Jesus, Master, I take thee to be mine for ever! May all in this house, through the rich grace of God, be led to do the same, and may they all be thine, great Son of God, in the day of thine appearing, for thy love's sake. Amen.

God With Us

"They shall call his name Emmanuel, which being interpreted is, God with us."
—Matthew i. 23.

THOSE words, "being interpreted," salute my ear with much sweetness. Why should the word " Emmanuel " in the Hebrew, be interpreted at all ? Was it not to show that it has reference to us Gentiles, and therefore it must needs be interpreted into one of the chief languages of the then existing Gentile world, namely, the Greek. This "being interpreted " at Christ's birth, and the three languages employed in the inscription upon the cross at his death, show that he is not the Saviour of the Jews only, but also of the Gentiles. As I walked along the quay at Marseilles, and marked the ships of all nations gathered in the port, I was very much interested by the inscriptions upon the shops and stores. The announcements of refreshments or of goods to be had within were not only printed in the French language, but in English, in Italian, in German, in Greek, sometimes in Russian and Swedish. Upon the shops of the sail-makers, the boat-builders, the ironmongers, or the dealers in ship stores, you read a polyglot announcement, setting forth the information to men of many lands. This was a clear indication that persons of all nations were invited to come and purchase, that they were expected to come, and that provision was made for their peculiar wants. " Being interpreted " must mean that different nations are addressed. We have the text put first in the Hebrew " Emmanuel," and afterwards it is translated into the Gentile tongue, " God with us; " " being interpreted," that we may know that we are invited, that we are welcome, that God has seen our necessities and has provided for us, and that now we may freely come, even we who were sinners of the Gentiles, and far off from God. Let us preserve with reverent love both forms of the precious name and wait the happy day when our Hebrew brethren shall unite their " Emmanuel " with our " God with us."

Our text speaks of a name of our Lord Jesus. It is said, "They shall call his name Emmanuel." In these days we call children by names which have no particular meaning. They are the names, perhaps, of father or mother or some respected relative, but there is no special meaning as a general rule in our children's names. It was not so in the olden times. Then names meant something. Scriptural names, as a general rule, contain teaching, and especially is this the case in every name ascribed to the Lord Jesus. With him names indicate things. "His name shall be called Wonderful, Counsellor, the Mighty God, the everlasting Father, the Prince of Peace," because he really is all these. His name is called Jesus, but not without a reason. By any other name Jesus would not be so sweet, because no other name could fairly describe his great work of saving his people from their sins. When he is said to be called this or that, it means that he really is so. I am not aware that anywhere in the New Testament our Lord is afterwards called Emmanuel. I do not find his apostles, or any of his disciples, calling him by that name literally ; but we find them all doing so in effect, for they speak of him as " God manifest in the flesh ", and they say, "The word was made flesh and dwelt among us, and we beheld his glory, the glory as of the only-begotten of the Father, full of grace and truth." They do not use the actual word, but they again interpret and give us free and instructive renderings, while they proclaim the sense of the august title and inform us in divers ways what is meant by God being with us in the person of the Lord Jesus Christ. It is a glorious fact, of the highest importance, that since Christ was born into the world God is with us.

You may divide the text, if you please, into two portions :—" GOD," and then " God WITH US." We must dwell with equal emphasis upon each word. Never let us for a moment hesitate as to the Godhead of our Lord Jesus Christ, for his Deity is a fundamental doctrine of the Christian faith. It may be we shall never understand fully how God and man could unite in one person, for who can by searching find out God. These great mysteries of godliness, these " deep things of God," are beyond our measurement : our little skiff might be lost if we ventured so far out upon this vast, this infinite ocean, as to lose sight of the shore of plainly revealed truth. But let it remain as a matter of faith that Jesus Christ, even he who lay in Bethlehem's manger, and was carried in a woman's arms, and lived a suffering life and died on a malefactor's cross, was, nevertheless, " God over all, blessed for ever," " upholding all things by the word of his power." He was not an angel—that the apostle has abundantly disproved in the first and second chapters of the epistle to the Hebrews : he could not have been an angel, for honours are ascribed to him which were never bestowed on angels. He was no subordinate deity or being elevated to the Godhead, as some have absurdly said—all these things are dreams and falsehoods; he was as surely God as God can be, one with the Father and the ever-blessed Spirit. If it were not so, not only would the great strength of our hope be gone, but as to this text the sweetness had evaporated altogether. The very essence and glory of the incarnation is that he was God who was veiled in human flesh: if it was any other being who thus came to us in human flesh, I see nothing very remarkable in it, nothing comforting, certainly. That an angel should become a man is a matter of no great consequence to me : that some other superior being should assume the nature of man brings no joy to my heart, and opens no well of consolation to me. But " God with us " is exquisite delight. " GOD with us ": all that " God" means, the Deity, the infinite Jehovah with us ; this, this is worthy of the burst of midnight song, when angels startled the shepherds with their carols, singing " Glory to God in the highest, and on earth peace, good will to men." This was worthy of the foresight of seers and prophets, worthy of a new star in the heavens, worthy of the care which inspiration has manifested to preserve the record. This, too, was worthy of the martyr deaths of apostles and confessors who counted not their lives dear unto them for the sake of the incarnate God ; and this, my brethren, is worthy at this day of your most earnest endeavours to spread the glad tidings, worthy of a holy life to illustrate its blessed influences, and worthy of a joyful death to prove its consoling power. Here is the first truth of our holy faith—" Without controversy great is the mystery of godliness, God was manifest in the flesh." He who was born at Bethlehem is God, and " God with us." God—there lies the majesty ; " God with us," there lies the mercy. *God*—therein is glory; " God *with us*," therein is grace. God alone might well strike us with terror ; but " God with us " inspires us with hope and confidence. Take my text as a whole, and carry it in your bosoms as a bundle of sweet spices to perfume your hearts with peace and joy. May the Holy Spirit open to you the truth, and the truth to you. I would joyfully say to you in the words of one of our poets—

> " Veil'd in flesh the Godhead see ;
> Hail the incarnate Deity !
> Pleased as man with men to appear,
> Jesus our Immanuel here."

First, *let us admire this truth;* then *let us consider it more at lengt.* and after that *let us endeavour personally to appropriate it.*

I. LET US ADMIRE THIS TRUTH. " God with us." Let us stand at a reverent distance from it as Moses when he saw God in the bush stood a little back, and put his shoes from off his feet, feeling that the place whereon he stood was holy ground. This is a wonderful fact, God the Infinite once dwelt in the frail body of a child, and tabernacled in the suffering form of a lowly man. " God was in Christ." " He made himself of no reputation, and took upon him the form of a servant, and was made in the likeness of men."

Observe first, the wonder *of condescension* contained in this fact, that God who made all things should assume the nature of one of his own creatures, that the self-existent should be united with the dependent and derived, and the Almighty linked with the feeble and mortal. In the case before us the Lord descended to the very depth of humiliation, and entered into alliance with a nature which did not occupy the chief place in the scale of existence. It would have been great condescension for the infinite and incomprehensible Jehovah to have taken upon himself the nature of some noble spiritual being, such as a seraph or a cherub ; the union of the divine with a created spirit would have been an unmeasurable stoop, but for God to be one with man is far more. Remember that in the person of Christ manhood was not merely quickening spirit, but also suffering, hungering, dying, flesh and blood. There was taken to himself by our Lord all that materialism which makes up a body, and a body is after all but the dust of the earth, a structure fashioned from the materials around us. There is nothing in our bodily frame but what is to be found in the substance of the earth on which we live. We feed upon that which groweth out of the earth, and when we die we go back to the dust from whence we were taken. Is not this a strange thing that this grosser part of creation, this meaner part, this dust of it, should nevertheless be taken into union, with that pure, marvellous, incomprehensible, divine being of whom we know so little, and can comprehend nothing at all? Oh, the condescension of it! I leave it to the meditations of your quiet moments. Dwell on it with awe. I am persuaded that no man has any idea how wonderful a stoop it was for God thus to dwell in human flesh, and to be "God with us."

Yet, to make it appear still more remarkable, remember that the creature whose nature Christ took was a being that had sinned. I can more readily conceive the Lord's taking upon himself the nature of a race which had never fallen; but, lo, the race of man stood in rebellion against God, and yet a man did Christ become, that he might deliver us from the consequences of our rebellion, and lift us up to something higher than our pristine purity. "God sending his own Son in the likeness of sinful flesh, has condemned sin in the flesh." "Oh, the depths," is all that we can say, as we look on and marvel at this stoop of divine love.

Note, next, as you view this marvel at a distance, what *a miracle of power* is before us. Have you ever thought of the power displayed in the Lord's fashioning a body capable of union with Godhead? Our Lord was incarnate in a body, which was truly a human body, but yet in some wondrous way was prepared to sustain the indwelling of Deity. Contact with God is terrible; "He looketh on the earth and it trembleth; he toucheth the hills and they smoke." He puts his feet on Paran, and it melts, and Sinai dissolves in flames of fire. So strongly was this truth inwrought into the minds of the early saints, that they said, "No man can see God's face and live;" and yet here was a manhood which did not merely see the face of God, but which was inhabited by Deity. What a human frame was this which could abide the presence of Jehovah! "A body hast thou prepared me." This was indeed a body curiously wrought, a holy thing, a special product of the Holy Spirit's power. It was a body like our own, with nerves as sensitive, and muscles as readily strained, with every organization as delicately fashioned as our own, and yet God was in it. It was a frail barque to bear such a freight. Oh, man Christ, how couldst thou bear the Deity within thee! We know not how it was, but God knoweth. Let us adore this hiding of the Almighty in human weakness, this comprehending of the Incomprehensible, this revealing of the Invisible, this localization of the Omnipresent. Alas, I do but babble! What are words when we deal with such an unutterable truth? Suffice it to say, that the divine power was wonderfully seen in the continued existence of the materialism of Christ's body, which else had been consumed by such a wondrous contact with divinity. Admire the power which dwelt in "God with us."

Again, as you gaze upon the mystery, consider what *an ensign of good will* this must be to the sons of men. When the Lord takes manhood into union with himself in this matchless way it must mean good to man. God cannot mean to destroy that race which he thus weds unto himself. Such a marriage as this, between man and God, must mean peace ; war and destruction are never thus predicted. God incarnate in Bethlehem, to be adored by shepherds, augurs nothing but "peace on earth and mercy mild." O ye sinners who tremble at the thought of the divine wrath, as well you may, lift up your heads with joyful hope of mercy and favour, for God must be full of grace and mercy to that race which he so distinguishes above all others by taking it into union with himself. Be of good cheer, O men of women born, and expect untold blessings for "unto us a child is born, unto us a Son is given." If you look at rivers you can often tell whence they come, and the soil over which they have flowed by their colour : those which flow from melting glaciers are known at once. There is a text concerning a heavenly river which you will understand if you look at it in this light : " He showed me a pure river of the water of life, clear as crystal, proceeding out of the throne of God, and *of the Lamb*." Where the throne is occupied by Godhead, and the appointed Mediator, the incarnate God, the once bleeding Lamb, then the river must be pure as crystal, and be a river, not of molten lava of devouring wrath, but a river of the water of life. Look you to "God with us " and you will see that the consequences of incarnation must be pleasant, profitable, saving, and ennobling to the sons of men.

I pray you to continue your admiring glance, and look upon God with us once more *as a pledge of our deliverance.* We are a fallen race, we are sunken in the mire, we are sold under sin, in bondage and in slavery to Satan ; but if God comes to our race, and espouses its nature, why then we must retrieve our fall, it cannot be possible for the gates of hell to keep those down who have God with them. Slaves under sin and bondsmen beneath the law, hearken to the trump of jubilee, for one has come among you, born of a woman, made under the law, who is also mighty God, pledged to set you free. He is a Saviour, and a great one : able to save, for he is Almighty, and pledged to do it, for he has entered the lists and put on the harness for the battle. The champion of his people is one who will not fail nor be discouraged till the battle is fully fought and won. Jesus coming down from heaven is the pledge that he will take his people up to heaven, his taking our nature is the seal of our being lifted up to his throne. Were it an angel that had interposed, we might have some fears ; were it a mere man, we might go beyond fear, and sit down in despair ; but if it be "God with us," and God has actually taken manhood into union with himself, then let us "ring the bells of heaven " and be glad ; there must be brighter and happier days, there must be salvation to man, there must be glory to God. Let us bask in the beams of the Sun of Righteousness, who now has risen upon us, a light to lighten the Gentiles, and to be the glory of his people Israel.

Thus we have admired at a distance.

II. And, now, in the second place, let us come nearer and CONSIDER THE SUBJECT MORE CLOSELY. What is this? What means this, "God with us"? I do not expect this morning to be able to set forth all the meaning of this short text, "God with us," for indeed, it seems to me to contain the whole history of redemption. It hints at man's being without God, and God's having removed from man on account of sin. It seems to tell me of man's spiritual life, by Christ's coming to him, and being formed in him the hope of glory. God communes with man, and man returns to God, and receives again the divine image as at the first. Yea, heaven itself is "God with us." This text might serve for a hundred sermons without any wire drawing; yea, one might continue to expatiate upon its manifold meanings for ever. I can only at this time give mere hints of lines of thought which you can pursue at your leisure, the Holy Spirit enabling you.

This glorious word Emmanuel means, first, that God in Christ is *with us in very near association.* The Greek particle here used is very forcible, and expresses the strongest form of "*with.*" It is not merely "in company with us" as another Greek word would signify, but "with," "together with," and "sharing with." This preposition is a close rivet, a firm bond, implying, if not declaring, close fellowship. God is peculiarly and closely "with us." Now, think for a while, and you will see that God has in very deed come near to us in very close association. He must have done so, for *he has taken upon himself our nature,* literally our nature,—flesh, blood, bone, everything that made a body; mind, heart, soul, memory, imagination, judgment, everything that makes a rational man. Christ Jesus was the man of men, the second Adam, the model representative man. Think not of him as a deified man any more than you would dare to regard him as a humanized God, or demigod. Do not confound the natures nor divide the person : he is but one person, yet very man as he is also very God. Think of this truth then, and say, "He who sits on the throne is such as I am, sin alone excepted." No, 'tis too much for speech, I will not speak of it ; it is a theme which masters me, and I fear to utter rash expressions. Turn the truth over and over, and see if it be not sweeter than honey and the honey-comb.

> "Oh joy! there sitteth in our flesh,
> Upon a throne of light,
> One of a human mother born,
> In perfect Godhead bright!"

Being with us in our nature, God was with us in *all our life's pilgrimage.* Scarcely can you find a halting-place in the march of life at which Jesus has not paused, or a weary league which he has not traversed. From the gate of entrance even to the door which closes life's way the footprints of Jesus may be traced. Were you in the cradle? He was there. Were you a child under parental authority? Christ was also a boy in the home at Nazareth. Have you entered upon life's battle? Your Lord and Master did the same ; and though he lived not to old age, yet through incessant toil and suffering he bore the marred visage which attends a battered old age. Are you alone? So was he, in the wilderness, and on the mountain's side, and in the garden's gloom. Do you mix in public society? So did he labour in the thickest press. Where can you find yourself, on the hill top, or in the valley, on the land or on the sea, in the daylight or in darkness,— where, I say, can you be without discovering that Jesus has been there before you? What the world has said of her great poet we might with far more truth say of our Redeemer—

> "A man so various that he seemed to be
> Not one, but all mankind's epitome."

One harmonious man he was, and yet all saintly lives seem to be condensed in his. Two believers may be very unlike each other, and yet both will find that Christ's life has in it points of likeness to their own. One shall be rich and another shall be poor, one actively laborious and another patiently suffering, and yet each man in studying the history of the Saviour shall be able to say—his pathway ran hard by my own. He was made in all points like unto his brethren. How charming is the fact that our Lord is " God with us," not here and there, and now and then, but evermore.

Especially does this come out with sweetness in his being " God with us " *in our sorrows*. There is no pang that rends the heart, I might almost say not one which disturbs the body, but what Jesus Christ has been with us in it all. Feel you the sorrows of poverty? He "had not where to lay his head." Do you endure the griefs of bereavement? Jesus " wept " at the tomb of Lazarus. Have you been slandered for righteousness' sake, and has it vexed your spirit? He said " Reproach hath broken mine heart." Have you been betrayed? Do not forget that he too had his familiar friend, who sold him for the price of a slave. On what stormy seas have you been tossed which have not also roared around his boat? Never glen of adversity so dark, so deep, apparently so pathless, but what in stooping down you may discover the footprints of the Crucified One. In the fires and in the rivers, in the cold night and under the burning sun, he cries, " I am with thee. Be not dismayed, for I am both thy companion and thy God."

Mysteriously true is it that when you and I shall come to *the last, the closing scene,* we shall find that Emmanuel has been there. He felt the pangs and throes of death, he endured the bloody sweat of agony and the parching thirst of fever. He knew the separation of the tortured spirit from the poor fainting flesh, and cried, as we shall, " Father, into thy hands I commend my spirit." Ay, and the grave he knew, for there he slept, and left the sepulchre perfumed and furnished to be a couch of rest, and not a charnel-house of corruption. That new tomb in the garden makes him God with us till the resurrection shall call us from our beds of clay to find him God with us in newness of life. We shall be raised up in his likeness, and the first sight our opening eyes shall see shall be the incarnate God. " I know that my Redeemer liveth, and though after my skin worms devour this body, yet in my flesh shall I see God." " God with us." I in my flesh shall see him as the man, the God. And so *to all eternity* he will maintain the most intimate association with us. As long as ages roll he shall be " God with us." Has he not said, " Because I live ye shall live also"? Both his human and divine life will last on for ever, and so shall our life endure. He shall dwell among us and lead us to living fountains of waters, and so shall we be for ever with the Lord.

Now, my brethren, if you will review these thoughts, you shall find good store of food; in fact, a feast even under that one head. God in Christ is with us in the nearest possible association.

But, secondly, *God in Christ is with us in the fullest reconciliation.* This, of course, is true, if the former be true. There was a time when we were parted from God; we were without God, being alienated from him by wicked works, and God also was removed from us by reason of the natural rectitude of character which thrusts iniquity far from him. He is of purer eyes than to behold iniquity, neither can evil dwell with him. That strict justice with which he rules the world requires that he should hide his face from a sinful generation. A God who looks with complacency upon guilty men is not the God of the Bible, who is in multitudes of places set forth as burning with indignation against the wicked. "The wicked and him that loveth violence his soul hateth." But, now the sin which separated us from God has been put away by the blessed sacrifice of Christ upon the tree, and the righteousness, the absence of which must have caused a gulf between unrighteous man and righteous God, that righteousness, I say, has been found, for Jesus has brought in everlasting righteousness. So that now in Jesus God is with us, reconciled to us, the sin which caused his wrath being for ever put away from his people. There are some who object to this view of the case, and I, for one, will not yield one jot to their objections. I do not wonder that they cavil at certain unwise statements, which I like no better than they do; but, nevertheless, if they oppose the atonement as making a recompense to injured justice, their objections shall have no force with me. It is most true that God is always love, but his stern justice is not opposed thereto. It is also most certainly true that towards his people he always was, in the highest sense, love, and the atonement is the result and not the cause of divine love; yet, still viewed in his rectoral character, as a judge and lawgiver, God is " angry with the wicked every day," and apart from the reconciling sacrifice of Christ, his own people were " heirs of wrath even as others." There was anger in the heart of God, as a righteous judge, against those who have broken his holy law, and the reconciliation has a bearing upon the position of the judge of all the earth as well as upon man. I for one shall never cease to say, " O Lord, I will praise thee, for though thou wast angry with me, thine anger is turned away, and thou comfortest me." God can now be with man, and embrace sinners as his children, as he could not have righteously done had not Jesus died. In this sense, and in this sense only, did Dr. Watts write some of his hymns which have been so fiercely condemned. I take leave to quote two verses, and to commend them as setting forth a great truth if the Lord be viewed as a judge, and represented as the awakened conscience of man rightly perceives him. Our poet says of the throne of God :

" Once 'twas the seat of dreadful wrath,
    And shot devouring flame ;
Our God appeared, consuming fire,
    And vengeance was his name.

> "Rich were the drops of Jesus' blood,
> Which calmed his frowning face,
> Which sprinkled o'er the burning throne,
> And turn'd the wrath to grace."

So that now Jehovah is not God against us, but "God with us," he has "reconciled us to himself by the death of his Son."

A third meaning of the text "God with us" is this, *God in Christ is with us in blessed communication.* That is to say, now he has come so near to us as to enter into commerce with us, and this he does in part by hallowed conversation. Now he speaks to us and in us. He has in these last days spoken to us by his Son and by the Divine Spirit with the still small voice of warning, consolation, instruction, and direction. Are you not conscious of this? Since your souls have come to know Christ, have you not also enjoyed intercourse with the Most High? Now, like Enoch, you "walk with God," and, like Abraham, you talk with him as a man talketh with his friend. What are those prayers and praises of yours but the speech which you are permitted to have with the Most High; and he replies to you when his Spirit seals home the promise or applies the precept, when with fresh light he leads you into the doctrine or bestows brighter confidence as to good things to come. Oh yes, God is with us now, so that when he cries, "Seek ye my face" our heart says to him, "Thy face, Lord, will I seek." These Sabbath gatherings, what mean they to many of us but "God with us." That communion table, what means it but "God with us"? Oh, how often in the breaking of bread and the pouring forth of the wine in the memory of his atoning death have we enjoyed his real presence, not in a superstitious, but in a spiritual sense, and found the Lord Jesus to be "God with us." Yes, in every holy ordinance, in every sacred act of worship, we now find that there is a door opened in heaven and a new and living way by which we may come to the throne of grace. Is not this a joy better than all the riches of earth could buy?

And it is not merely in speech that the Lord is with us, but God is with us now by powerful *acts* as well as words. "God with us," why it is the inscription upon our royal standard which strikes terror to the heart of the foe, and cheers the sacramental host of God's elect. Is not this our war cry, "The Lord of hosts is with us, the God of Jacob is our refuge." As to our foes within, God is with us to overcome our corruptions and frailties; and as to the adversaries of truth without, God is with his church, and Christ has promised that he ever will be with her "even to the end of the world." We have not merely God's word and promises, but we have seen his acts of grace on our behalf, both in providence and in the working of his blessed Spirit. "The Lord hath made bare his holy arm in the eyes of all the people." "In Judah is God known: his name is great in Israel. In Salem also is his tabernacle, and his dwelling place in Zion. There brake he the arrows of the bow, the shield, and the sword, and the battle." "God with us"—oh, my brethren, it makes our hearts leap for joy, it fills us with dauntless courage. How can we be dismayed when the Lord of hosts is on our side?

Nor is it merely that God is with us in acts of power on our behalf, but in emanations of his own life into our nature by which we are at first new born, and afterwards sustained in spiritual life. This is more wonderful still. By the Holy Spirit the divine seed which "liveth and abideth for ever" is sown in our souls, and from day to day we are strengthened with might by his Spirit in the inner man.

Nor is this all, for as the masterpiece of grace, the Lord, by his Spirit, even dwells in his people. God is not incarnate in us as in Christ Jesus, but only second in wonder to the incarnation is the indwelling of the Holy Spirit in believers. Now is it "God with us" indeed, for God dwelleth in us. "Know ye not," says the apostle, "that your bodies are the temples of the Holy Ghost." "As it is written, I will dwell in them, and I will walk in them." Oh, the heights and depths then comprehended in those few words, "God with us."

I had many more things to say unto you, but time compels me to sum them up in brief. The Lord becomes "God with us" *by the restoration of his image in us.* "God with us" was seen in Adam when he was perfectly pure, but Adam died when he sinned, and God is not the God of the dead but of the living. Now we, in receiving back the new life and being reconciled to God in Christ Jesus, receive also the restored image of God, and are renewed in knowledge and true holiness. "God with us" means sanctification, the image of Jesus Christ imprinted upon all his brethren.

God is with us, too, let us remember, and leave the point, *in deepest sympathy.* Brethren, are you in sorrow? God is in Christ sympathetic to your grief. Brethren, have you a grand object? I know what it is, it is God's glory; therein also you are sympathetic with God, and God with you. What, let me inquire, is your greatest joy? Have you not learned to rejoice in the Lord? Do you not joy in God by Jesus Christ? Then God also joyeth in you. He rests in his love, and rejoices over you with singing, so that there is God with us in a very wonderful respect, inasmuch as through Christ our aims and desires are like those of God. We desire the same thing, press forward with the same aim, and rejoice in the same objects of delight. When the Lord says, "This is my beloved Son, in whom I am well pleased," our heart answers, "Ay, and in him we are well pleased too." The pleasure of the Father is the pleasure of his own chosen children, for we also joy in Christ; our very soul exults at the sound of his name.

III. I must leave this delightful theme when I have said two or three things about OUR PERSONAL APPROPRIATION of the truth before us.

"God with us." Then, if Jesus Christ be "God with us," let us come to God without any question or hesitancy. Whoever you may be you need no priest or intercessor to introduce you to God, for God has introduced himself to you. Are you children? Then come to God in the child Jesus, who slept in Bethlehem's manger. Oh, ye grey-heads, ye need not keep back, but like Simeon come and take him in your arms, and say, "Lord, now lettest thou thy servant depart in peace according to thy word, for mine eyes have seen thy salvation." God sends an ambassador who inspires no fear: not with helmet and coat of mail, bearing lance, does heaven's herald approach us, but the white flag is held in the hand of a child, in the hand of one chosen out of the people, in the hand of one who died, in the hand of one who though he sits in glory wears the nail-print still. O man, God comes to you as one like yourself. Do not be afraid to come to the gentle Jesus. Do not imagine that you need to be prepared for an audience with him, or that you want the intercession of a saint, or the intervention of priest or minister. Anyone could have come to the babe in Bethlehem. The horned oxen, methinks, ate of the hay on which he slept and feared not. Jesus is the friend of each one of us, sinful and unworthy though we be. You, poor ones, you need not fear to come, for, see, in a stable he is born, and in a manger he is cradled. You have not worse accommodation than his, you are not poorer than he. Come and welcome to the poor man's Prince, to the peasants' Saviour. Stay not back through fear of your unfitness; the shepherds came to him in all their deshabille. I read not that they tarried to put on their best garments, but in the clothes in which they wrapped themselves that cold midnight they hastened just as they were to the young child's presence. God looks not at garments, but at hearts, and accepts men when they come to him with willing spirits, whether they be rich or poor. Come, then; come, and welcome, for God indeed is " God with us."

But, oh, let there be no delay about it. It did seem to me, as I turned this subject over, yesterday, that for any man to say, "I will not come to God," after God has come to man in such a form as this, were an unpardonable act of treason. Peradventure, you knew not God's love when you sinned, as you did ; peradventure, though you persecuted his saints, you did it ignorantly in unbelief ; but, behold your God extends the olive branch of peace to you, extends it in a wondrous way, for he himself comes here to be born of a woman, that he may meet with you who were born of women too, and save you from your sin. Will you not hearken now that he speaks by his Son ? I can understand that you ask to hear no more of his words when he speaks with the sound of a trumpet, waxing exceeding loud and long, from amidst the flaming crags of Sinai ; I do not wonder that you are afraid to draw near when the earth rocks and reels before his awful presence ; but now he restrains himself and veils the splendour of his face, and comes to you as a child of humble mien, a carpenter's son. Oh, if he comes so, will you turn your backs upon him ? Can ye spurn him ? What better ambassador could you desire ? This embassage of peace is so tenderly, so gently, so kindly, so touchingly put, that surely you cannot have the heart to resist it. Nay, do not turn away, let not your ears refuse the language of his grace, but say, "If God is with us, we will be with him." Say it, sinner, say, "I will arise and go to my Father and will say unto him, Father, I have sinned."

And as for you who have given up all hope, you that think yourselves so degraded and fallen that there can be no future for you,—there is hope for you yet, for you are a man, and the next being to God is a man. He that is God is also man, and there is something about that fact which ought to make you say, "Yes, I may yet discover, mayhap, brotherhood to the Son of man who is the Son of God, I, even I, may yet be lifted up to be set among princes, even the princes of his people, by virtue of my regenerated manhood which brings me into relation with the manhood of Christ, and so into relation with the Godhead." Fling not yourself away, oh man, you are something too hopeful after all to be meat for the worm that never dies, and fuel for the fire that never can be quenched. Turn you to your God with full purpose of heart, and you shall find a grand destiny in store for you.

And now, my brethren, to you the last word is, let us be with God since God is with us. I give you for a watchword through the year to come, "Emmanuel, God with us." You, the saints redeemed by blood, have a right to all this in its fullest sense, drink into it and be filled with courage. Do not say, "We can do nothing." Who are ye that can do nothing? God is with you. Do not say "The church is feeble and fallen upon evil times,"—nay, "God is with us." We need the courage of those ancient soldiers who were wont to regard difficulties only as whetstones upon which to sharpen their swords. I like Alexander's talk—when they said there were so many thousands, so many millions perhaps of Persians. "Very well," says he, "it is good reaping where the corn is thick. One butcher is not afraid of a thousand sheep." I like even the talk of the old Gascon, who said when they asked him, "Can you and your troops get into that fortress? it is impregnable." "Can the sun enter it?" said he. "Yes." "Well, where the sun can go we can enter." Whatever is possible or whatever is impossible, Christians can do at God's command, for God is with us. Do you not see that the word, "God with us," puts impossibility out of all existence? Hearts that never could else be broken will be broken if God be with us. Errors which never else could be confuted can be overthrown by "God with us." Things impossible with men are possible with God. John Wesley died with that upon his tongue, and let us live with it upon our hearts.—"The best of all is God with us." Blessed Son of God, we thank thee that thou hast brought us that word. Amen.

The Great Birthday

" The angel said unto them, Fear not : for, behold, I bring you good tidings of great joy, which shall be to all people."—Luke ii. 10.

THERE is no reason upon earth beyond that of ecclesiastical custom why the 25th of December should be regarded as the birthday of our Lord and Saviour Jesus Christ any more than any other day from the first of January to the last day of the year; and yet some persons regard Christmas with far deeper reverence than the Lord's-day. You will often hear it asserted that " The Bible and the Bible alone is the religion of Protestants," but it is not so. There are Protestants who have absorbed a great deal beside the Bible into their religion, and among other things they have accepted the authority of what they call " the Church," and by that door all sorts of superstitions have entered. There is no authority whatever in the word of God for the keeping of Christmas at all, and no reason for keeping it just now except that the most superstitious section of Christendom has made a rule that December 25th shall be observed as the birthday of the Lord, and the church by law established in this land has agreed to follow in the same track. You are under no bondage whatever to regard the regulation. We owe no allegiance to the ecclesiastical powers which have made a decree on this matter, for we belong to an old-fashioned church which does not dare to make laws, but is content to obey them. At the same time the day is no worse than another, and if you choose to observe it, and observe it unto the Lord, I doubt not he will accept your devotion : while if you do not observe it, but unto the Lord observe it not, for fear of encouraging superstition and will-worship, I doubt not but what you shall be as accepted in the non-observance as you could have been in the observance of it. Still, as the thoughts of a great many Christian people will run at this time towards the birth of Christ, and as this cannot be wrong, I judged it meet to avail ourselves of the prevailing current, and float down the stream of thought. Our minds will run that way, because so many around us are following customs suggestive of it, therefore let us get what good we can out of the occasion. There can be no reason why we should not, and it may be helpful that we should, now consider the birth of our Lord Jesus. We will do that voluntarily which we would refuse to do as a matter of obligation: we will do that simply for convenience sake which we should not think of doing because enjoined by authority or demanded by superstition.

The shepherds were keeping their flocks by night; probably a calm, peaceful night, wherein they felt the usual difficulty of keeping their weary eyelids still uplifted as sleep demanded its due of them. On a sudden, to their amazement, a mighty blaze lit up the heavens, and turned midnight into midday. The glory of the Lord, by which, according to the idiom of the language, is meant the greatest conceivable glory as well as a divine glory, surrounded and alarmed them, and in the midst of it they saw a shining spirit, a form the like of which they had never beheld before, but of which they had heard their fathers speak, and of which they had read in the books of the prophets, so that they knew it to be an angel. It was indeed no common messenger from heaven, but "the angel of the Lord," that choice presence angel, whose privilege it is to stand nearest the heavenly majesty, "'mid the bright ones doubly bright," and to be employed on weightiest errands from the eternal throne. "The angel of the Lord came upon them." Are you astonished that at first they were afraid? Would not you be alarmed if such a thing should happen to you? The stillness of the night, the suddenness of the apparition, the extraordinary splendour of the light, the supernatural appearance of the angel—all would tend to astound them, and to put them into a quiver of reverential alarm; for I doubt not there was a mixture both of reverence and of fear in that feeling which is described as being "sore afraid." They would have fallen on their faces to the ground in fright, had there not dropped out of that "glory of the Lord" a gentle voice, which said, "Fear not." They were calmed by that sweet comfort, and enabled to listen to the announcement which followed. Then that voice, in accents sweet as the notes of a silver bell, proceeded to say, "Behold, I bring you good tidings of great joy, which shall be to all people. For unto you is born this day in the city of David a Saviour, which is Christ the Lord." They were bidden to shake off all thoughts of fear, and to give themselves up to joy. Doubtless they did so, and amongst all mankind there were none so happy at that dead of night as were these shepherds, who had seen an amazing sight, which they would never forget, and now were consulting whether they should not haste away to gaze upon a sight which would be more delightful still, namely, the Babe whereof the angel spoke.

May great joy be upon us also while our thought shall be that *the birth of Christ is the cause of supreme joy.* When we have spoken upon this we shall have to enquire, *to whom does that joy belong;* and thirdly, we shall consider, *how they shall express that joy* while they possess it. May the Holy Spirit now reveal the Lord Jesus to us, and prepare us to rejoice in him.

I. THE BIRTH OF CHRIST SHOULD BE THE SUBJECT OF SUPREME JOY. Rightly so. We have the angelic warrant for rejoicing because Christ is born. It is a truth so full of joy that it caused the angel who came to announce it to be filled with gladness. He had little to do with the fact, for Christ took not up angels, but he took up the seed of Abraham; but I suppose that the very thought that the Creator should be linked with the creature, that the great Invisible and Omnipotent should come into alliance with that which he himself had made, caused the angel as a creature to feel that all creatureship was elevated, and this made him glad. Beside, there was a sweet benevolence of spirit in the angel's bosom which made him happy because he had such gladsome tidings to bring to the fallen sons of men. Albeit they are not our brethren, yet do angels take a loving concern in all our affairs. They rejoice over us when we repent, they are ministering spirits when we are saved, and they bear us aloft when we depart; and sure we are that they can never be unwilling servants to their Lord, or tardy helpers of his beloved ones. They are friends of the Bridegroom and rejoice in his joy, they are household servants of the family of love, and they wait upon us with an eager diligence, which betokens the tenderness of feeling which they have towards the King's sons. Therefore the angel delivered his message cheerfully, as became the place from which he came, the theme which brought him down, and his own interest therein. He said, " I bring you good tidings of great joy," and we are sure he spake in accents of delight. Yea, so glad were angels at this gospel, that when the discourse was over, one angel having evangelized and given out the gospel for the day, suddenly a band of choristers appeared and sang an anthem loud and sweet that there might be a full service at the first propounding of the glad tidings of great joy. A multitude of the heavenly host had heard that a chosen messenger had been sent to proclaim the new-born King, and, filled with holy joy and adoration, they gathered up their strength to pursue him, for they could not let him go to earth alone on such an errand. They overtook him just as he had reached the last word of his discourse, and then they broke forth in that famous chorale, the only one sung of angels that was ever heard by human ears here below, " Glory to God in the highest, and on earth peace, good will toward men." Thus, I say, they had full service; there was gospel ministry in rich discourse concerning Christ, and there was hearty and devout praise from a multitude all filled with heavenly joy. It was so glad a message that they could not let it be simply spoken by a solitary voice, though that were an angel's, but they must needs pour forth a glad chorus of praise, singing unto the Lord a new song. Brothers, if the birth of Jesus was so gladsome to our cousins the angels, what should it be to us? If it made our neighbours sing who had comparatively so small a share in it, how should it make us leap for joy? Oh, if it brought heaven down to earth, should not our songs go up to heaven? If heaven's gate of pearl was set open at its widest, and a stream of shining ones came running downward to the lower skies, to anticipate the time when they shall all descend in solemn pomp at the glorious advent of the great King; if it emptied heaven for a while to make earth so glad, ought not our thoughts and praises and all our loves to go pouring up to the eternal gate, leaving earth a while that we may crowd heaven with the songs of mortal men? Yea, verily, so let it be.

"Glory to the new-born King!
Let us all the anthem sing,
'Peace on earth, and mercy mild ;
God and sinners reconciled.'"

For, first, *the birth of Christ was the incarnation of God:* it was God taking upon himself human nature—a mystery, a wondrous mystery, to be believed in rather than to be defined. Yet so it was that in the manger lay an infant, who was also infinite, a feeble child who was also the Creator of heaven and earth. How this could be we do not know, but that it was so we assuredly believe, and therein do we rejoice : for if God thus take upon himself human nature, then manhood is not abandoned nor given up as hopeless. When manhood had broken the bonds of the covenant, and snatched from the one reserved tree the fruit forbidden, God might have said, " I give thee up, O Adam, and cast off thy race. Even as I gave up Lucifer and all his host, so I abandon thee to follow thine own chosen course of rebellion !" But we have now no fear that the Lord has done this, for God has espoused manhood and taken it into union with himself. Now manhood is not put aside by the Lord as an utterly accursed thing, to be an abomination unto him for ever, for Jesus, the Well-beloved, is born of a virgin. God would not so have taken manhood into union with himself if he had not said, " Destroy it not, for a blessing is in it." I know the curse has fallen upon men because they have sinned, but evidently not on manhood in the abstract, for else had not Christ come to take upon himself the form of man and to be born of woman. The word made flesh means hope for manhood, notwithstanding its fall. The race is not to be outlawed, and marked with the brand of death and hell, and to be utterly abandoned to destruction, for, lo, the Lord hath married into the race, and the Son of God has become the Son of man. This is enough to make all that is within us sing for joy.

Then, too, if God has taken manhood into union with himself, he loves man and means man's good. Behold what manner of love God hath bestowed upon us that he should espouse our nature ! For God had never so united himself with any creature before. His tender mercy had ever been over all his works, but they were still so distinct from himself that a great gulf was fixed between the Creator and the created, so far as existence and relationship are concerned. The Lord had made many noble intelligences, principalities, and powers of whom we know little ; we do not even know what those four living creatures may be who are nearest the eternal presence ; but God had never taken up the nature of any of them, nor allied himself with them by any actual union with his person. But, lo, he has allied himself with man, that creature a little lower than the angels, that creature who is made to suffer death by reason of his sin ; God has come into union with man, and therefore full sure he loves him unutterably well, and has great thoughts of good towards him. If a king's son doth marry a rebel, then for that rebel race there are prospects of reconciliation, pardon, and restoration. There must be in the great heart of the Divine One wondrous thoughts of pity and condescending love, if He deigns to take human nature into union with himself. Joy, joy for ever, let us sound the loud cymbals of delight, for the incarnation bodes good to our race.

If God has taken manhood into union with himself then God will feel for man, he will have pity upon him, he will remember that he is dust, he will have compassion upon his infirmities and sicknesses. You know, beloved, how graciously it is so, for that same Jesus who was born of a woman at Bethlehem is touched with the feelings of our infirmities, having been tempted in all points like as we are. Such intimate practical sympathy would not have belonged to our great High Priest if he had not become man. Not even though he be divine could he have been perfect in sympathy with us if he had not also become bone of our bone and flesh of our flesh. The Captain of our salvation could only be made perfect through suffering ; it must needs be that since the children were partakers of flesh and blood he himself also should take part of the same. For this again we may ring the silver bells, since the Son of God now intimately sympathizes with man because he is made in all points like unto his brethren.

Further, it is clear that if God condescends to be so intimately allied with manhood, he intends to deliver man, and to bless him. Incarnation prophesies salvation. Oh, believing soul, thy God cannot mean to curse thee. Look at God incarnate ! What readest thou there but salvation ? God in human flesh must mean that God intends to set man above all the works of his hands, and to give him dominion, according to his first intent, over all sheep and oxen and all that pass through the paths of the sea and the air ; yea it must mean that there is to be a man beneath whose feet all things shall be placed, so that even death itself shall be subject unto him. When God stoops down to man it must mean that man is to be lifted up to God. What joy there is in this ! Oh that our hearts were but half alive to the incarnation ! Oh that we did but know a thousandth part of the unutterable delight which is hidden in this thought, that the Son of God was born a man at Bethlehem ! Thus you see that there is overflowing cause for joy in the birth of Christ, because it was the incarnation of the Deity.

But further, the angel explained our cause for joy by saying that *he who was born was unto us a Saviour.* " Unto you is born this day a Saviour." Brothers and sisters, I know who will be gladdest to-day to think that Christ was born a Saviour. It will be those who are most conscious of their sinnership. If you would draw music out of that ten-stringed harp, the word " Saviour," pass it over to a sinner. " Saviour" is the harp, but " sinner " is the finger that must touch the strings and bring forth the melody. If thou knowest thyself lost by nature and lost by practice, if thou feelest sin like a plague at thy heart, if evil wearies and worries thee, if thou hast known of iniquity the burden and the shame, then will it be bliss to thee even to hear of that Saviour whom the Lord has provided. Even as a babe, Jesus the Saviour will be precious to thee, but most of all because he has now finished all the work of thy salvation. Thou wilt look to the commencement of that work, and then survey it even to its close, and bless and magnify the name of the Lord. Unto you, O ye who are of sinners the chief, even unto you, ye consciously guilty ones, is born a Saviour. He is a Saviour by birth : for this purpose is he born. To save sinners is his birthright and office. It is henceforth an institution of the divine dominion, and an office of the divine nature to save the lost. Henceforth God has laid help upon One that is mighty, and exalted One chosen out of the people, that he may seek and save that which was lost. Is there not joy in this? Where else is there joy if not here?

Next the angel tells us that *this Saviour is Christ the Lord,* and there is much gladness in that fact. "Christ" signified *anointed.* Now when we know that the Lord Jesus Christ came to save, it is most pleasant to perceive in addition that the Father does not let him enter upon his mission without the necessary qualification. He is anointed of the Highest that he may carry out the offices which he has undertaken : the Spirit of the Lord rested upon him without measure. Our Lord is anointed in a threefold sense, as prophet, priest, and king. It has been well observed that this anointing, in its threefold power, never rested upon any other man. There have been kingly prophets, David to wit; there was one kingly priest, even Melchisedec ; and there have also been priestly prophets, such as Samuel. Thus it has come to pass that two of the offices have been united in one man, but the whole three,—prophet, priest, and king, never met in one thrice anointed being until Jesus came. We have the fullest anointing conceivable in Christ, who is anointed with the oil of gladness above his fellows, and as the Messiah, the sent One of God, is completely prepared and qualified for all the work of our salvation. Let our hearts be glad. We have not a nominal Saviour, but a Saviour fully equipped ; one who in all points is like ourselves, for he is man, but in all points fit to help the feebleness which he has espoused, for he is the anointed man. See what an intimate mingling of the divine and human is found in the angel's song. They sing of him as "a Saviour," and a Saviour must of necessity be divine, in order to save from death and hell; and yet the title is drawn from his dealings with humanity. Then they sing of him as " Christ," and that must be human, for only man can be anointed, yet that unction comes from the Godhead. Sound forth the jubilee trumpets for this marvellously Anointed One, and rejoice in him who is your priest to cleanse you, your prophet to instruct you, and your king to deliver you. The angels sang of him as Lord, and yet as born ; so here again the godlike in dominion is joined with the human in birth. How well did the words and the sense agree.

The angel further went on to give these shepherds cause for joy by telling them that while their Saviour was born to be the Lord yet he was so *born in lowliness* that they would find him a babe, wrapped in swaddling clothes, lying in a manger. Is there cause of joy there ? I say, ay, indeed there is, for it is the terror of the Godhead which keeps the sinner oftentimes away from reconciliation ; but see how the Godhead hath graciously concealed itself in a babe, a little babe,— a babe that needed to be wrapped in swaddling bands like any other new-born child. Who feareth to approach him ? Who ever heard of trembling in the presence of a babe ? Yet is the Godhead there. My soul, when thou canst not for very amazement stand on the sea of glass mingled with fire, when the divine glory is like a consuming fire to thy spirit, and the sacred majesty of heaven is altogether overpowering to thee, then come thou to this babe, and say, " Yet God is here, and here can I meet him in the person of his dear Son, in whom dwelleth all the fulness of the Godhead bodily." Oh, what bliss there is in incarnation if we remember that herein God's omnipotence cometh down to man's feebleness, and infinite majesty stoops to man's infirmity.

Now mark, the shepherds were not to find this babe wrapped in Tyrian purple nor swathed in choicest fabrics fetched from afar.

> " No crown bedecks his forehead fair,
> No pearl, nor gem, nor silk is there."

Nor would they discover him in the marble halls of princes, nor guarded by prætorian legionaries, nor lackied by vassal sovereigns, but they would find him the babe of a peasant woman, of princely lineage it is true, but of a family whose stock was dry and forgotten in Israel. The child was reputed to be the son of a carpenter. If you looked on the humble father and mother, and at the poor bed they had made up, where aforetime oxen had come to feed, you would say " This is condescension indeed." O ye poor, be glad, for Jesus is born in poverty, and cradled in a manger. O ye sons of toil rejoice, for the Saviour is born of a lowly virgin, and a carpenter is his foster father. O ye people, oftentimes despised and downtrodden, the Prince of the Democracy is born, one chosen out of the people is exalted to the throne. O ye who call yourselves the aristocracy, behold the Prince of the kings of the earth, whose lineage is divine, and yet there is no room for him in the inn. Behold, O men, the Son of God, who is bone of your bone, intimate with all your griefs, who in his after life hungered as ye hunger, was weary as ye are weary, and wore humble garments like your own; yea, suffered worse poverty than you, for he was without a place whereon to lay his head. Let the heavens and the earth be glad, since God hath so fully, so truly come down to man.

Nor is this all. The angel called for joy, and I ask for it too, on this ground, that *the birth of this child was to bring glory to God in the highest, on earth peace, good will toward men.* The birth of Christ has given such glory to God as I know not that he could ever have had here by any other means. We must always speak in accents soft and low when we talk of God's glory; in itself it must always be infinite and not to be conceived by us, and yet may we not venture to say that all the works of God's hands do not glorify him so much as the gift of his dear Son, that all creation and all providence do not so well display the heart of Deity as when he gives his Only Begotten and sends him into the world that men may live through him? What wisdom is manifested in the plan of redemption of which the incarnate God is the centre! What love is there revealed! What power is that which brought the Divine One down from glory to the manger; only omnipotence could have worked so great a marvel! What faithfulness to ancient promises! What truthfulness in keeping covenant! What grace, and yet what justice! For it was in the person of that newborn child that the law must be fulfilled, and in his precious body must vengeance find recompense for injuries done to divine righteousness. All the attributes of God were in that little child most marvellously displayed and veiled. Conceive the whole sun to be focussed to a single point and yet so softly revealed as to be endurable by the tenderest eye, even thus the glorious God is brought down for man to see him born of a woman. Think of it. The express image of God in mortal flesh! The heir of all things cradled in a manger! Marvellous is this! Glory to God in the highest! He has never revealed himself before as he now manifests himself in Jesus.

It is through our Lord Jesus being born that there is already a measure of peace on earth and boundless peace yet to come. Already the teeth of war have been somewhat broken, and a testimony is borne by the faithful against this great crime. The religion of Christ holds up its shield over the oppressed, and declares tyranny and cruelty to be loathsome before God. Whatever abuse and scorn may be heaped upon Christ's true minister he will never be silent while there are downtrodden nationalities and races needing his advocacy, nor will God's servants anywhere, if faithful to the Prince of Peace, ever cease to maintain peace among men to the utmost of their power. The day cometh when this growing testimony shall prevail, and nations shall learn war no more. The Prince of Peace shall snap the spear of war across his knee. He, the Lord of all, shall break the arrows of the bow, the sword and the shield and the battle, and he shall do it in his own dwelling-place, even in Zion, which is more glorious and excellent than all the mountains of prey. As surely as Christ was born at Bethlehem he will yet make all men brothers, and establish a universal monarchy of peace, of which there shall be no end. So let us sing if we value the glory of God, for the new-born child reveals it ; and let us sing if we value peace on earth, for he is come to bring it. Yea, and if we love the link which binds glorified heaven with pacified earth,—the good will towards men which the Eternal herein manifests, let us give a third note to our hallelujah and bless and magnify Immanuel, God with us, who has accomplished all this by his birth among us. "Glory to God in the highest, and on earth peace, good will toward men."

I think I have shown you that there was room enough for joy to the shepherds, but you and I, who live in later days, when we understand the whole business of salvation, ought to be even more glad than they were, though they glorified and praised God for all the things that they had heard and seen. Come, my brethren, let us at least do as much as these simple shepherds, and exult with our whole souls.

II. Secondly, let us consider TO WHOM THIS JOY BELONGS. I was very heavy yesterday in spirit, for this dreary weather tends greatly to depress the mind.

> "No lark could pipe to skies so dull and grey."

But a thought struck me and filled me with intense joy. I tell it out to you, not because it will seem anything to you, but as having gladdened myself. It is a bit all for myself to be placed in a parenthesis ; it is this, that the joy of the birth of Christ in part *belongs to those who tell it,* for the angels who proclaimed it were exceedingly glad, as glad as glad could be. I thought of this and whispered to my heart, "As I shall tell of Jesus born on earth for men, I will take license to be glad also, glad if for nothing else that I have such a message to bring to them." The tears stood in my eyes, and stand there even now, to think that I should be privileged to say to my fellow men, "God has condescended to assume your nature that he might save you." These are as glad and as grand words as he of the golden mouth could have spoken. As for Cicero and Demosthenes, those eloquent orators had no such theme to dwell upon. Oh, joy, joy, joy, joy ! There was born into this world a man who is also God. My heart dances as David danced before the ark of God.

This joy was meant, not for the tellers of the news alone, but *for all who heard it.* The glad tidings " shall be unto all people." Read " all *the* people," if you like, for so, perhaps, the letter of the original might demand. Well, then, it meant that it was joy to all the nation of the Jews ; but assuredly our version is truer to the inner spirit of the text ; it is joy to all people upon the face of the earth that Christ is born. There is not a nation under heaven but what has a right to be glad because God has come down among men. Sing together, ye waste places of Jerusalem. Take up the strain, O ye dwellers in the wilderness, and let the multitude of the isles be glad thereof ! Ye who beneath the frigid zone feel in your very marrow all the force of God's north wind, let your hearts burn within you at this happy truth. And ye whose faces are scorched by the heat of the torrid sun, let this be as a well of water unto you. Exult and magnify Jehovah that his Son, his Only Begotten, is also brother to mankind.

> " O wake our hearts, in gladness sing !
> And hail each one the newborn King ,
> Till living song from loving souls
> Like sound of mighty waters rolls."

But brethren they do not all rejoice, not even all of those who know this glorious truth, nor does it stir the hearts of half mankind. To whom, then, is it a joy ? I answer, *to all who believe it,* and especially to all who believe it as the shepherds did, with that faith which staggers not through unbelief. The shepherds never had a doubt : the light, the angels, and the song were enough for them ; they accepted the glad tidings without a single question. In this the shepherds were both happy and wise, ay, wiser than the would-be wise whose wisdom can only manifest itself in cavilling. This present age despises the simplicity of a childlike faith, but how wonderfully God is rebuking its self-conceit. He is taking the wise in their own craftiness. I could not but notice in the late discovery of the famous Greek cities and the sepulchres of the heroes, the powerful rebuke which the spirit of scepticism has received. These wise doubters have been taken on their own ground and put to confusion. Of course they told us that old Homer was himself a myth, and the poem called by his name was a mere collection of unfounded legends and mere tales. Some ancient songster did but weave his dreams into poetry and foist them upon us as the blind minstrel's song : there was no fact in it, they said, nor indeed in any current history ; everything was mere legend. Long ago these gentlemen told us that there was no King Arthur, no William Tell, no anybody indeed. Even as they questioned all sacred records, so have they cast suspicion upon all else that common men believe. But lo, the ancient cities speak, the heroes are found in their tombs ; the child's faith is vindicated. They have disinterred the king of men, and this and other matters speak in tones of thunder to the unbelieving ear, and say, "Ye fools, the simpletons believed and were wiser than your 'culture' made you. Your endless doubts have led you into falsehood and not into truth."

The shepherds believed and were glad as glad could be, but if Professor —— (never mind his name) had been there on that memorable night he would certainly have debated with the angel, and denied that a Saviour was needed at all. He would coolly have taken notes for a lecture upon the nature of light, and have commenced a disquisition upon the cause of certain remarkable nocturnal phenomena, which had been seen in the fields near Bethlehem. Above all he would have assured the shepherds of the absolute non-existence of anything superhuman. Have not the learned men of our age proved that impossibility scores of times with argument sufficient to convince a wooden post? They have made it as plain as that three times two are eighteen that there is no God, nor angel, nor spirit. They have proved beyond all doubt, as far as their own dogmatism is concerned, that everything is to be doubted which is most sure, and that nothing is to be believed at all except the infallibility of pretenders to science. But these men find no comfort, neither are they so weak as to need any, so they say. Their teaching is not glad tidings but a wretched negation, a killing frost which nips all noble hopes in the bud, and in the name of reason steals away from man his truest bliss. Be it ours to be as philosophical as the shepherds, for they did not believe too much, but simply believed what was well attested, and this they found to be true upon personal investigation. In faith lies joy. If our faith can realize we shall be happy now. I want this morning to feel as if I saw the glory of the Lord still shining in the heavens, for it was there, though I did not see it. I wish I could see that angel, and hear him speak ; but, failing this, I know he did speak, though I did not hear him. I am certain that those shepherds told no lies, nor did the Holy Ghost deceive us when he bade his servant Luke write this record. Let us forget the long interval between and only recollect that it was really so. Realize that which was indeed matter of fact, and you may almost hear the angelic choir up in yonder sky singing still, "Glory to God in the highest, and on earth peace, good will toward men." At any rate, our hearts rehearse the anthem and we feel the joy of it, by simply believing, even as the shepherds did.

Mark well, that believing what they did these simple-minded shepherds *desired to approach nearer* the marvellous babe. What did they do but consult together and say, " Let us now go even unto Bethlehem and see this thing which has come to pass"? O beloved, if you want to get the joy of Christ, come near to him. Whatever you hear about him from his own book, believe it ; but then say, " I will go and find him." When you hear the voice of the Lord from Sinai draw not nigh unto the flaming mountain, the law condemns you, the justice of God overwhelms you. Bow at a humble distance and adore with solemn awe. But when you hear of God in Christ hasten hither. Hasten hither with all confidence, for you are not come unto the mount that might be touched, and that burned with fire, but ye are come unto the blood of sprinkling, which speaketh better things than that of Abel. Come near, come nearer, nearer still. " Come," is his own word to those who labour and are heavy laden, and that selfsame word he will address to you at the last—" Come, ye blessed of my Father, inherit the kingdom prepared for you from before the foundation of the world." If you want joy in Christ come and find it in his bosom, or at his feet; there John and Mary found it long ago.

And then, my brethren, do what the shepherds did when they came near. *They rejoiced to see the babe of whom they had been told.* You cannot see with the physical eye, but you must meditate, and so see with the mental eye this great, and grand, and glorious truth that the Word was made flesh and dwelt among us. This is the way to have joy to-day, joy such as fitly descends from heaven with the descent of heaven's King. Believe, draw near, and then fixedly gaze upon him, and so be blest.

> " Hark how all the welkin rings
> Glory to the King of kings!
> Peace on earth and mercy mild,
> God and sinners reconciled.

> " Veil'd in flesh the Godhead see;
> Hail the incarnate Deity,
> Pleased as man with men to appear,
> Jesus our Immanuel here."

III. My time has fled, else I desired to have shown, in the third place, HOW THAT JOY SHOULD BE MANIFESTED. I will only give a hint or two. The way in which many believers in Christmas keep the feast we know too well. This is a Christian country, is it not? I have been told so so often that I suppose it must be true. It is a Christian country! But the Christianity is of a remarkable kind! It is not only that in the olden time " Christmas broached the mightiest ale," but nowadays Christmas keepers must needs get drunk upon it. I slander not our countrymen when I say that drunkenness seems to be one of the principal items of their Christmastide delight. If Bacchus were born at this time I do think England keeps the birthday of that detestable deity most appropriately, but tell me not that it is the birth of the holy child Jesus that they thus celebrate. Is he not crucified afresh by such blasphemy? Surely to the wicked, Jesus saith, " What hast thou to do to keep my birthday and mention my name in connection with thy gluttony and drunkenness?" Shame that there should be any cause for such words. Tenfold shame that there should be so much.

You may keep his birthday all the year round, for it were better to say he was born every day of the year than on any one, for truly in a spiritual sense he is born every day of every year in some men's hearts, and that to us is a far weightier point than the observation of holy days. Express your joy, first, as the angels did, by public ministry. Some of us are called to speak to the many. Let us in the clearest and most earnest tones proclaim the Saviour and his power to rescue man. Others of you cannot *preach*, but you can *sing*. Sing then your anthems, and praise God with all your hearts. Do not be slack in the devout use of your tongues, which are the glory of your frames, but again and again and again lift up your joyful hymns unto the new-born King. Others of you can neither preach nor sing. Well, then, you must do what the shepherds did, and what did they? You are told twice that they *spread the news*. As soon as they had seen the babe they made known abroad the saying that was told them, and as they went home they glorified God. This is one of the most practical ways of showing your joy. Holy conversation is as acceptable as sermons and anthems. There was also one who said little, but thought the more: "Mary *pondered* all these things in her heart." Quiet, happy spirit, weigh in thy heart the grand truth that Jesus was born at Bethlehem. Immanuel, God with us;—weigh it if you can; look at it again and again, examine the varied facets of this priceless brilliant, and bless, and adore, and love, and wonder, and yet adore again this matchless miracle of love.

Lastly, *go and do good to others.* Like the wise men, bring your offerings, and offer to the new-born King your heart's best gold of love, and frankincense of praise, and myrrh of penitence. Bring everything of your heart's best, and somewhat of your substance also, for this is a day of good tidings, and it were unseemly to appear before the Lord empty. Come and worship God manifest in the flesh, and be filled with his light and sweetness by the power of the Holy Spirit. Amen.

Out of Egypt

" When he arose, he took the young child and his mother by night, and departed into Egypt: and was there until the death of Herod: that it might be fulfilled which was spoken of the Lord by the prophet, saying, Out of Egypt have I called my son."— Matthew ii. 14, 15.

"When Israel was a child, then I loved him, and called my son out of Egypt."— Hosea xi. 1.

EGYPT occupies a very singular position towards Israel. It was often the shelter of the seed of Abraham. Abraham himself went there when there was a famine in the land of his sojourn. To Egypt Joseph was taken that he might escape from the death intended for him by his envious brethren, and become the foster-father of the house of Israel. Into Egypt, as we all right well know, went the whole family of Jacob, and there they sojourned in a strange land. There Moses acquired the learning which was so useful to him. It was out of the spoils of Egypt that the furniture of the Tabernacle was made, as if to show that God intended to take out of heathen hands an offering to his own glory, just as afterwards the timber of the Temple was hewn by Hiram the Phœnician, that the Gentiles might have a share in building the Temple, in token that they would one day be made fellow heirs with Israel. But while Egypt was for awhile the shelter of the house of Israe. it became afterwards the house of bondage, and a country fraught with danger to the very existence of the elect nation. There was a very useful purpose to be served by their going down into Egypt for awhile, that they might be consolidated into a nation, and might acquire many useful arts which they could not have learned while they were wandering about in Palestine : the lesson was valuable, but it was learned in much misery. They had to smart beneath the lash, and faint beneath their labour : the iron bondage entered into Israel's soul, so that an exceeding great and bitter cry went up unto heaven. Yet, when the heaviest burdens were laid on their shoulders, the day of liberty was dawning : when the tale of bricks was doubled, Moses was born. When man had come to his extremity of persecution, then God took his opportunity of salvation, and led his Israel out of Egypt in the teeth of their tyrant master. It had been at first a Goshen to them, a place of great abundance in the Delta of the Nile; but afterwards it became a Mizriam to them, for that is the Hebrew word for Egypt, and it means a place of straits and tribulations. The point that is meant to be brought forward by the prophet is that they were called out of Egypt, for it was not possible for them to mingle with the sons of Ham and lose their separate existence. They were on the banks of the Nile, and at first dwelt there in much comfort, but this seductive ease was not allowed to hold them: full soon they were heavily oppressed, and their existence was threatened; yet both from the comfort of Egypt and from the captivity of Egypt they were called, and at the call of God they came forth. The living seed may go into strange places, but it can never be destroyed. The host of God may walk through fire, but it shall not be burned. God has made the living seed immortal, and it cannot die, for it is born of God. Out of deadly lands, where every breath is disease, they shall be called by the eternal voice. Those whom God has chosen may be cast far, but they shall never be cast away; they may dwell among a people like the Egyptians, most superstitious and debased, a nation of whom even the heathen Juvenal made sport when he said, " Oh, happy people who grow their gods in their kitchen gardens," for they worshipped leeks and onions, and all kinds of beasts and fowls, and creeping things; but the children of the Lord cannot be suffered to remain among such a people, for the Lord desires to make of Israel, and of all believers, a people separated unto himself. Out of the midst of guilty Egypt the Lord called his people, whom he had formed for himself, to show forth his praise. The abundance of superstition, though it be like the sea, shall not quench the spark of the divine life in the living family of God : it shall burn on amidst the waves until the God who first enkindled it shall by his own right hand pluck it from among the billows, and set it as a light upon a candlestick that it may give light to all that are in the house. Neither Egypt of old, nor Babylon, nor Rome can destroy the seed royal; out of all dangers the church must emerge the better for her affliction. " Out of Egypt have I called my son," is a text worthy to be made a proverb, for it is true all through the history of the chosen seed. They are called out from amongst the surrounding race of rebels, and when the call comes none can hold them back. It were easier to restrain the sun from rising than to hold the redeemed of the Lord in perpetual servitude. "The Breaker has gone up before them, and their King at the head of them": who shall block up their road? God is still calling them out, and until the very last of his elect shall be ingathered it shall still stand true, " Out of Egypt "—and out of anywhere else that is like to Egypt, out of the worst and vilest places, out of the places where they are held fast in bitter bondage, out of these—" have I called my son."

At this time I shall first call your attention to the text in Hosea according to the sense in which the prophet first uttered it. He speaks of *the natural seed called out from the sheltering world,* for Egypt was a sheltering world to Israel, the natural seed, and they were called out of it by the omnipotent power of God. Secondly, we shall notice *the divine seed called out literally from a sheltering Egypt,* and brought up from it into the land of Judea, that he might be the glory of his people Israel. Thirdly, we shall spend a little time in considering *the chosen seed,* those who are given unto Christ of the Father: these also must come out from the world, whether it be friendly or hostile. The Lord hath said to them, " This is not your rest, for it is polluted": he is saying the same to-day. Still is it true of the spiritual seed as of our Lord Jesus and of the natural seed, "Out of Egypt have I called my son." May the Holy Spirit be our teacher while we handle this great subject.

I. Let us think of THE NATURAL SEED of Israel, as called out of Egypt, for with them this wonderful text began to be expounded. It is well worth considering, for this constituted one of the loftiest lyrics of Hebrew poetry. The deliverance of the people of God out of Egypt " with a high hand and with an outstretched arm " is a song which the nation never wearied of singing, and which we ought never to weary of singing either, for at the close of all things we and all the spirits redeemed shall sing the song of Moses, the servant of God and of the Lamb. The great redemption of the Exodus shall always be so eminent a type of the greater redemption upon the cross that the two may be blended together, and words that were sung concerning the first deliverance may be readily enough used as expressions of our joy in our salvation from death and hell.

> " From Egypt lately come,
> Where death and darkness reign,
> We seek our new, our better home,
> Where we our rest shall gain.
> Hallelujah !
> We are on our way to God."

While speaking upon this natural seed I want you to notice, first, that if they are to be called out of Egypt *they must first go down into Egypt.* They cannot come out of it if they have not first gone into it. I do not know of anything that could have tempted them down into Egypt, for it had nothing to offer which was better than Canaan ; but the fathers of the tribes were driven there by a famine which troubled the whole world. The Lord sent a man before them, even Joseph, who laid up in store food for the seven years of famine, and Israel went down into Egypt that they might not die, but might be cherished by Joseph, who had become lord of the land.

The Lord may, in order to prevent his people falling into a worse evil, permit them to go into that which seems hopeful, but ultimately turns out to be a great trial to them. Suffering is infinitely preferable to sinning ; the Lord may therefore send us sorrow to keep us from iniquity. Dear friend, the Lord who reads your heart may know that it is absolutely necessary for you to be tried, and so spiritually to go down into Egypt. He may send a famine to drive you there ; he may place you under great tribulations, and so he may bring you down both mentally and spiritually into a sad condition, where you shall sigh and cry by reason of bondage. Do not look upon this as a strange thing, for all God's gold must pass through the fire. It is one of the marks of God's elect that they are afflicted. The Lord Jesus saith. " As many as I love I rebuke and chasten." Depend upon it that if you are one of the true seed you must go down into Egypt : for the Lord said to Abraham,

"Know of a surety that thy seed shall be a stranger in a land that is not theirs." The escutcheon of the chosen bears the emblem of a smoking furnace and a burning lamp. Even if the world shelters you, it will sooner or later become to you the house of bondage: yet into that house of bondage you must go, for there is a great educational process going on in affliction to prepare us for the land which floweth with milk and honey. Egypt is one of the early lessons; strangely early with some; their religious life begins with a cloudy morning and threatening of storm. This will work them lasting good. "It is good for a man that he bear the yoke in his youth;" hence we have "When Israel was a child, then I loved him and called my son out of Egypt." The earliest days of Israel were in Egypt, the nation in its infancy was called from thence. While the divine life has not yet attained to maturity we meet with straits and troubles, and have to go down into Egypt and feel the weight of the yoke upon our shoulders. This is one of God's ways of preparing us for freedom, for he that has never tasted of the bitterness of bondage will never be able to appreciate the sweets of the liberty wherewith Christ makes men free. So Israel must first go down into Egypt; he descends that he may rise to greater heights.

Note next, that *it was while in Egypt, and at the worst time of their bondage in Egypt, that they received the first notification that the nation was to be called the son of God.* Israel is not called a son until Moses comes to Pharaoh and says, "Israel is my son, even my firstborn: and I say unto thee, Let my son go, that he may serve me." God had been with Abraham, and called him his friend, but I do not perceive that he called him his son, or that Abraham addressed the Lord as "Our Father which art in heaven." Neither do I find similar sweet words flowing from the lips of Isaac or of Jacob; but when Israel was in bondage, then it was that the Lord revealed Israel's adoption, and openly declared, "Israel is my son, even my firstborn." He scourgeth every son whom he receiveth, and he receives them even while the scourge is sorely bruising them. They were a poor down-trodden nation—a nation of slaves begrimed with brick-earth, and bleeding beneath the lash of their taskmasters! The Egyptians must have utterly despised a people who yielded so readily to all their exactions: they looked upon them as a herd of slaves, who had not the spirit to rebel, whatever cruelties they might endure. But now it is, while they are lying among the pots, and their faces are stained with tears, that the Lord openly before proud Pharaoh owns the nation as his son, saying, "Israel is my son, even my first-born." I think I see Pharaoh's grim, sardonic smile as he seems to say, "Those slaves, those wretched brickmakers, whom the lowest of my people despise,—if these are Jehovah's firstborn, what care I for him or them?" Learn hence, dear brothers and sisters, that God is not ashamed of his children when they are in their worst estate. We are told concerning our Lord Jesus, "For which cause he is not ashamed to call them brethren." Ay, and not when they put on their beautiful array, and when the jewels are in their ears, and when they are led forth with music and dancing, and when they shout over Egyptian chivalry drowned in the Red Sea, will they be more the Lord's children than they are in the house of bondage. The Lord God speaks of their adoption for the first time when they are still under the oppressor, and when it seems impossible that they can be rescued. The Lord' speaks very plainly to the haughty Pharaoh, "Let my son go that he may serve me; and if thou refuse to let him go, behold I will slay thy son, even thy firstborn." Oh, but is it not a blessed thing to go down into the Egypt of tribulation if there for the first time we learn our adoption of the Lord? Is it not a sweet thing even to be under the heaviest bondage if you are by such means made to understand better than ever you did before what it is to be a son and a heir, a joint heir with Jesus Christ? The firstborn of every creature is he, and we are the church of the firstborn whose names are written in heaven. The heritage of the firstborn belongs to Jesus, and to us in him; and we often know this best when our heart is broken for sin, and when our troubles are overwhelming our spirit. "Fear not," saith he, "I will help thee." "Fear not, thou worm Jacob, and ye men of Israel; I will help thee, saith the Lord, and thy Redeemer the Holy One of Israel." Yes, it was in Egyptian bondage that they received the first witness of the Spirit that they were as a people the sons of God.

When it became clear that they were really the sons of God, then *they suffered persecution* for it. A place which, as I have said, was at first their shelter, now became the iron furnace of oppression. Their hard labours are doubled, their male children were ordered to be cast into the river, and edicts of the most intolerable kind were fulminated against them. Now, brethren, Satan soon knows the man that God has owned to be his son, and he seeks to slay him even as Herod sought to kill Jesus. When the man-child was born, the Dragon knew who that man-child was, and sought to destroy him, and vomited forth floods to sweep him away, until we read that the earth helped the woman, and there were given to her wings of a great eagle that she might fly into the wilderness, into her place, where she is nourished from the face of the serpent. No sooner is the child of God really acknowledged to be such, than at once the seed of the serpent will hiss about him, and if they can will cast their venom upon him: at any rate, they will bite at his heel, till God has taught him in the name of Jesus to break the serpent's head. Rest assured that this is another mark of the election of grace. All that will live godly in Christ Jesus must suffer persecution. In Ishmael's case it was seen that he that is born after the flesh persecuteth him that is born after the Spirit, and so it is now. You cannot expect to pass through this Vanity Fair without exciting the jeers and sneers of the ungodly; for the Lord's inheritance is unto him as a speckled bird: the birds round about her are against her. Every David has his Saul, every Nehemiah his Sanballat, and every Mordecai his Haman.

But now comes the crown of the text, that is, "I have called my son out of Egypt," and *out of Egypt Israel must come*. For Egypt was not Israel's portion: it was "a land that was not theirs." My brethren, we are not citizens of "the great city which spiritually is called Sodom and Egypt, where also our Lord was crucified"; and the best thing in this present evil world is not your portion nor mine. Friendly Egypt, sheltering Egypt, was not Israel's inheritance. He gave them no portion even in the land of Goshen by a covenant of salt. They might tarry there for awhile, but out of it they must come, as it is written "thou hast brought a vine out of Egypt." The best side of the world when it seems warmest and tenderest to us is not the place whereon we may lie down with comfort. The bosom of our God—that is the true shelter of his people, and there we must find rest. If we are dwelling in the world, and are tempted to be of the world, and to take up with the riches of Egypt, we must by grace be taught to cast all this behind our back, for we have not our portion in this life, neither can we have our inheritance until we enter upon the life that is to come. Jacob said on his death-bed, "Bury me not, I pray thee, in Egypt," and Joseph gave commandment concerning his bones that they should not remain in Pharaoh's land. Even so the saints of God are weary of the world's dominions; they tremble like a bird out of Egypt.

Not in Egypt would God reveal himself to his people. What saith he? "Come ye out from among them : be ye separate, and I will be a Father unto you, and ye shall be my sons and daughters." When he called Israel his son it is in connection with this coming out. "Out of Egypt have I called my son." And you and I must be fetched out from the world and all its associations, and truly severed from it, if we are ever to come to know the Lord our God. In Egypt God was not known, but "in Judah is God known : his name is great in Israel." His people must not permanently reside in a strange country. The land of tombs was no fit home for a living people whose God was the living God : therefore it is written, "Out of Egypt have I called my son"; and the heathen knew it, for they said one to another, "Behold, there is a people come out of Egypt."

There were many difficulties in connection with this calling of Israel out of Egypt. Perhaps one of the chief obstacles was their own wish to stop there; for, strange as it may seem, though it was a house of bondage to them, they did not wish to stir from it at the first. Their spirit was broken by their sore bondage, so that they did not receive Moses and Aaron as they ought to have done, but they even chided with them. Ah, brethren, the chief work of God with us is to make us willing to go out, willing by faith to follow Jesus, willing to count the reproach of Christ greater riches than all the treasures of Egypt. He did make them willing, and they went out at last right joyfully, marching in rank, like a trained army; not needing to be driven, but hasting to escape out of the enemy's country. Moreover, the Lord made them *able* to go, as well as willing, for it is very beautiful to think that there were no sick people in the whole nation of Israel at that time of the going out. We read,—"There was not one feeble person in all their tribes." What a splendid thing for a whole nation to have no weaklings! There was no need to carry any in the ambulance, but they all went marching forth with steady foot out of the dominions of Pharaoh. O child of God, has God given you the will to get out of the bondage of the sin and the corruption of this crooked generation? He that gives you the will will give you the power. Perhaps you are crying, "Who shall deliver me? To will is present with me, but how to perform that which I would I find not." Rest assured that God the Holy Spirit, who has given you the will, will also give you the strength, and you shall come marching out of Egypt, having eaten of the Paschal Lamb. The Lord stunned their enemies, so that they begged them to be gone, and bribed them to make haste. With blow upon blow he smote the Egyptians, till on that dreadful night, when shrieks of pain went up from every house in Egypt, the Egyptians hastened them to go. " We be all dead men," said they, " unless you go "; and even their taskmasters urged them to immediate flight. Our God knows how to make even the wicked men of the world cast out the Christian : they cannot endure him when once his adoption is made known; they grow tired of his melancholy presence, tired of his convictions of sin, and of that gloomy face which he carries about with him, and they say, " Go out, go out, we cannot endure you." They perceive something in him which is foreign to themselves, and so they thrust him out. Egypt was glad when they departed, and so even the world itself seems glad to be rid of the Lord's elect when God's time is come to set a difference between Israel and Egypt.

The spiritual meaning of all this is, that from under the power of sin, of Satan, and of the world God will certainly call his own redeemed. They shall not abide in the land of Egypt ; sin shall not be pleasant to them ; they shall not continue under Satan's power, but they shall break his yoke from off their neck. The Lord will help them, and strengthen them, so that they shall clean escape from their former slavery. With a high hand and an outstretched arm brought he up Israel out of the land of Egypt, and with that same high hand and outstretched arm will he save his own elect, whom he has loved from before the foundations of the world, and whom he has purchased with his most precious blood. They, too, shall sing as Israel did, " Sing unto the Lord, for he hath triumphed gloriously, ' in the day when God shall deliver them. So far we have spoken of the natural seed.

II. Now we turn with pleasure to THE DIVINE SEED, the man Christ Jesus. He had to be called out by an angel from the sheltering Egypt into which Joseph and his mother had fled with him. I dare say when you have read that passage in Hosea, you have said, " I cannot see that it has anything to do with Christ." The passage in Hosea is about Israel evidently, for God is speaking of Israel both before and after the verse ; but look ye : the natural seed of Israel is the shell of the egg of which the divine seed is the life. God calls Israel his son. What for ? Because within that nation lay that seed which afterwards was known as the Well-beloved, the Son of the Highest. They were the shell, and therefore to be preserved for the sake of the Blessed One who, according to the flesh, lay within the race. I do not think the Lord would have cared about the Jews more than for any other nation, if it had not been that in due time He was to be born of them, even he in whom is his delight, that choice one of the Father, the Son whom he loveth. So when he brought his son out of Egypt, it means first that he rescued the external, nominal, outward sonship ; but the core, the living core within, is this Son, this true Son, of whom the Lord said, putting all others aside, " This is my beloved Son, in whom I am well pleased." And the passage, if I had time to show you, could not be limited to Israel, for if it had been it would lose much of its accuracy. Why, think you, was the passage made so obscure, for it is obscure confessedly, and anyone reading it without the spiritual teaching which Matthew received would never have perceived that Christ was going down into Egypt to fulfil that word ? I take it, the reason of the obscurity was this,—that its fulfilment might be of the Lord alone. Suppose his father and mother had known these prophecies, and had purposely set themselves to fulfil them, there would have existed a kind of collusion which would have beclouded the wonderful wisdom of God in bearing testimony to his Son. Mary and Joseph may have known of this prophecy, but I greatly question whether they perceived that it referred to their son at all, or to the Son of the Highest: but now they must do the very thing that God says shall be done, without knowing that they are fulfilling a Scripture. One of the worst things you and I can ever attempt is to try and fulfil a prophecy. Good mistress Rebecca wanted to fulfil a prophecy, and what a mess she made of it! She endeavoured to make her second son the heir, and in the attempt she brought upon him and herself a world of sorrow. Had she not better have let the prophecy alone? Surely, if a prophecy is made of God, God will see that it comes to pass. If it is a Chaldaic prophecy, a prophecy of soothsayers and magi, no doubt they will try to make their own oracle true; but the Lord, who seeth the end from the beginning and ordaineth all things, can speak positively of the future. If any of you set up for prophets, beware of prophesying till you know that you can make it good. God doth not need such petty provision: he wants no help from us: his word will surely be established. Mary and Joseph did not try to fulfil the prophecy, for they could not have understood it to mean what it did mean. It was purposely put in a dark and cloudy form, but still the Lord knew what he was doing: "That it might be fulfilled, which was spoken of the Lord by the prophet, saying, Out of Egypt have I called my Son."

Remember one thing, that all the words of God in the Old Testament and the New refer to Christ; and what is more, that all the works of God have an opened window towards Christ. Yes, I say that in the creation of the world the central thought of God was his Son Jesus, and he made the world with a view to his death, resurrection, and glorious reign. From every midge that dances in the summer sunbeam up to the great leviathan in the sea, the whole design of the world worketh toward the seed in whom the earth is blessed. In providence it is just the same: every event, from the fall of a leaf to the rise of a monarchy, is linked with the kingdom of Jesus. I have not time to show this, but it is so; and if you choose to think it over, you will clearly perceive it. He set the bounds of the nations according to the number of the children of Israel, and everything that has happened or ever shall happen in the outside world, all has a look towards the Christ, and that which comes of the Christ. I love to find Jesus everywhere,—not by twisting the Psalms and other Scriptures to make them speak of Christ when they do nothing of the kind, but by seeing him where he truly is. I would not err as Cocceius did, of whom they said his greatest fault was that he found Christ everywhere; but I would far rather err in his direction than have it said of me, as of another divine of the same period, that I found Christ nowhere. Would it not be better to see him where he is not than to miss him where he is? The pattern of the things on earth is in heaven; is, in fact, in Jesus, the Son of God. He is the pattern according to which the Tabernacle and the Temple were builded; ay, and the pattern according to which this brave world was made, and worlds which are yet to be revealed. All the treasures of the wisdom of God are hidden in Christ, and in Christ they are made manifest. I do not wonder therefore that this passage in Hosea should point to him.

It is certain that our blessed Lord is in the hightest sense the Son of God. " Out of Egypt have I called my son." Write the word SON in capitals,—and it must mean him : it cannot with emphasis mean anyone else. I would rather give up the idea that Hosea even thought of Israel, than think that the Holy Spirit did not intend that we should see Jesus in those memorable words, " My son."

It came to pass that our Lord must find no room in Israel, and so must go down into Egypt. There was no room for the young child in the inn ; and now the Edomite, the child-devouring Herod, has risen, and there is no room for the new-born King anywhere in Palestine. Alas, how sad a picture of the visible church, where Christ, at times, can find no room ! What with contending sects, Pharisees and Sadducees, there would seem to be no more room for Christ in the church to-day than there used to be. By fear of Herod his parents are made anxious, and by angelic direction they must go down into Egypt, where Herod's warrant would not run. Heathen Egypt will shield while hypocritical Judea will slay. Jesus, like another Joseph, must be carried down into Egypt, that the young child's life may be preserved. Here he has a foretaste of his life-trials, and early begins his life of affliction. The King of the Jews flees from his own dominions, the Lord of all must know the heart of a stranger in the land of Egypt. The poet represents his mother as saying—

> "Through the desert wild and dreary,
>   Following tracts explored by few,
> Sad at heart, and worn, and weary,
>   We our toilsome march pursue.
> Israel's homes lie far behind us,
>   Yet we pause not to look back,
> Lest the keen pursuer find us,
>   Lest grim murder scent our track.
>
> " Eagles o'er our heads are whirling,
>   Each careering towards her nest ;
> E'en the wolf and fox are stealing
>   To the covert of their rest ;
> Every fowl and noxious creature
>   Finds on earth its lair and bed ;
> But the infant Lord of Nature
>   Hath not where to lay his head.
>
> " Yes, my babe, sweet sleep enfolds thee
>   On thy fainting mother's arm ;
> God in his great love beholds thee,
>   Angels guard thy rest from harm.
> Earth and hell in vain beset thee,
>   Kings against thy life conspire ;
> But our God can ne'er forget thee,
>   Nor his arm that shields thee, tire."

Mark well, that, if the Lord Jesus Christ had willed it, even though but a babe, he might have blasted Herod as he did another Herod in

111

after days, and he might have made him to be eaten of worms. The glorious Jehovah could have sent a legion of angels, and have driven the Idumæan dynasty from off the throne, if so it had pleased him; but no violence was used—a gentler course was chosen. When Jesus stands up to fight he wars by non-resistance. He says, "My kingdom is not of this world, else would my servants fight." He conquers by flight rather than by fight. He taught his people when persecuted in one city to flee to another; and never did he bid them form bands, and battle with their persecutors. That is not according to Christ's law or example. A fighting church is the devil's church, but a bearing and enduring church—that is Christ's church. His parents fled with him by night, and took him down into Egypt, that he might be sheltered there. Traditions tell us wonderful stories about what happened when Jesus went into Egypt, but as none of them are inspired, I need not waste your time with them. The only one that might look like fact is, that his parents sheltered themselves in a temple wherein idol gods were ranged, and when the child entered all the images fell down. Certainly, if not actually true, it is a poetical description of that which happens wherever the holy child puts in an appearance. Every idol god falls before him. Down he must go, whether it be Dagon, or Baal, or Ashtaroth, or whatever the god may be called; ay, and he that wears the triple tiara on the seven hills, and calls himself the vicar of God on earth, must come down, and all his empire must sink like a millstone in the flood. We do not know how the young child and Joseph and Mary lived in Egypt, except that they had received gold from the Magi, and that being a carpenter, not a hedge carpenter, but one skilled in joinery and wheelwrighting, Joseph could find plenty of work in Egypt, where vast multitudes of Jews were already settled. Whether our Lord was carried to Alexandria or not we cannot tell. The probability is that there he was housed, for it was the great rendezvous of his nation and the centre of their learning: there had the Bible been translated into the Greek tongue by the seventy, and there flourished schools of Jews much more liberal than those in Judea. It is, therefore, not unlikely that the Prince of Peace went to that region where we have most unhappily illustrated Christianity with cuts—not all of wood, nor all innocent of blood. But Jesus could not stop in Egypt. "Out of Egypt have I called my son." His parents by a brave act of faith went back at the command of the angel to the Holy Land: thy land, O Immanuel! Jesus could not stay in Egypt, for he was no Egyptian. He did not come to exercise a ministry among the Egyptians. He was sent only to the lost sheep of the house of Israel, in his public working. Being called out of Egypt the heavenly vision was not disobeyed. His foster-parent Joseph took him back, and they settled in Nazareth. Yet remember he had been in Egypt, and this was a prophecy of blessing to that land; for wherever Jesus goes the air is sweetened. Every plot of land that his foot hath ever trodden on shall be his for ever. What said God to Jacob? "The land whereon thou liest will I give thee." And the same is true to Jacob's great descendant. Jesus has slept in Egypt, and Egypt is his own. God has given it to him, and his it shall be; glory be to his blessed name.

III. Let us turn to think of THE CHOSEN SEED that shall be brought out of Egypt. Here I would remark that this passage may be taken, and should be taken literally. God has a chosen people who shall assuredly come out of the very Egypt which now exists. It is remarkable that early in the gospel day the truth was gladly received in Egypt. Egypt became the land of saints and divines, and as it had once been the source and home of civilization, so it became an active camp for the soldiers of the cross. Under the successors of Mahomet all this was swept away, and now the Crescent's baneful beam falls where once the heavenly sun shed out its infinite glory, and scattered health among the sons of men. Egypt did turn to God, and it will turn again. Let me read you this passage (Isaiah xix.) : " In that day shall five cities in the land of Egypt speak the language of Canaan, and swear to the Lord of hosts ; one shall be called, The city of destruction. In that day shall there be an altar to the Lord in the midst of the land of Egypt, and a pillar at the border thereof to the Lord. And it shall be for a sign and for a witness unto the Lord of hosts in the land of Egypt : for they shall cry unto the Lord because of the oppressors, and he shall send them a saviour, and a great one, and he shall deliver them. And the Lord shall be known to Egypt, and the Egyptians shall know the Lord in that day, and shall do sacrifice and oblation ; yea, they shall vow a vow unto the Lord, and perform it. And the Lord shall smite Egypt : he shall smite and heal it : and they shall return even to the Lord, and he shall be intreated of them, and shall heal them. In that day shall there be a highway out of Egypt to Assyria, and the Assyrian shall come into Egypt, and the Egyptian into Assyria, and the Egyptians shal' serve with the Assyrians. In that day shall Israel be the third with Egypt and with Assyria, even a blessing in the midst of the land : whom the Lord of hosts shall bless, saying, Blessed be Egypt my people, and Assyria the work of my hands, and Israel mine inheritance."

So that we feel clear that our God has yet a son to call out of Egypt, and he will call him. There shall be a seed to serve him even in the midst of the down-trodden people who live by the Nile-floods, for God hath said it. There is one passage to which I should like to refer you, because it is so full of comfort. (Jeremiah xliii. 12): "And he shall array himself with the land of Egypt,"—think of that—putting it on as Joseph put on his coat of many colours,—" as a shepherd putteth on his garment ; and he shall go forth from thence in peace." Yet shall Christ wear as a robe of honour this land of Egypt, and again shall it be true, " Out of Egypt have I called my son."

Let us learn from this that, out of the strangest and oddest places God will call his son. Certain brethren among us go to the lodging-houses in Mint-street, Kent-street, and other places. Can any good thing come out of them ? Assuredly, it can, for " Out of Egypt have I called my son." Out of Thieves' Acre and Ketch's Warren saints shall come. Some of you perhaps know of holes and corners in London where a decent person scarcely dares to be seen : do not pass by these abominable haunts, for out of such Egypts will the Lord call his sons. The worst field is often the most hopeful. Here is virgin soil, unploughed, untilled. What harvests may be won by willing workers! Oh ye brave hands, thrust in the ploughshare and break up this neglected soil, for thus saith the Lord, " Out of Egypt have I called my son." Many of you who live in the midst of Israel, and hear the gospel every day, remain disobedient; but some from the lowest and vilest parts of the earth shall yet be called with an effectual calling, and they shall obey, for it is written, "Out of Egypt have I called my son."

But we will take the text, and conclude with it, in a *spiritual* sense. All men are in Egypt spiritually, but God calls out his own sons. Sin is like Pharaoh, a tyrant that will not yield: he will not let men go; but he shall let them go, for God saith, "Out of Egypt have I called my son." We are in a world which is the destroyer of grace as Pharaoh was the destroyer of Israel's little ones. You do not think a good thought but what it is laughed out of you: you scarcely catch a word of Scripture, but as soon as you get home you are compelled to forget it. Nevertheless out of that,—"Out of Egypt have I called my son." You shall be delivered yet. Put you your trust in Jesus Christ, for "to as many as received him, to them gave he power to become the sons of God," and out of Egypt will he call every son of his.

Perhaps you are in the dark, as the Egyptians were during the plague, or as when God turned the dark side of the pillar to Egypt. Ah, but if you are one of his, if you will but trust Jesus, which is the mark of being God's elect, out of darkness will God call you; out of thick Egyptian night will he fetch you, and your eyes shall be made glad with the light of the gospel of Christ.

Perhaps you dwell in the midst of superstition, for the Egyptians were horribly given to superstition, but yet out of that will God call his people. I look to see priests converted. I hope yet to see leaders of the gospel found among men that were once steeped to the throat in superstition. Why not? "Out of Egypt have I called my son." Where did Luther come from but from the monastery, and he preached the word with thunder and lightning from heaven, and God blessed it to the emancipation of nations. He will bring others of that kind; out of all sorts of ignorance and superstition he will fetch them, to the praise of the glory of his grace. I feel encouraged to pray for those who appear to be hopeless: I feel as if I must cry to God, "Bring them out of Egypt, Lord, the worst, the vilest." You here that know what Egypt is, and are in it, and know you are in it, oh, believe that the Emancipator has come, the Redeemer has appeared; with an offering of blood has he stood before God, and given Egypt for a ransom, Ethiopia and Seba for you. Oh, that he might win those with power whom he has bought with price, and to him be glory, world without end. Amen.

"He Shall Be Great"

"He shall be great."—Luke i. 32.

STRICTLY speaking, I suppose these words refer to the human nature of our Lord Jesus Christ, for it is as to his humanity that Christ was born of Mary. The context runs thus—" Behold, thou shalt conceive in thy womb, and bring forth a son, and shalt call his name JESUS. He shall be great, and shall be called the Son of the Highest: and the Lord God shall give unto him the throne of his father David: And he shall reign over the house of Jacob for ever; and of his kingdom there shall be no end." The angel of the Lord thus spake concerning the manhood of "that holy thing" that should be born of the favoured virgin by the overshadowing of the power of the Highest. As to his divinity, we must speak concerning him in another style than this: but, as a man, he was born of the virgin, and it was said to her before his birth, "He shall be great."

The man Christ Jesus stooped very low. In his first estate he was not great; he was very little when he hung upon his mother's breast. In his after estate he was not great; but despised, rejected, and crucified. Indeed, he was so poor that he had not where to lay his head; and he was so cast out by the tongues of men that they called him a " fellow," mentioned him among drunken men and wine-bibbers, and even accused him of having a devil, and being mad. In the esteem of the great ones of the earth he was an ignorant Galilean of whom they said, " We know not whence he is." His life binds up more fitly with the lowly annals of the poor than with the court-circular or whatever stood for that in Cæsar's day. In his own time his enemies could not find a word base enough to express their contempt of him. He was brought very low in his trial, condemnation, and suffering. Who thought him great when he was covered with bloody sweat, or when he was sold at the price of a slave, or when a guard came out against him with swords, and with lanterns, and with torches, as if he had been a thief? Who thought him great when they bound him and led him to the judgment-seat as a malefactor?

or when the abjects smote him, blindfolded him, and spat in his face? or when he was scourged, led through the streets bearing his cross, and afterwards hung up between two thieves to die? Truly he was brought very low, and a sword pierced through his mother's heart as she saw the sufferings of her holy Son. When she knew that he was dead, and buried in a borrowed tomb, she must have painfully pondered in her heart the words from heaven concerning him, and thought within herself, "The angel said he should be great, but who is made so vile as he? He said that he should be called the 'Son of the Highest,' but, lo! he is brought into the dust of death; and men seal his sepulchre, and cast out his name as evil."

Still, while I think that our text most fitly applies to the manhood of Christ in the first place, I rejoice to think that—

> "He who on earth as man was known,
>   And bore our sins and pains,
> Now, seated on th' eternal throne,
>   The God of glory reigns."

The very man who was despised and spat upon sits glorious on his Father's throne. As man he is anointed "King of kings, and Lord of lords." As man he has been lifted up from the lowest depths, and set in the greatest heights to reign for ever and ever. Peter and the apostles testified, "This Jesus hath God raised up, whereof we all are witnesses, he being by the right hand of God exalted." Stephen also said, "Behold, I see the heavens opened, and the Son of man standing on the right hand of God." While we believe that, and rejoice in it, we shall be wise never to dissociate the deity of Christ from his humanity, for they make up one person. I cannot help remarking that in the New Testament you find a disregard of all rigid distinction of the two natures in the person of our Lord when the Spirit speaks concerning him. The two natures are so thoroughly united in the person of Christ that the Holy Ghost does not speak of the Lord Jesus with theological exactness, like one who writes a creed, but he speaks as to men of understanding, who know and rejoice in the truth of the one indivisible person of the Mediator. For instance, we read in Scripture of "the blood of God": Paul saith in Acts xx. 28, "Feed the church of God, which he hath purchased with his own blood." Now, strictly speaking, there can be no blood of God, and the expression looks like a confusion of the two natures; but this is intentional, that we may clearly see that the two natures are so joined together that the Holy Ghost does not stop to dissect and set out differences; but he says of the united person of our blessed Lord that which is strictly true either of his humanity or of his deity. He is called both "God, our Saviour," and "the man Christ Jesus." The combined natures of the man, the God, Christ Jesus our Lord, are one person; and all the acts of either nature may be ascribed to that one person. Hence I, for one, do not hesitate to sing such verses as these—

> "He that distributes crowns and thrones,
> Hangs on a tree, and bleeds and groans:
> The Prince of Life resigns his breath;
> The King of Glory bows to death."

> "Well might the sun in darkness hide,
> And shut his glories in,
> When God, the mighty Maker, died
> For man, the creature's sin."

> "See how the patient Jesus stands,
> Insulted in his lowest case!
> Sinners have bound the Almighty hands,
> And spit in their Creator's face."

We shall not labour, therefore, to preserve the niceties of theology, but we shall at this time freely speak of our Lord as he is in his Godhead and in his manhood, and apply our text to the whole Christ, declaring the divine promise that "He shall be great."

While my brother was praying for me I was wishing that I had the tongues of men and of angels with which to set forth my theme to-night; and yet I shall retract my wish, for the subject is such, that if my words were the commonest that could be found—yea, if they were ungrammatical, and if they were put together most uncouthly, it would little matter; for a failure awaits me in any case: the subject far transcends all utterance. Jesus is such a one that no oratory can ever reach the height of his glory, and the simplest words are best suited to a subject so sublime. Fine words would be but tawdry things to hang beside the unspeakably glorious Lord. I can say no more than that *he is great*. If I could tell forth his greatness with choral symphonies of cherubim, yet should I fail to reach the height of this great argument. I will be content if I can touch the hem of the garment of his greatness. If the Lord will but set us in a cleft of the rock, and only make us see the back parts of his character, we shall be overcome by the vision. As yet, even of Jesus, the face of his full glory cannot be seen, or if seen, it cannot be described. Were we caught up to the third heaven we should have little to say on coming back, for we should have seen things which it were not lawful for us to utter. I shall not therefore fail with loss of honour if I tell you that my utmost success at this time will but touch the fringe of the splendour of the Son of man. This is not the time of his clearest revealing. The day is coming for the manifestation of the Lord; as yet he shineth not forth among men in his noontide. His second advent shall more fully reveal him. Then shall his people "shine forth as the sun in the kingdom of their Father," because he also shall rise in the clear face of heaven as the Sun of Righteousness, greatly blessing the sons of men.

I. Let me touch my theme as best I can by, first of all, saying of our adorable Lord Jesus that HE IS GREAT FROM MANY POINTS OF VIEW. I might have said from *every* point of view; but that is too large a truth to be surveyed at one sitting. Mind would fail us, life would fail us, time would fail us: eternity and perfection will alone suffice for that boundless meditation. But from the points of view to which I would conduct you for a moment, the Lord Jesus Christ is emphatically great.

First, *in the perfection of his nature*. Think, my brethren. There was never such a being as our Well-Beloved. He is peerless and incomparable. He is divine, and therefore unique. He is "Light of light, very God of very God." Jesus is truly equal with God, one with

117

the Father. Oh, the greatness of Godhead! Jehovah is a being infinite, immeasurable, incomprehensible, inconceivable! He filleth all things, and yet is not contained by all things. He is indeed great beyond any idea of greatness that has ever dawned upon us. All this is true of the Only-Begotten. "In the beginning was the Word, and the Word was with God, and the Word was God. The same was in the beginning with God. All things were made by him; and without him was not anything made that was made." "For of him, and through him, and to him, are all things: to whom be glory for ever. Amen." "He is before all things, and by him all things consist."

But our Lord Jesus is also man, and this makes the singularity of his person, that he should be perfectly and purely God, and as truly and really man. He is not humanity deified: he is not Godhead humanized. I have admitted latitude of expression; but there is, in fact, no confusion of the substance. He is God. He is man. He is all that God is, and all that man is as God created him. He is as truly God as if he were not man, and yet as completely and perfectly man as if he were not God. Think of this wondrous combination! a perfect manhood without spot or stain of original or actual sin, and then the glorious Godhead combined with it! Said I not truly that Jesus stands alone? He is not greatest of the great; but great where all else are little. He is not something among all; but all where all else are nothing. Who shall be compared with him? He counts it not robbery to be equal with God, and among men he is the Firstborn of every creature; among the risen ones he is the Firstborn by his resurrection from the dead; among the glorified he is the source and object of glory. I cannot compass his nature: who shall declare his generation? He is one with us, and yet inconceivably beyond us. Our nature is limited, sinful, fallen; but his nature is unbounded, holy, divine. When Jehovah looks on us we ask, "What is man, that thou art mindful of him? and the son of man, that thou visitest him?" But "when he bringeth in the firstbegotten into the world, he saith, And let all the angels of God worship him." Shall it not truly be said as to his nature, "He is great"?

He is great also *in the grandeur of his offices*. Remember that he has for our sakes undertaken to be our Redeemer. You see your bondage, brethren. You know it, for some of you have worn the fetters till they have entered into your soul: from such slavery he came to redeem us. Behold his Zion in ruins, heaps on heaps, smoking, consumed! He comes to rebuild and to restore. This is his office—to build up the old wastes, and to restore the temple of the living God, which had been cast down by the foe. To accomplish this he came to be our Priest, our Prophet, and our King; in each office glorious beyond compare. He came to be our Saviour, our Sacrifice, our Substitute, our Surety, our Head, our Friend, our Lord, our Life, our All. Pile up the offices, and remember that each one is worthy of a God. Mention them as you may, and truly you shall never remember them all; for he, the express image of his Father's glory, has undertaken every kind of office, that he might perfectly redeem his people, and make them to be his own for ever. In each office he has gained the summit of glory, and therein he is and shall be great.

Have you ever stood in Westminster Abbey when some great warrior was being buried, and when the herald pronounced his various titles? He has been greatly honoured of his queen, and of the nation, for which he has fought so valiantly, and he is prince of this, and duke of that, and count of the other, and earl of something else : and the titles are many and brilliant. What a parade it is! "Vanity of vanities! All is vanity!" What boots it to the senseless clay that it is buried with pomp of heraldry? But I stand at the tomb of Christ, and I say of his offices that they are superlatively grand; and, moreover, that they are not buried, neither is he among the dead. He lives and bears his honours still in the fulness of their splendour. He is all to his people still; every office he still carries on, and will carry on till he shall deliver up the kingdom to God, even the Father, and God shall be all in all. Oh, the splendour of this Christ of God in the mighty offices which he sustains! He is the Standard-bearer among ten thousand. Who is like unto him in all eternity? "The government shall be upon his shoulder : and his name shall be called Wonderful, Counsellor, the Mighty God, the Everlasting Father, the Prince of Peace." "Hosanna to the son of David : Blessed is he that cometh in the name of the Lord!" Let our hearts give him our adoring praise to-night, for he is great in the glorious offices which God has heaped upon him.

His nature and his offices would alone furnish us with a lengthened theme ; but oh! my brethren, the Lord Jesus is great *in the splendour of his achievements.* He does not wear an office whose duty is neglected ; but his name is faithful and true. He is no holder of a sinecure ; he claims to have finished the work which his Father gave him to do. He has undertaken great things, and, glory be to his name, he has achieved them. His people's sins were laid upon him, and he bore them up to the cross, and on the cross he made an end of them, so that they will never be mentioned against them any more for ever. Then he went down into the grave, and slept there for a little season ; but he tore away the bars of the sepulchre and left death dead at his feet, bringing life and immortality to light by his resurrection. This was his high calling, and he has fulfilled it. His victory is complete, the defeat of the foe is perfect. "O death, where is thy sting? O grave, where is thy victory?" Springing upward from the tomb when the appointed days were come, he opened heaven's gates to all believers, according to the word,—"The breaker is come up before them, and their king shall pass before them, and the Lord on the head of them." As he opened the golden gates, he led captivity captive; and, receiving gifts for men, he cast down a royal largess among the poorest of his people that they might be enriched thereby. This was his object, and the design has been carried out without flaw or failure. Within the veil he went, our Representative, to take possession of our crowns and thrones, which he holds for us to this day by the tenure of his own cross. Having purchased the inheritance, and paid off the heavy mortgage that lay upon it, he has taken possession of the Canaan wherein our souls shall dwell at the end of the days when we shall stand in our lot. Is it not proven that he is great? Conquerors are great, and he is the greatest of them. Deliverers are great, and he is the greatest of them. Liberators are great, and he is the greatest of them. Saviours are great, and he is the greatest of them. They that multiply the joys of men are truly great, and what shall I say of him who has bestowed everlasting joy upon his people, and entailed it upon them by a covenant of salt for ever and ever? Well didst thou say, O Gabriel, " He shall be great," for great indeed he is!

He shall be great, again, *in the prevalence of his merits.* Never being had such merit as Christ. His life and death cover all believers from head to foot with a perfect obedience to the law. With royal vesture are they clad: Solomon in all his glory was not arrayed like one of these. His blood has washed believers white as the driven snow, and his righteousness has made them to be " accepted in the Beloved." He has such merit with God that he deserves of the Most High whatsoever he wills to ask ; and he asks for his people that they shall have every blessing needful for eternal life and perfection. He is great, indeed, my brethren, when we think that he has clothed us all in his righteousness, and washed us all in his blood. Nor us alone, but ten thousand times ten thousand of his redeemed stand to-day in the wedding-dress of his eternal merit, and plead before God a claim that never can be denied —the claim of a perfect obedience which must always please the Father's heart. Oh, what mercy is that which has turned our hell to heaven, transformed our disease into health, and lifted us from the dunghill, and set us among the princes of his people! In infinite power to remove sin, to perfume with acceptance, to clothe with righteousness, to win blessings, to preserve saints, and to save to the uttermost, the Lord Jesus is great beyond all greatness.

My theme will never be exhausted, though I may be. Let me not delay to add that our Lord Jesus Christ is great *in the number of his saved ones.* I do not believe in a little Christ, or a little heaven, or a little company before the throne, or a few that shall be saved. Hear you this, for I would fain reply to a lie that is often stated, and is the last resort of those who assail the doctrines of grace. They say that we believe that God has left the great mass of his creatures to perish, and has arbitrarily chosen an elect few. We have never thought such a thing. We believe that the Lord has an elect many ; and it is our joy and delight to think of them as a number that no man can number. " Oh," they say, " you think that the few who go to your little Bethel or Salem are the elect of God." That, sirs, is what you invent for your own purposes, but *we* have never said anything of the sort. We rejoice to believe that as many as the stars of heaven shall the redeemed of Christ be—that as many as the sands that are upon the sea-shore, even an innumerable company, are those for whom Christ has shed his precious blood that he might effectually redeem them. As I look up to the heaven of the sanctified, my mind's eye does not see a few dozen saints met together in select circles of exclusiveness ; but my eyes are dazzled with the countless lights which shine each one from the lustrous brows of the redeemed; lustrous I say, for each glorified one wears upon his forehead the name of the Most High. My heart is glad to turn away from the multitude that throng the broad way, and to see a greater multitude that throng the heavenly fields, and, day without night, celebrate redemption by the blood of the Lamb. Have they not washed their robes, and made them white in his blood ? In all things our Lord will have the pre-eminence, and this shall be the case in the number of his followers: he shall therein vanquish his great enemy. His redeemed shall fly as a cloud, and as doves to their windows. Countless as the drops of morning dew shall his people be in the day of his power. He shall be great in the host of his adherents in glory.

Multitudes upon earth are even now pursuing their road to heaven, and greater hosts are yet to follow them. A day shall be when the people of God shall be increased exceedingly, above anything that we see at this present; they shall spring up as the grass and as willows by the water-courses, as if every stone that heard the ripple of the brook had been turned into a man. The seed of the Lord Jesus Christ shall multiply till arithmetic shall be utterly baffled, and numeration shall fail. He is great—a great Saviour of a great mass of great sinners, who shall by his redeeming arm be brought safely, without fail, to his right hand in the endless glory. As the tribes of the natural Israel increased exceedingly, so also shall the spiritual Israel. The Lord shall multiply his Zion with men as with a flock, and thus shall the King of Israel be great.

Brethren and sisters, the Lord Jesus Christ shall be great *in the estimation of his people.* If I were to try to-night to praise my Lord to the highest heavens, my brother might well follow me, and extol our Lord much more. Then I would get up from my seat again, and I would not rest until I found yet loftier praises for my Lord and God. Then might my dear brother return to the happy task, and excel me yet again; and then, for sure, I would be on my feet a third time, and keep up the hallowed rivalry, lauding and magnifying Jesus to my mind's utmost; and, if the Lord permitted, we would never leave off, for I would give in to no man in my desire to extol my Lord Jesus. I am sure that none of his people would give way to others in a humble sense of supreme indebtedness; but each one would say, "There is something which he has done for me which he never did for you. There is some point of view in which he is greater to me than he is to you." Brothers, I admit that there are many points in which he is greater to you than he is to me; but yet to me he is higher than heaven, vaster than eternity, more delightful than Paradise, more blessed than blessedness itself. If I could speak of him according to my soul's desire, I would speak in great capital letters, and not in the small italics which I am compelled to use. If I could speak as I would, I would make winds and waves my orators, and cause the whole universe to become one open mouth with which to tell out the praises of Emmanuel. If all eternity would speak, as though it, too, were but one tongue, yet it could not tell out all the charms of his love and the sureness of his faithfulness and his truth. We must leave off somewhere, but, truly, if it be the point of our estimation of him we never can express our overwhelming sense of his honour, his excellence, his sweetness. Oh, that he were praised by every creature that has breath! Oh, that every minute placed another gem in his crown! Oh, that every soul that breathes did continue to breathe out nothing but hosannas and hallelujahs unto him, for he deserves all possible praises! Do you hear the crash of the multitudinous music of heaven? It is like many waters, and like the mighty waves of the sea; but it is all for him. Can you catch the charming notes of "harpers harping with their harps"? Their harpings are all for him. Can you conceive the unutterable joys of the glorified? Every felicity of eternity is a song to his honour. Heaven and earth shall yet be full of the out-shinings of his glory. Who can look the sun in the face in the height of his noontide? Who can tell the illimitable greatnesses of the Son of God? To him, even to him, let all praises be, for he has redeemed our souls with blood, and set the captives free: he has made us unto our God both kings and priests, and we shall reign with him for ever and for ever. Truly, he is great, and shall be great eternally.

But, oh, brethren, how great must Christ be *in the glory of heaven!* We have never seen that. Some of us shall see it full soon.

> " For we are in the border-land,
> The heavenly country's near at hand :
> A step is all 'twixt us and rest,
> E'en now we converse with the blest."

But the greatness of Christ in heaven—surely this is the grand sight for which we long to go to heaven,—that we may behold his glory, "the glory which he had with the Father before the world was," and the glory which he has gained by his service of the Father here below. Has he not said, "Father, I will that they also, whom thou hast given me, be with me where I am; that they may behold my glory"? What honour and majesty surround our Prince in the metropolis of his empire! What is this city? Whence comes its brightness? The sun is dim, the moon no more displays herself. "The glory of God did lighten it, and the Lamb is the light thereof": the whole city shines in the Redeemer's glory. And who are these that come trooping down the golden streets?—these shining ones. each one comparable to a living, moving sun? each one as bright as the star of the morning? Ask them whence comes their brightness, and they tell you that the glory of Christ has risen upon them, and they are reflecting his brightness as the moon reflects the effulgence of the sun. If you sit down with one of these shining ones, and hear him tell his story, the sum of the matter will be, "Not unto us; but unto him that loved us, be honour and glory." This will be the substance of every testimony,—"He loved me, and gave himself for me;" only they will put it something like this—"HE loved *me.* He, that great HE." How they will pronounce it as they point to his glory—"HE loved me—that little *me.*" They will sink their voices, oh, so low, as with wonder and surprise they express their admiration that ever he could have loved such unworthy ones as they were.

But I must not—dare not—try to touch upon the *glory of Christ upon the throne of the Father.* Certain great divines have written upon the glory of Christ, but I will warrant you that, when they died and went to heaven, they half wished that they could come back again to amend their most glowing pages. Ah me, what can ignorance say of the All-wise? What do blinking owls know of high noon? What do we poor limited creatures, babes of yesterday, know of the Infinite, the Ancient of days, and of the splendour that flames from the Firstborn at the right hand of the Most High? It would need an angel to tell us that; but, peradventure, if he did, either we should not understand, or else what we did understand would overpower us, and we should fall before our Lord as dead. The heavens are now telling the glory of our Lord, but the half of it will never be told throughout ages of ages. Assuredly, concerning our adorable Lord Jesus it is true—" He shall be great."

II. Now, by your leave, I want to turn the subject a little round, and look at it in another light. " He shall be great," and he is so, for HE DEALS WITH GREAT THINGS.

He is a Saviour, and a great one. As I have already said, it was a *great ruin* which he came to restore. The wind came from the abyss and smote the four corners of the house of manhood, and it fell and lay along. Devils laughed and triumphed as they saw God's handiwork despoiled. Human nature sank in shame, Paradise was blasted, sin was triumphant, and the fiery sword was set at Eden's gate to exclude us. It was a hideous ruin. But, oh! when Christ came, he brought a great salvation. He came to prepare a better Paradise, and to plant in it a better tree of life, and to give us possession of it upon a better tenure than before. Oh, he is a great Saviour; he wrought amid the chaos of the fall, and restored what Adam had destroyed!

And, beloved, we were covered with *great sin*—some of us especially so. But "he shall be great," and therefore he makes short work of great sin. Great sinners, what a joy it ought to be to you to think that he is great, and, therefore, has come to rescue such as you are, and deal with such difficulties as beset and surround *you;* for what if sin be great? His arrangement for its removal is great too. Look there at Calvary, and, if you can see it through your blinding tears, behold the sacrifice he offered once for all to put away sin. Regard the old Tabernacle and its faulty types:—Aaron has offered his bullock which has smoked to heaven, but no result has followed. Aaron has brought his lambs, and goats, and rams, and their blood in basins is thrown at the altar foot: the whole soil of the Tabernacle is saturated with the blood of bullocks and of goats: but no result has come of it. These can never take away sin. See now the greater sacrifice which Jesus brings. That great High Priest of ours is great indeed, for he has offered up *himself* without spot unto God! Lo, on his great altar there smokes to heaven no longer clouding incense or burning flesh, but the body and soul of the appointed Substitute are offered up in sacrifice for men. We have none of us a due conception of the grandeur of that vicarious offering, which at once and for ever made an end of sin. Think of it carefully and in detail. Count it no light thing that he who was the Father's equal, that he who was pure and perfect in both natures, became a curse for us, and was made sin for us, and presented himself as a victim to justice on our behalf. This is a wonder among wonders, as much exceeding miracle as miracle exceeds the most common-place fact. It overtops the highest Alps of thought, that he who was offended should expiate the offence, he who was perfect should suffer punishment, he who was all goodness should be made sin, and he who was all love should be forsaken of the God of love. What merit and majesty are found in his glorious oblation! Great is the sin, but greater is the sacrifice. The atonement has covered the guilt, and left a margin of abounding righteousness.

Beloved, what a mercy it is for us that we have such a High-Priest, for if you and I are burdened to-night with great transgression, there is *great pardon* to be had—pardon so great that it actually annihilates the sin—pardon so great that the sin is cast behind Jehovah's back, while the pardon rings out perpetual notes of joy and peace in the soul.

> " His the pardon, ours the sin,—
> Great the sin, the pardon great ;
> Great his good which healed our ill,
> Great his love which killed our hate."

He shall be great indeed who has wrought us so great salvation.

And now, dear friends, you and I, being greatly pardoned through the great sacrifice, are journeying through the wilderness toward Canaan, and we have *great wants* and many, pressing upon us every day. We are poverty itself, and only All-sufficiency can supply us; but that is found in Jesus. We need great abundance of food : the heavenly bread lies around about the camp, and each may fill his omer. We require rivers of living water : the smitten rock yields us a ceaseless flood ; the out-flow never ceases. We have great demands, but Christ has *great supplies*. Between here and heaven we shall have, perhaps, greater wants than we have yet known; but, all along, every halting-place is ready, provender is laid up, good cheer is stored, nothing has been overlooked. The commissariat of the Eternal is absolutely perfect. Do you feel sometimes so thirsty for grace that like Behemoth you could drink up Jordan at a draught ? more than that river could hold is given you. Drink abundantly, for Christ has prepared you a bottomless sea of grace to fill you with all the fulness of God. Stint not yourselves, and doubt not your Saviour : wherefore should you limit the Holy One of Israel ? Be great in your experience of his all-sufficiency, and great in your praises of his bounty, and then in heaven you shall pour at his feet great treasures of gratitude for ever and ever.

Yes, and he is a Christ *of great preparations*. He is engaged before the throne to-day in preparing a *great heaven* for his people ; it will be made up of great deliverance, great peace, great rest, great joy, great victory, great discovery, great fellowship, great rapture, great glory. He is preparing for his redeemed no little heaven, no starveling banquet, no narrow delight. He is a great Creator, and he is creating a great Paradise wherein a great multitude shall be greatly happy for ever and ever. " He shall be great "—great in the bliss of his innumerable elect. If we once get within the pearly gates, and walk those golden streets, we are not ashamed to-night to vow that he shall be great ; we will make him glorious before his holy angels. If praises can make him great, our praises shall ring out day and night at the very loudest, and ten thousand times ten thousand of the glorified shall join with us in perpetual hallelujahs to him who loved us before all worlds, and will love us when all worlds shall cease to be. " He shall be great." He must be great. If we live it shall be our business to sing like the Virgin, " My soul doth magnify the Lord, and my spirit hath rejoiced in God my Saviour."

III. I have come to a close when I have said a few words upon the last point, which is this : HIS GREATNESS WILL SOON APPEAR. It now lies under a cloud to men's blear eyes. They still belittle him with their vague and vain thoughts ; but it shall not always be so. It is midnight with his honour here just now ; or if it be not midnight, it is much the same, for men are stone blind. But it will not be darkness long, nor shall human minds be blinded for ever. My eyes foresee the dawning. Did you hear the clarion just now ? I dream not that ears of flesh can catch the sound as yet ; but the ears of faith can hear it. The trumpet rings out exceeding loud and long, and after the trumpet there is heard this voice : " Behold, the Bridegroom cometh ! Go ye forth to meet him." Hear ye not the shouts of armies,—" Lo, he cometh ! Lo, he cometh ! Lo, he cometh !" Right gladly I hear the cry. Let the world ring with the joy-note. He comes. That trumpet proclaims him. I shall propound no order now as to how predicted events shall happen ; but I know this, that the Lord shall reign for ever and ever, King of kings, and Lord of lords. Hallelujah ! " He shall be great." The nations shall bow at his feet. Rebellious enemies shall own him as their King. The whole universe shall be filled with the glory of God. There shall be left no space where his light shall not shine. " He shall be great." To him " every knee shall bow, and every tongue confess that Jesus Christ is Lord, to the glory of God the Father."

Fret not yourselves, brethren, because of the false doctrine which roams through the world to-day. Worry not your hearts as though the Christ were defeated. He is clad in shining armour, through which no dart of error can ever pierce. He lingers for a little while upon the hills, surveying the battle-field with eagle-eye. He leaves his poor servants to prove how weak they are, as they almost turn their backs in the day of battle. He lets heaven and earth see the weakness of an arm of flesh. But courage, brethren ! The Prince Emmanuel hastens ! You may hear his horse hoofs on the road. He is near to come. On white horses shall his chosen follow him, going forth " conquering and to conquer," for the battle is the Lord's, and he will deliver the enemy into our hands. The Lord shall reign for ever and ever; King of kings ! Hallelujah ! "He must reign, till he hath put all enemies under his feet."

The day is coming when the mighty progress of the gospel shall make Christ to be great among men ; and then you need not listen long to hear that other trumpet which shall wake the sleeping dead. The Risen One descends. *Resurrection* is at hand ! Oh, what greatness will be upon Christ in that hour when all shall leave their graves, even the whole multitude of the slain of death ! He shall be glorious among them, the Firstfruits of the resurrection, illustrious in those who rise by virtue of his rising. Oh, what honour will he have that day ! Jesus, thou art he whom thy brethren shall praise as they see thee victorious over death in all those quickened myriads.

Then shall come the *Judgment;* and oh, how great will Christ be in men's eyes in that day when he sits upon the throne and holds the scales of justice, and judges men for the deeds done in the body ! I warrant you that none will deny his Godhead in that day. None will proclaim themselves his adversaries in that dread hour. The earth is reeling ! The sky is crumbling ! The stars are falling ! The sun is quenched ! The moon is black as sackcloth of hair ! and Jesus is sitting on the throne ! A cry is heard from all his enemies, " Hide us, mountains. Rocks fall upon us. Hide us from his face." That face of his—calm, quiet, and triumphant, shall be terrible to them. They will cry in horror, " Hide us from the face of him that sitteth on the throne, and from the wrath of the Lamb." But they cannot be hidden. Fly whither they may, those eyes pursue them—those eyes of love more terrible than flames of wrath. Oil, though it be soft, yet burns full furiously ; and love on fire is hell. Fiercer than a lion on his prey is love when once it groweth angry for holiness' sake and truth's sake. In that day those who know his love shall admire him beyond measure ; but those who know his wrath shall equally feel that "he is great." Though it be their hell to feel it, yet shall they know that there is none so great as he, when he shall take the iron rod, and dash them in pieces like a potter's vessel. Their cries of remorse and despair, as they rise up to the throne of his awful majesty, shall proclaim to an awe-struck universe that Jesus is great. "Kiss the Son, lest he be angry, and ye perish from the way, when his wrath is kindled but a little. Blessed are all they that put their trust in him."

He shall be great, finally, *when he shall gather all his elect about him—* when all the souls redeemed by blood shall assemble within his palace-gate to worship him. Oh, what a sight it will be when he is seen as the centre, while, far away from north, south, east, and west, a blazing host of shining ones, all glorious in his glory, shall in ever-widening circles surround his person and his throne, all bowing down before the Son of God, and crying, "Hallelujah!" as they adore him! Not one will doubt him there, nor oppose him there. Oh, what a sight it shall be when every one shall praise him to the uttermost ; when from every heart shall leap up reverent love, when every tongue shall sound forth his honours, when there shall be no division, no discord, no jarring notes ; but countless armies shall as one man adore the Lord whom they love! Again they say, "Hallelujah!" and the incense of their adoration goeth up for ever and ever. Oh, for that grandest of cries, "Hallelujah! Hallelujah! the Lord God omnipotent reigneth, and his Son is exalted to sit with him upon the throne of his glory for ever and ever." Truly, he shall be great.

Oh, make him great to-night, poor sinner, by trusting him! Make him great to-night, dear child of God, by longing for him. Make him great as you come to the table by hungering after him. Count it a great privilege to eat and drink with him with overflowing delight. Come with a great hunger and a great thirst after him, and take him into your very self, and say, "He is my bread: he is my drink: he is my life : he is my all." All the while let your spirit live by adoring, and let every pulse of your body beat to his honour. Tune your hand, your heart, your tongue to this one song, "Hallelujah, hallelujah, hallelujah! Unto him that loved us and died for us, and rose again, be glory for ever and ever!"

> "To the Lamb that was slain all honour be paid,
> Let crowns without number encircle his head :
> Let blessing, and glory, and riches, and might,
> Be ascribed evermore by angels of light."

The Great Birthday and Our Coming of Age

"Even so we, when we were children, were in bondage under the elements of the world: but when the fulness of the time was come, God sent forth his Son, made of a woman, made under the law, to redeem them that were under the law, that we might receive the adoption of sons. And because ye are sons, God hath sent forth the Spirit of his Son into your hearts, crying, Abba, Father."—Galatians iv. 3—6.

THE birth of our Lord Jesus Christ into this world is a wellspring of pure, unmingled joy. We associate with his crucifixion much of sorrowful regret, but we derive from his birth at Bethlehem nothing but delight. The angelic song was a fit accompaniment to the joyful event, and the filling of the whole earth with peace and good will is a suitable consequence of the condescending fact. The stars of Bethlehem cast no baleful light: we may sing with undivided joy, "Unto us a child is born, unto us a son is given." When the Eternal God stooped from heaven and assumed the nature of his own creature who had rebelled against him, the deed could mean no harm to man. God in our nature is not God against us but God with us. We may take up the young child in our arms and feel that we have seen the Lord's salvation; it cannot mean destruction to men. I do not wonder that the men of the world celebrate the supposed anniversary of the great birthday as a high festival with carols and banquets. Knowing nothing of the spiritual meaning of the mystery, they yet perceive that it means man's good, and so in their own rough way they respond to it. We who observe no days which are not appointed of the Lord, rejoice continually in our Prince of Peace, and find in our Lord's manhood a fountain of consolation.

To those who are truly the people of God the incarnation is the subject of a thoughtful joy, which ever increases with our knowledge of its meaning, even as rivers are enlarged by many trickling brooks. The Birth of Jesus not only brings us hope, but the certainty of good things. We do not merely speak of Christ's coming into relation with our nature, but of his entering into union with ourselves, for he has become one flesh with us for purposes as great as his love. He is one with all of us who have believed in his name.

Let us consider by the light of our text the special effect produced upon the church of God by the coming of the Lord Jesus Christ in human flesh. You know, beloved, that his coming a second time will produce a wonderful change upon the church. "Then shall the righteous shine forth as the sun." We are looking forward to his second advent for the uplifting of the church to a higher platform than that upon which it now stands. Then shall the militant become triumphant, and the labouring become exultant. Now is the time of battle, but the second advent shall bring both victory and rest. To-day our King commands us to conflict, but soon he shall reign upon Mount Zion, with his ancients gloriously. When he shall appear we shall be like him, for we shall see him as he is. Then shall the bride adorn herself with her jewels, and stand ready for her Husband. The whole waiting creation which now groaneth and travaileth together in harmony with the birth-pangs of the church shall then come to her time of deliverance, and enter into the glorious liberty of the children of God. This is the promise of the second advent ; but what was the result of the first advent? Did that make any difference in the dispensation of the church of God? Beyond all doubt it did. Paul here tells us that we were minors, in bondage under the elements of the world, until the fulness of time was come, when "God sent forth his Son, made of a woman, made under the law." Some will say, "He is speaking here of the Jews"; but he expressly guards us in the previous chapter against dividing the church into Jews and Gentiles. To him it is only one church, and when he says we were in bondage he is talking to the Galatian Christians, who were many of them Gentiles ; but in truth he regards them neither as Jews nor Gentiles, but as part of the one and indivisible church of God. In those ages in which election mainly embraced the tribes of Israel there were always some chosen ones beyond that visible line, and in the mind of God the chosen people were always regarded as neither Jews nor Gentiles, but as one in Christ Jesus. So Paul lets us know that the church up to the time of the coming of Christ was like a child at school under tutors and governors ; or like a young man not yet arrived at years of discretion, and therefore most fitly kept under restraint. When Jesus came his great birthday was the day of the coming of age of the church : then believers remained no more children, but became men in Christ Jesus. Our Lord by his first advent brought the church up out of her nonage and her pupilage into a condition of maturity, in which it was able to take possession of the inheritance, and claim and enjoy its rights and liberties. It was a wonderful step from being under the law as a schoolmaster, to come from under its rod and rule into the freedom and power of a full-grown heir ; but such was the change for believers of the old time, and in consequence there was a wonderful difference between the highest under the Old Testament and the lowest under the New. Of them that are born of woman there was not born a greater than John the Baptist, and yet the least in the kingdom of heaven was greater than he. John the Baptist may be compared to a youth of nineteen, still an infant in law, still under his guardian, still unable to touch his estate ; but the least believer in Jesus has passed his minority, and is "no more a servant, but a son ; and if a son, then an heir of God through Christ."

May the Holy Spirit bless the text to us while we use it thus. First, let us *consider in itself the joyful mission of the Son of God,* and then let us consider *the joyful result which has come of that mission,* as it is expressed in our text.

I. I invite you to CONSIDER THE JOYFUL MISSION OF THE SON OF GOD. The Lord of heaven has come to earth; God has taken upon himself human nature. Hallelujah !

This great transaction was accomplished at the right time : "When the fulness of the time was come, God sent forth his Son, made of a woman." The reservoir of time had to be filled by the inflowing of age after age, and when it was full to the brim the Son of God appeared. Why the world should have remained in darkness for four thousand years, why it should have taken that length of time for the church to attain her full age, we cannot tell ; but this we are told, that Jesus was sent forth when the fulness of time was come. Our Lord did not come before his time nor behind his time : he was punctual to his hour, and cried to the moment,—" Lo, I come." We may not curiously pry into the reasons why Christ came when he did ; but we may reverently muse thereon. The birth of Jesus is the grandest light of history, the sun in the heavens of all time. It is the pole-star of human destiny, the hinge of chronology, the meeting-place of the waters of the past and the future. Why happened it just at that moment ? Assuredly it was so predicted. There were prophecies many which pointed exactly to that hour. I will not detain you just now with them ; but those of you who are familiar with the Old Testament Scriptures well know that, as with so many fingers, they pointed to the time when the Shiloh should come, and the great sacrifice should be offered. He came at the hour which God had determined. The infinite Lord appoints the date of every event ; all times are in his hand. There are no loose threads in the providence of God, no stitches are dropped, no events are left to chance. The great clock of the universe keeps good time, and the whole machinery of providence moves with unerring punctuality. It was to be expected that the greatest of all events should be most accurately and wisely timed, and so it was. God willed it to be when and where it was, and that will is to us the ultimate reason.

If we might suggest any reasons which can be appreciated by ourselves, we should view the date in reference to the church itself as to the time of her coming of age. There is a measure of reason in appointing the age of twenty-one as the period of a man's majority, for he is then mature, and full grown. It would be unwise to make a person to be of age while only ten, eleven, or twelve ; everybody would see that such boyish years would be unsuitable. On the other hand, if we were detained from being of age till we were thirty, every one would see that it was a needless and arbitrary postponement. Now, if we were wise enough, we should see that the church of God could not have endured gospel light earlier than the day of Christ's coming ; neither would it have been well to keep her in gloom beyond that time. There was a fitness about the date which we cannot fully understand, because we have not the means of forming so decided an estimate of the life of a church as of the life of a man. God alone knows the times and seasons for a church, and no doubt to him the four thousand years of the old dispensation made up a fit period for the church to abide at school, and bear the yoke in her youth.

The time of coming of age of a man has been settled by law with reference to those that are round about him. It were not meet for servants that the child of five or six should be master: it were not meet in the world of commerce that an ordinary boy of ten or twelve should be a trader on his own account. There is a fitness with reference to relatives, neighbours, and dependants. So was there a fitness in the time when the church should come to her age with regard to the rest of mankind. The world must know its darkness that it might value the light when it should shine forth; the world must grow weary of its bondage that it might welcome the great Emancipator. It was God's plan that the world's wisdom should prove itself to be folly; he meant to permit intellect and skill to play themselves out, and then he would send his Son. He would allow man to prove his strength to be perfect weakness, and then he would become his righteousness and strength. Then, when one monarch governed all lands, and when the temple of war was shut after ages of bloodshed, the Lord whom the faithful sought suddenly appeared. Our Lord and Saviour came when time was full, and like a harvest ready for his reaping, and so will he come again when once more the age is ripe and ready for his presence.

Observe, concerning the first advent, that *the Lord was moving in it towards man.* "When the fulness of the time was come, God sent forth his Son." We moved not towards the Lord, but the Lord towards us. I do not find that the world in repentance sought after its Maker. No; but the offended God himself in infinite compassion broke the silence, and came forth to bless his enemies. See how spontaneous is the grace of God. All good things begin with him.

It is very delightful that God should take an interest in every stage of the growth of his people from their spiritual infancy to their spiritual manhood. As Abraham made a great feast when Isaac was weaned, so doth the Lord make a feast at the coming of age of his people. While they were as minors under the law of ceremonial observances, he led them about and instructed them. He knew that the yoke of the law was for their good, and he comforted them in the bearing of it; but he was glad when the hour came for their fuller joy. Oh, how truly did the Psalmist say, "How precious are thy thoughts unto me, O God! how great is the sum of them!" Tell it out with joy and gladness, that the blessings of the new dispensation under which we dwell are the spontaneous gifts of God, thoughtfully bestowed in great love, wherein he hath abounded towards us in all wisdom and prudence. When the fulness of time was come, God himself interposed to give his people their privileges; for it is not his will that any one of his people should miss a single point of blessedness. If we are babes it is not his wish; he would have us men. If we are famished it is not by his desire, he would fill us with the bread of heaven.

Mark the divine interposition,—"God sent forth his Son." I hope it may not seem wearisome to you if I dwell upon that word "sent,"—"God *sent* forth his Son." I take great pleasure in that expression, for it seals the whole work of Jesus. Everything that Christ did was done by commission and authority of his Father. The great Lord, when he was born at Bethlehem, and assumed our nature, did it under divine authorization; and when he came and scattered gifts with both his hands among the sons of men he was the messenger and ambassador of God. He was the Plenipotentiary of the Court of Heaven. At the back of every word of Christ there is the warrant of the Eternal; at the back of every promise of Christ there is the oath of God. The Son doeth nothing of himself, but the Father worketh with him and in him. O soul, when thou dost lean on Christ thou dost rely upon no amateur Saviour, no uncommissioned Redeemer; but upon One who is sent of the Most High, and therefore is authorised in everything that he does. The Father saith, "This is my beloved Son; hear ye him:" for in hearing him you are hearing the Most High. Let us find joy, then, in the coming of our Lord to Bethlehem, because he was sent.

Now run your eye to the next word: "When the fulness of time was come, God sent forth *his Son." Observe the Divine person who was sent.* God sent not an angel, nor any exalted creature, but "his Son." How there can be a Son of God we know not. The eternal filiation of the Son must for ever remain one of those mysteries into which we must not pry. It were something like the sin of the men of Beth-shemesh if we were to open the ark of God to gaze upon the deep things of God. It is quite certain that Christ is God; for here he is called "his Son." He existed before he was born into this world; for God "sent" his Son. He was already in being or he could not have been "sent." And while he is one with the Father, yet he must be distinct from the Father, and have a personality separate from that of the Father, otherwise it could not be said that God sent his Son. God the Father was not made of a woman, nor made under the law, but only God the Son; therefore, while we know and are assured that Christ is one with the Father, yet is his distinctness of personality most clearly to be observed.

Admire that God should have only one begotten Son, and should have sent him to uplift us. The messenger to man must be none other than God's own Son. What dignity is here! It is the Lord of angels that is born of Mary; it is he without whom was not anything made, who deigns to hang at a woman's breast and to be wrapped in swaddling bands. Oh, the dignity of this, and consequently, oh, the efficiency of it! He that has come to save us is no weak creature like ourselves; he that has taken upon himself our nature is no being of limited strength, such as an angel or a seraph might have been; but he is the Son of the Highest. Glory be to his blessed name! Let us dwell on this with delight.

"If some prophet had been sent
    With salvation's joyful news,
Who that heard the blest event
    Could their warmest love refuse?

But 'twas he to whom in heaven
    Hallelujahs never cease;
He, the mighty God, was given—
    Given to us—a Prince of Peace.

None but he who did create us
    Could redeem from sin and hell;
None but he could reinstate us
    In the rank from which we fell."

Press on, still keeping to the very words of the text, for they are very sweet. *God sent his Son in real humanity*—"made of a woman." The Revised Version properly hath it, "born of a woman." Perhaps you may get nearer to it if you say, "Made to be born of a woman," for both ideas are present, the *factum* and the *natum*, the being made and the being born. Christ was really and truly of the substance of his mother, as certainly as any other infant that is born into the world is so. God did not create the human nature of Christ apart, and then transmit it into mortal existence by some special means; but his Son was made and born of a woman. He is, therefore, of our race, a man like ourselves, and not man of another stock. You are to make no mistake about it; he is not only of humanity, but of your humanity; for that which is born of a woman is brother to us, be it born when it may. Yet there is an omission, I doubt not intentional, to show how holy was that human nature, for he is born of a woman, not of a man. The Holy Spirit overshadowed the Virgin, and "that holy thing" was born of her without the original sin which pertains to our race by natural descent. Here is a pure humanity though a true humanity; a true humanity though free from sin. Born of a woman, he was of few days and full of trouble; born of a woman, he was compassed with our physical infirmities; but as he was not born of man he was altogether without tendency to evil or delight therein. I beg you to rejoice in this near approach of Christ to us. Ring out the glad bells, if not in the spires and steeples, yet within your own hearts; for gladder news did never greet your ear than this, that he that is the Son of God was also "made of a woman."

Still further it is added, that God sent his Son "*made under the law,*" or born under the law; for the word is the same in both cases; and by the same means by which he came to be of a woman he came under the law. And now admire and wonder! The Son of God has come under the law. He was the Law-maker and the Law-giver, and he is both the Judge of the law and the Executioner of the law, and yet he himself came under the law. No sooner was he born of a woman than he came under the law: this voluntarily and yet necessarily. He willed to be a man, and being a man he accepted the position, and stood in the place of man as subject to the law of the race. When they took him and circumcised him according to the law, it was publicly declared that he was under the law. During the rest of his life you will observe how reverently he observed the commands of God. Even to the ceremonial law as it was given by Moses he had scrupulous regard. He despised the traditions and superstitions of men, but for the rule of the dispensation he had a high respect.

By way of rendering service unto God on our behalf, he came under the moral law. He kept his Father's commandments. He obeyed to the full both the first and the second tables; for he loved God with all his heart, and his neighbour as himself. "I delight to do thy will, O my God," saith he, "yea, thy law is within my heart." He could truly say of the Father, "I do always those things that please him." Yet it was a marvellous thing that the King of kings should be under the law; and especially that he should come under the penalty of the law as well as the service of it. "Being found in fashion as a man, he humbled himself, and became obedient unto death, even the death of the cross." As our Surety and Substitute he came under the curse of the law;

132

being made a curse for us. Having taken our place and espoused our nature, though without sin himself, he came under the rigorous demands of justice, and in due time he bowed his head to the sentence of death. "He laid down his life for us." He died the just for the unjust, to bring us to God. In this mystery of his incarnation, in this wonderful substitution of himself in the place of sinful men, lies the ground of that wonderful advance which believers made when Jesus came in the flesh. His advent in human form commenced the era of spiritual maturity and freedom.

II. I ask you now, therefore, in the second place, to CONTEMPLATE THE JOYOUS RESULT WHICH HAS COME OF OUR LORD'S INCARNATION.

I must return to what I have said before—*this coming of Christ has ended the minority of believers.* The people of God among the Jews were before Christ came the children of God ; but they were mere babes or little children. They were instructed in the elements of divine knowledge by types, emblems, shadows, symbols : when Jesus was come there was an end of that infantile teaching. The shadows disappear when the substance is revealed ; the symbols are not wanted when the person symbolized is himself present. What a difference between the teaching of our Lord Jesus Christ when he shows them plainly of the Father and the teaching of the priests when they taught by scarlet wool and hyssop and blood ! How different the teaching of the Holy Ghost by the apostles of our Lord, and the instruction by meats and drinks and holy days. The old economy is dim with smoke, concealed with curtains, guarded from too familiar an approach ; but now we come boldly to the throne, and all with unveiled face behold as in a glass the glory of God. The Christ has come, and now the Kindergarten school is quitted for the college of the Spirit, by whom we are taught of the Lord to know even as we are known. The hard governorship of the law is over. Among the Greeks, boys and youths were thought to need a cruel discipline : while they went to school they were treated very roughly by their pedagogues and tutors. It was supposed that a boy could only imbibe instruction through his skin, and that the tree of knowledge was originally a birch ; and therefore there was no sparing the rod, and no mitigation of self-denials and hardships. This fitly pictures the work of the law upon those early believers. Peter speaks of it as a yoke, which neither they nor their fathers were able to bear (Acts xv. 10). The law was given amid thunder and flaming fire ; and it was more fitted to inspire a wholesome dread than a loving confidence. Those sweeter truths, which are our daily consolation, were hardly known, or but seldom spoken. Prophets did speak of Christ, but they were more frequently employed in pouring out lamentations and denunciations against children that were corrupters. Methinks, one day with Christ was worth a half century with Moses. When Jesus came, believers began to hear of the Father and his love, of his abounding grace, and the kingdom which he had prepared for them. Then the doctrines of eternal love, and redeeming grace, and covenant faithfulness were unveiled ; and they heard of the tenderness of the Elder Brother, the grace of the great Father, and the indwelling of the ever-blessed Spirit. It was as if they had risen from servitude to freedom, from infancy to manhood. Blessed were they who in their day shared the privilege of the old economy, for it was wonderful light as compared with heathen darkness; yet, for all that, compared with the noontide that Christ brought, it was mere candle-light. The ceremonial law held a man in stern bondage : you must not eat this, and you must not go there, and you must not wear this, and you must not gather that. Everywhere you were under restraint, and walked between hedges of thorn. The Israelite was reminded of sin at every turn, and warned of his perpetual tendency to fall into one transgression or another. It was quite right that it should be so, for it is good for a man that, while he is yet a youth, he should bear the yoke, and learn obedience ; yet it must have been irksome. When Jesus came what a joyful difference was made. It seemed like a dream of joy, too glad to be true. Peter could not at first believe in it, and needed a vision to make him sure that it was even so. When he saw that great sheet let down, full of all manner of living creatures and four-footed things, and was bidden to kill and eat, he said, " Not so, Lord; for I have never eaten anything that is common or unclean." He was startled indeed when the Lord said, " What God hath cleansed, that call not thou common." That first order of things " stood only in meats and drinks, and divers washings, and carnal ordinances, imposed on them until the time of reformation ;" but Paul saith, " I know, and am persuaded by the Lord Jesus, that there is nothing unclean of itself." Prohibition upon mere ceremonial points, and commands upon carnal matters are now abolished, and great is our liberty : we shall be foolish indeed if we suffer ourselves to be again entangled with the yoke of bondage. Our minority was ended when the Lord, who had aforetime spoken to us by his prophets, at last sent his Son to lead us up to the highest form of spiritual manhood.

Christ came, we are told next, *to redeem those who were under the law;* that is to say, the birth of Jesus, and his coming under the law, and his fulfilling the law, have set all believers free from it as a yoke of bondage. None of us wish to be free from the law as a rule of life ; we delight in the commands of God, which are holy, and just, and good. We wish that we could keep every precept of the law, without a single omission or transgression. Our earnest desire is for perfect holiness ; but we do not look in that direction for our justification before God. If we be asked to-day, are we hoping to be saved by ceremonies ? we answer, " God forbid." Some seem to fancy that baptism and the Lord's Supper have taken the place of circumcision and the Passover, and that while Jews were saved by one form of ceremonial we are to be saved by another. Let us never give place to this idea ; no, not for an hour. God's people are saved, not by outward rites, nor forms, nor priestcraft, but because " God sent forth his Son, made of a woman, made under the law," and he has so kept the law that by faith his righteousness covers all believers, and we are not condemned by the law. As to the moral law, which is the standard of equity for all time, it is no way of salvation for us. Once we were under it, and strove to keep it in order to earn the divine favour ; but we have now no such motive. The word was, " This do and thou shalt live," and we therefore strove like slaves to escape the lash, and earn our wage ; but it is so no longer. Then we strove to do the Lord's will that he might love us, and that we might be rewarded for what we did; but we have no design of purchasing that favour now, since we freely and securely enjoy it on a very different ground. God loves us out of pure grace, and he has freely forgiven us our iniquities, and this out of gratuitous goodness. We are already saved, and that not by works of righteousness which we have done, or by holy acts which we hope to perform, but wholly of free grace. If it be of grace it is no more of works, and that it is all of grace from first to last is our joy and glory. The righteousness that covers us was wrought out by him that was born of a woman, and the merit by which we enter heaven is the merit, not of our own hands or hearts, but of him that loved us, and gave himself for us. Thus are we redeemed from the law by our Lord's being made under the law ; and we become sons and no more servants, because the great Son of God became a servant in our stead.

"What!" saith one; "then do you not seek to do good works?" Indeed we do. We talked of them before, but we actually perform them now. Sin shall not have dominion over us, for we are not under law, but under grace. By God's grace we desire to abound in works of holiness, and the more we can serve our God the happier we are. But this is not to save ourselves, for we are already saved. O sons of Hagar, ye cannot understand the freedom of the true heir, the child born according to promise! Ye that are in bondage, and feel the force of legal motives, ye cannot understand how we should serve our Father who is in heaven with all our heart and all our soul, not for what we get by it, but because he has loved us, and saved us, irrespective of our works. Yet it is even so; we would abound in holiness to his honour, and praise, and glory, because the love of Christ constraineth us. What a privilege it is to cease from the spirit of bondage by being redeemed from the law! Let us praise our Redeemer with all our hearts.

We are redeemed from the law in its operation upon our mind: it breeds no fear within us now. I have heard children of God say sometimes, " Well, but don't you think if we fall into sin we shall cease to be in God's love, and so shall perish?" This is to cast a slur upon the unchangeable love of God. I see that you make a mistake, and think a child is a servant. Now, if you have a servant, and he misbehaves himself, you say, "I give you notice to quit. There is your wage ; you must find another master." Can you do that to your son? Can you do that to your daughter? "I never thought of such a thing," say you. Your child is yours for life. Your boy behaved very badly to you: why did you not give him his wages and start him? You answer, that he does not serve you for wages, and that he is your son, and cannot be otherwise. Just so. Then always know the difference between a servant and a son, and the difference between the covenant of works and the covenant of grace.

I know how a base heart can make mischief out of this; but I cannot help it: the truth is the truth. Will a child rebel because he will always be a child? Far from it; it is this which makes him feel love in return. The true child of God is kept from sin by other and better forces than a slavish fear of being turned out of doors by his Father. If you are under the covenant of works, then, mind you, if you do not fulfil all righteousness you will perish: if you are under that covenant, unless you are perfect you are lost; one sin will destroy you, one sinful thought will ruin you. If you have not been perfect in your obedience, you must take your wages and be gone. If God deals with you according to your works, there will be nothing for you but, "Cast out this bond-woman and her son." But if you are God's child, that is a different matter; you will still be his child even when he corrects you for your disobedience.

"Ah," saith one, "then I may live as I like." Listen! If you are God's child, I will tell you how you will like to live. You will desire to live in perfect obedience to your Father, and it will be your passionate longing from day to day to be perfect even as your Father which is in heaven is perfect. The nature of sons which grace implants is a law unto itself : the Lord puts his fear into the hearts of the regenerate so that they do not depart from him. Being born again and introduced into the family of God, you will render to the Lord an obedience which you would not have thought of rendering to him if you had only been compelled by the idea of law and penalty. Love is a master force, and he that feels its power will hate all evil. The more salvation is seen to be all of grace, the deeper and more mighty is our love, and the more does it work towards that which is pure and holy. Do not quote Moses for motives of Christian obedience. Do not say, "The Lord will cast me away unless I do this and that." Such talk is of the bondwoman and her son; but it is very unseemly in the mouth of a true-born heir of heaven. Get it out of your mouth. If you are a son you disgrace your Father when you think that he will repudiate his own; you forget your spiritual heirship and liberty when you dread a change in Jehovah's love. It is all very well for a mere babe to talk in that ignorant fashion, and I don't wonder that many professors know no better, for many ministers are only half-evangelical; but you that have become men in Christ, and know that he has redeemed you from the law, ought ιot to go back to such bondage. "God sent forth his Son, made of a woman, made under the law, to redeem them that were under the law."

What else has he come for? Notice further, "*That we might receive the adoption of sons.*" The Lord Jesus Christ has come in human flesh that his people might to the full realise, grasp, and enjoy, "the adoption of sons." I want you this morning to see if you can do that. May the Holy Spirit enable you. What is it to receive the adoption of sons? Why to feel, Now I am under the mastery of love, as a dear child, who is both loved and loving. I go in and out of my Father's house not as a casual servant, called in by the day or the week, but as a child at home. I am not looking for hire as a servant, for I am ever with my Father, and all that he has is mine. My God is my Father, and his countenance makes me glad. I am not afraid of him, but I delight in him, for nothing can separate me from him. I feel a perfect love that casteth out fear, and I delight myself in him. Try now and enter into that spirit this morning. That is why Christ has come in the flesh—on purpose that you, his people, may be to the full the adopted children of the Lord, acting out and enjoying all the privileges which sonship secures to you.

And then, next, exercise your heirship. One who is a son, and knows he is an heir of all his father's estates, does not pine in poverty, nor act like a beggar. He looks upon everything as his own ; he regards his father's wealth as making him rich. He does not feel that he is stealing if he takes what his father has made to be his own, but he makes free with it. I wish believers would make free with the promises and blessings of their God. Help yourselves, for no good thing will the Lord withhold from you. All things are yours : you only need to use the hand of faith. Ask what thou wilt. If you appropriate a promise it will not be pilfering : you may take it boldly and say, " This is mine." Your adoption brings with it large rights : be not slow to use them. " If children, then heirs; heirs of God, and joint heirs with Christ." Among men, sons are only heirs, heirs in possession, when the father is dead ; but our Father in heaven lives, and yet we have full heirship in him. The Lord Jesus Christ was made of a woman on purpose that his dear people might at once enter into their heirship.

You ought to feel a sweet joy in the perpetual relationship which is now established between you and God, for Jesus is still your brother. You have been adopted, and God has never cancelled adoption yet. There is such a thing as regeneration, but there is not such a thing as the life then received dying out. If you are born unto God you are born unto God. The stars may turn to coals, and the sun and moon may become clots of blood, but he that is born of God has a life within him which can never end: he is God's child, and God's child he shall be. Therefore let him walk at large like a child, an heir, a prince of the blood royal, who bears a relationship to the Lord which neither time nor eternity can ever destroy. This is why Jesus was made of a woman and made under the law, that he might give us to enjoy the fulness of the privilege of adopted sons.

Follow me a minute a little further. The next thing that Christ has brought us by being made of a woman is, " Because ye are sons, God *hath sent forth the Spirit of his Son into your hearts.*" Here are two sendings. God sent his Son, and now he sends his Spirit. Because Christ has been sent, therefore the Spirit is sent ; and now you shall know the Holy Ghost's indwelling because of Christ's incarnation. The Spirit of light, the Spirit of life, the Spirit of love, the Spirit of liberty, the same Spirit that was in Christ Jesus is in you. That same Spirit which descended upon Jesus in the waters of baptism has also descended upon you. You, O child of God, have the Spirit of God as your present guide and Comforter ; and he shall be with you for ever. The life of Christ is your life, and the Spirit of Christ is your Spirit ; wherefore, this day be exceeding glad, for you have not received the spirit of bondage again to fear, but ye have received the Spirit of adoption.

There we finish, for Jesus has come *to give us the cry* as well as the spirit of adoption, " whereby we cry, Abba, Father." According to ancient traditions no slave might say, " Abba, Father," and according to the truth as it is in Jesus none but a man who is really a child of God, and has received the adoption, can truly say, " Abba, Father." This day my heart desires for every one of you, my brethren, that because Christ has been born into the world you may at once come of age, and may at this hour confidently say, " Abba, Father." The great God, the Maker of heaven and earth, is my Father, and I dare avow it without fear that he will disown the kindred. The Thunderer, the ruler of the stormy sea, is my Father, and notwithstanding the terror of his power I draw near to him in love. He who is the Destroyer, who says, " Return, ye children of men," is my Father, and I am not alarmed at the thought that he will call me to himself in due time. My God, thou who shalt call the multitudes of the slain from their graves to live, I look forward with joy to the hour when thou shalt call and I shall answer thee. Do what thou wilt with me, thou art my Father. Smile on me; I will smile back and say, " My Father." Chasten me, and as I weep I will cry, " My Father." This shall make everything work good to me, be it never so hard to bear. If thou art my Father all is well to all eternity. Bitterness is sweet, and death itself is life, since thou art my Father. Oh, trip ye merrily home, ye children of the living God, saying each one within himself, " I have it, I have it. I have that which cherubim before the throne have never gained; I have relationship with God of the nearest and the dearest kind, and my spirit for her music hath this word, ' Abba, Father; Abba, Father.' "

Now, dear children of God, if any of you are in bondage under the law, why do you remain so? Let the redeemed go free. Are you fond of wearing chains? Are you like Chinese women that delight to wear little shoes which crush their feet? Do you delight in slavery? Do you wish to be captives? You are not under the law, but under grace; will you allow your unbelief to put you under the law? You are not a slave. Why tremble like a slave? You are a child; you are a son; you are an heir; live up to your privileges. Oh, ye banished seed, be glad! You are adopted into the household of God; then be not as a stranger. I hear Ishmael laughing at you : let him laugh. Tell your Father of him, and he will soon say, " Cast out this bondwoman and her son." Free grace is not to be mocked by human merit; neither are we to be made sad by the forebodings of the legal spirit. Our soul rejoices, and, like Isaac, is filled with holy laughter; for the Lord Jesus has done great things for us whereof we are glad. To him be glory for ever and ever. Amen.